A Longman Cultural Edition

Jane Austen's

NORTHANGER ABBEY

Edited by

Marilyn Gaull

New York University

PEARSON
Longman

New York   San Francisco   Boston
London   Toronto   Sydney   Tokyo   Singapore   Madrid
Mexico City   Munich   Paris   Cape Town   Hong Kong   Montreal

Vice President and Editor-in-Chief: Joseph P. Terry
Development Editor: Barbara Santoro
Executive Marketing Manager: Ann Stypuloski
Production Coordinator: Shafiena Ghani
Project Coordination, Text Design, and Electronic Page Makeup: Dianne Hall
Cover Designer/Manager: John Callahan
Manufacturing Buyer: Roy L. Pickering
Printer and Binder: R R Donnelley and Sons Company / Harrisonburg
Cover Printer: Coral Graphics Services, Inc.

Cover Illustration: James Gillray, *Tales of Wonder!*, published 1 February 1802.
Courtesy Harriet Guest, University of York, Centre for Eighteenth Century Studies.

Library of Congress Cataloging-in-Publication Data
CIP data is on file.

Please visit our website at http://www.ablongman.com

ISBN: 0-321-20208-2

7 8 9 10 - OPM - 10 09 08

Contents

List of Illustrations

About Longman Cultural Editions

Reading always seems to vibrate with the transformation of the day—now, yesterday, and centuries ago, when the presses first put printed language into wide circulation. Correspondingly, literary culture has always been a matter of change: of new practices confronting established traditions; of texts transforming under the pressure of new techniques of reading and new perspectives of understanding; of canons shifting and expanding; of informing traditions getting reviewed and renewed, recast and reformed by emerging cultural interests and concerns; of culture, too, as a variable "text"—a reading. Inspired by the innovative *Longman Anthology of British Literature*, Longman Cultural Editions respond creatively to the changes, past and recent, by presenting key texts in contexts that illuminate the lively intersections of literature, tradition, and culture. A principal work is made more interesting by materials that place it in relation to its past, present, and future, enabling us to see how it may be reworking traditional debates and practices, how it appears amid the conversations and controversies of its own historical moment, how it gains new significances in subsequent eras of reading and reaction. Readers new to the work will discover attractive paths for exploration, while those more experienced will encounter fresh perspectives and provocative juxtapositions.

Longman Cultural Editions serve not only several kinds of readers but also (appropriately) their several contexts, from various courses of study to independent adventure. Handsomely produced and affordably priced, our volumes offer appealing companions to *The Longman Anthology of British Literature,* in some cases enriching and expanding units originally developed for the *Anthology*, and in other cases presenting this wealth for the first time. The logic and composition of the contexts vary across the series. The constants are the complete text of an important literary work, reliably edited, headed by an inviting introduction, and supplemented by helpful annotation; a table of dates to track its composition, publication, and public reception in relation to biographical, cultural, and historical events; and a guide for further inquiry and study. With these common measures and uncommon assets, Longman Cultural Editions encourage your literary pleasures with resources for lively reflection and adventurous inquiry.

Susan J. Wolfson
General Editor
Professor of English
Princeton University

About This Edition

Written by 1798, *Northanger Abbey*, the first of Jane Austen's novels, was not published until 1818. During the twenty-year interval, Austen changed the title twice, from "Susan" to "Catherine," and wrote five other novels: *Sense and Sensibility* in 1811, *Pride and Prejudice* in 1813, a new edition of *Sense and Sensibility*, and *Mansfield Park* in 1814, and *Emma* published by John Murray, Byron's publisher, late in 1815, dated 1816. Six months after Austen's death, in July, 1817, her brother Henry titled the book *Northanger Abbey,* added a biographical notice, and Murray published it in December, 1817, along with *Persuasion,* printing 1,750 copies to sell at £1.4s (one pound, four shillings) for the set of four volumes (Le Faye [2004] 259).

In 1803, Jane Austen sold the manuscript of *Northanger Abbey,* then called "Susan," for £10 to the same firm that had published Ann Radcliffe's *Mysteries of Udolpho* (1794), Benjamin Crosby & Co., who advertised it as "in the press" in two volumes. When, by 1809, the novel had not appeared, Austen, under the name "Mrs. Ashton Dennis" (acronym "MAD"), wrote to Crosby asking that they either publish or return it so she could publish it elsewhere, offering to provide another copy. Crosby offered to return the manuscript in exchange for the original £10 and threatened to sue if she published the other copy. In 1815, after the success of her four other novels, Jane asked Henry to buy back the manuscript, to which she added the "Advertisement" accounting for the delay in publishing.

Since gothic novelists usually claimed that their books were either written overnight or found in manuscript many years after they were written, Austen's explanation, while true, also introduced both her voice and the mock-gothic machinery of the novel. Her claim, for example, that in the thirteen years "places, manners, books and opinions" had become "comparatively obsolete" is a brilliant and concise example of the exaggeration that characterizes her humor: how, after all, can anything be "comparatively obsolete," at all, especially an "opinion" in only thirteen years?

Although the text of *Northanger Abbey* remained relatively stable over the twenty years of Jane Austen's brief authorial life, it accurately reflects British society, culture, and literary production in both 1798 and 1818. She had moved from the politically revolutionary and experimental generation of William Wordsworth, Samuel Taylor Coleridge, William Blake, Mary Wollstonecraft, William Godwin, Ann Radcliffe, and "Monk" Lewis to the postwar generation of Percy Shelley, John Keats, Thomas Love Peacock, Leigh Hunt, Thomas DeQuincey, William Hazlitt, Charles Lamb, and Wordsworth, still, and the definitive presence of Lord Byron and Sir Walter Scott. The gothic style of the 1790's was still fashionable, dominating the stage in popular melodrama, parodied by Peacock in *Melincourt* (1817), and *Nightmare Abbey* (1818), and re-interpreted in the hauntings of Mary Shelley's *Frankenstein* (1818), John Polidori's *The Vampyre* (1819), and Charles Robert Maturin's *Melmouth, the Wanderer* (1820).

During that twenty-year period, battles still loomed in America and on the European continent, riots in London over food and machinery. Repressive laws still threatened writers and publishers while publishing itself expanded, and the reading public was viewed with a strange combination of fear and scorn. The threats to survival that Thomas Malthus described in 1798 in the *Essay on Population*, the warped ratio between people and provisions, the inevitable war, famine, and disease that followed were still in evidence everywhere. And while women's fashions were less revealing in 1818 than they had been in 1798—skirts billowing instead of clinging, breasts less exposed—men's fashions were approaching what would become the familiar standardized and impersonal ideal of the dandy (see p. 22). The education of women, indeed of everyone, the role and function of literature, the relation between literature and history, the conventions of marriage and property rights, were still unresolved; and the pursuit of happiness, to which everyone was entitled, was still undefined.

In 1798, Jane Austen defended the same "common feelings of common life," as Wordsworth in *Lyrical Ballads*, and objected to the same emotional excesses, the "frantic novels, sickly and stupid German tragedies, and deluges of idle and extravagant stories in verse," he cited in the Preface of 1800. While Austen described General Tilney's self-indulgent renovations to his estate, Wordsworth in "The Ruined Cottage" conveyed the social reality behind the ruins: an abandoned and desolate house and an innocent family destroyed by war and poverty. Like *Northanger Abbey*, "The Ruined Cottage" appeared under a new name years later, in 1814, as part of *The Excursion*, still apt, and now part of a new conversation, one that Scott entered with *Waverley*, also in 1814, another novel about a house, an estate, assimilating romance and history, subtitled *Sixty Years Since*, that had also spent at least a decade in manuscript. If anything had changed for any of these belatedly published works, it is the shift of emphasis from the property to the proprietor, to the protagonist, a new preoccupation with what constitutes a good citizen, a hero, a code of behavior in the post-war world.

After the first edition in 1818, sales of Jane Austen's novels declined, and, by 1820, the last 282 copies of the four-volume edition were remaindered (Gilson 82–86). *Northanger Abbey* appeared in Richard Bentley's less expensive Standard Novels in 1833, and in a scholarly edition, *The Novels of Jane Austen*, edited by R. W. Chapman in 1923, to which most subsequent texts are indebted. The publication of her letters and memoirs in 1870 raised a flurry of interest in her work, and a century later, in 1970, the novels remained unpredictably popular among young readers and in the thriving community of Jane Austen Societies in Great Britain and America. Academically, however, they were dismissed as frivolous, intellectually as unrespectable as popular romances. In David Lodge's satiric novel *Changing Places* (1975), for example, Professor Morris Zapp becomes a joke merely for choosing to be the "Jane Austen man," caught up in his "utterly exhaustive" study "examining the novels from every conceivable angle. . . . After Zapp, the rest would be silence." Within a decade, however, with the rise of feminist literary criticism, Jane Austen, like Joanna Baillie, Maria Edgeworth, and Mary Wollstonecraft, among others, acquired an academic status to complement her popular appeal.

In the 1990's, with films, television shows, and radio adaptations, Jane Austen became a cult, a brand: her novels on the bestseller list of the *New York Times*, her face on tee-shirts, tea sets, coffee mugs; her name associated with embroidery, cookbooks, fabrics, and costumes, even a bumper sticker that reads, "I would rather be reading Jane Austen" (Thompson [2003] 13–15). While only three films were made of *Northanger Abbey* (1971, 1986, and 1990), this novel was the subject of more radio programs, all on the BBC, than the other novels (1937, 1949, 1951, 1953, 1962, 1970, 1972), for reasons about which one can only speculate.

The mystery that every critic and reader confronts: how to account for Austen's perennial and universal appeal. I believe that her power lies in an emotional subtext that she gave voice to: the common and the exceptional feelings of common life to which everyone responds. Most of us live, as Jane Austen did, remote from great public events, from scientific, philosophical, and religious conflicts. Like Austen, we live tangentially, sometimes unaware or even against our will drawn into those cultural revolutions which change our lives forever. The Contexts materials I have chosen illustrate the experiences, emphases, and shadows we share, the feeling of living as she did and as we do, to quote Wordsworth in the *Ode: Intimations of Immortality*, "in worlds not realized." Beneath the surfaces and choices, the styles and substance of our different cultures, like Jane Austen, we are also concerned with making a life; with finding love in all its rich varieties; with seeing clearly, correctly, and acting appropriately; with the nature of happiness, of trust, and fear, how to assess and live with them—themes which, then and now, from nursery tales to the daily news, are never far away.

Since there is no surviving manuscript for *Northanger Abbey*, I have gone back to the first publication, corrected obvious typos, added italics for both titles and foreign words, updated spelling, punctuation, and footnotes. Similarly, most of the selections in the Contexts section are from first or early editions (lightly edited), cited by chapter or location rather than pages for ease of reference to contemporary editions. The letters are cited by dates to the Brabourne edition (1884) which, like all the novels, maps, links, allusions, illustrations, biography, jokes, songs, films, are available online at http://www.pemberley.com. My goal is an accurate text for students and for non-academic readers, the popular literate audience that Jane Austen addressed. I have chosen contextual materials to show how the novel reflected, avoided, and contributed to the larger cultural conversation it entered.

My gratitude and admiration to Anne Ehrenpreis, to Marilyn Butler, and to the generations of readers, editors, and critics who enriched our understanding of *Northanger Abbey*; to my colleagues at the Wordsworth Summer Conference; to my friends and colleagues in the English Department of New York University, for their inspiration and generosity; to Bobst Library, New York University, for access to its exceptional collection of early editions from which the Contexts materials are drawn; to Karl Kroeber, for his friendship, his "clearest insight and amplitude of mind"; and to the great goddess herself, Jane Austen, without whom there would be much less pleasure in the world.

Marilyn Gaull
New York University

Jane Austen's Life and Times

Born, the Rector's daughter, in Steventon, a small farming village in Hampshire, south of London, the seventh of eight children, the younger of two daughters, Jane Austen wrote six novels—*Sense and Sensibility* (1811), *Pride and Prejudice* (1813), *Mansfield Park* (1814), *Emma* (1815), *Northanger Abbey* and *Persuasion* (1818)—published four during her lifetime, 162 letters that survive, and an assortment of poems and parodies to amuse herself and her family. Six months after her death at age forty-one, on July 24, 1817, her brother Henry revealed her identity as an author in the biographical notice attached to *Northanger Abbey* and *Persuasion* (p. 2), admiring her "cheerfulness, sensibility, and benevolence, which," he says, "were her real characteristics": "Faultless . . . she always sought, in the faults of others, something to excuse, to forgive or forget." Her tombstone emphasized "The benevolence of her heart / the sweetness of her temper," and "the extraordinary endowments of her mind," and, according to her nephew, James Edward Leigh's memoir (1870), in spite of all these virtues, she "lived in entire seclusion from the literary world. . . . I doubt whether it would be possible to mention any other author of note, whose personal obscurity was so complete."

True, Austen was dutiful and loving to her family, attended her aging parents, moved to Bath when her father retired, and, after his death, lived in a cottage with her mother and sister on an estate her brother inherited. She travelled here and there visiting with brothers, nieces and nephews, and on occasional trips to London attended the theater, art exhibits, dinner parties, reporting in lively letters to her sister on everyone she met and what they wore. These same letters, however, so brisk and engaging, contradict the family legend of the "good Jane," someone she would not have liked at all: "Pictures of perfection," she wrote to her niece, Fanny, "as you know make me sick & wicked" (March 23, 1817).[1] In the letters, the ones that Cassandra and her nieces considered acceptable enough to preserve, she was judgmental, fretful, self-involved, envious, and insensitive, sometimes so nasty that even Virginia Woolf wrote, "I would rather not find myself alone in the room with her" (Halperin 186). Admittedly, in the privacy of her correspondence, her worldly wit and even cruelty were harmless and confidential: describing the ideal household staff, "We plan having a steady cook and a young, giddy housemaid, with a sedate, middle-aged man, who is to undertake the double office of husband to the former and sweetheart to the latter. No children, of course, to be allowed on either side" (Letter to Cassandra, January 1, 1803).

Although her biographers try to reconcile the legend with the letters, the public saint and a private shrew, like most people, Jane Austen remains a mystery, complex, profound, a life that mostly took place between the surviving bits and scraps, between what she said and what they said, in the quiet mental space where most authors live, occasionally either revealing herself or hiding in her fictions.

Jane Austen had one verifiable flirtation with Tom Lefroy who could not afford to marry her, one authentic marriage proposal from the wealthy but awkward and considerably younger Harris Bigg-Wither, which she accepted and rejected within hours, and one mysterious encounter in Lyme Regis that became a major literary event in Constance Pilgrim's *Dear Jane* (1991). According to an anecdote her sister Cassandra divulged late in life, Jane had met a gentleman while they were on holiday, a gentleman who became, in Miss Pilgrim's version, on no special evidence, William Wordsworth's

---

[1]Cassandra, to whom most of Jane's letters were written, first saved them and then destroyed those that were too personal. Some letters were printed in 1870, by her nephew, James Edward Austen-Leigh in his *Memoir*. But the first collected edition, from which the letters are quoted, appeared in 1884, edited by Edward Knatchbull-Hugessen, first baron Brabourne, son of Lady Knatchbull, born Fanny Knight, Jane Austen's favorite niece, who entrusted Brabourne with the legacy when she died at age ninety. The most complete and reliable collection: Deirdre Le Faye, *Jane Austen's Letters* (1995).

mariner brother, John, with whom she had an extended and hopeless romance that ended with his death in 1805.

Behind a characteristic self-mockery, the letters reveal her pleasures: parties, dinners, dancing, and, in this first age of fashion, being fashionably dressed, sewing many of her own clothes based on what she saw and conveying the details, right down to the cost of the ribbon: on October 27, 1798, "Next week I shall begin operations on my hat, on which you know my principal hopes of happiness depend," and on June 11, 1799, after searching all over Bath for hat trimming, "I cannot help thinking that it is more natural to have flowers grow out of the head than fruit. What do you think on that subject?" When anyone dies, her first question to Cassandra is what they should wear for mourning, but then, she seems curiously unmoved by death. "How horrible it is to have so many people killed," she comments on reading recent reports of the Peninsular War in Spain, where one of her brothers may have been engaged, "and what a blessing that one cares for none of them" (May 31, 1811). On the death of one lady she wrote, "Poor woman, she has done the only thing in the World she could . . . to make one cease to abuse her" (October 13, 1813), and another, "Poor Mrs. C. Miller, that she should die on the wrong day at last, after being about it so long!" (March 13, 1816). And when her sister-in-law, Edward's wife Elizabeth died suddenly, after regrets, prayers, consolations, "I am to be in Bombazen & Crape. . . . My Mourning however will not impoverish me": she will reline her pelisse and trim her bonnet (October 16, 1808).

Like most of her family, in her letters she casts a cold eye on the emotionally charged experiences of life. Of a friend who had five babies, "poor Woman! How can she be honestly breeding again?" (October 1, 1808) and, of another, after the eighteenth child, recommending "the simple regimen of separate rooms" (February 20, 1817). Of a new nephew, "if he ever comes to be hanged it will not be until we are too old to care about it" (October 27, 1798), and of another, "I shall think with tenderness and delight on his beautiful and smiling countenance . . . until a few years have turned him into an ungovernable, ungracious fellow" (April 25, 1811). Of marriage, "Single women have a dreadful propensity for being poor, which is one very strong argument in favour of matrimony" (March 13, 1816). Money was a great problem, of course, in the novels as well as her life, and everyone's life, and she was conscious of the cost of things, down to excruciating detail: on May 6, 1801, she encourages a friend to settle in Bath because "Meat is only 8d per pound, butter 12d & cheese 91/2 d. . . . salmon has been sold at 2s:9d pr. pound the whole fish," which even she called "vulgar economies"[2]

Although her novels are never boring, Jane is often bored, and conveys it well: "We live at home, quite confined, and our feelings prey upon us" (Anne Elliot, *Persuasion*) or, in her own words, from Bath, where, if anywhere, social activity abounded, she complained in a clever turn of phrase, "Bath is getting so very empty that I am not afraid of doing too little" (May 6, 1801); or, later, when one pictures her hovering over her desk turning out novels, "I have read The Corsair [Byron], mended my petticoat, and have nothing else to do" (March 5, 1814). While it is tempting to attribute her boredom to being the under-employed female intellectual that feminists such as Mary Wollstonecraft lamented, she actually enjoys the ordinary, the trivial, in being, she says on November 17, 1798, while she is writing *Northanger Abbey*, "a very good house-keeper," which Catherine Moreland's mother says she isn't: "I really think it is my peculiar excellence," Jane continued, "and for this reason—I always take care to provide such things as please my own appetite, which I consider the chief merit in housekeeping. I have had some ragout veal, and I mean to have some haricot mutton tomorrow. We are to kill a pig soon." Later, on September 18, 1816, now a published author, she found writing "impossible . . . with a head full of joints of mutton and doses of rhubarb."

Her self-portrait is in a letter to Fanny, her favorite niece, who reflected her contradictions and gifts:

You are inimitable, irresistible. You are the delight of my Life. Such Letters, such entertaining Letters as you have lately sent! Such a description of your queer little heart! Such lovely display of what Imagination does.—You are worth your weight in gold. . . . I cannot express to you what I felt in reading your history of yourself, how full of Pity & Concern & Admiration

---

[2]"d" = pence or pennies; "s" = shillings: 12d to a shilling, 20s to a pound, £1 = approx. $2.50.

& Amusement. . . . You are the Paragon of all that is Silly and
Sensible, common-place & eccentric, Sad & Lively, Provoking
& Interesting—Who can keep pace with the fluctuations of
your Fancy, the Capprizios of your Taste, the Contradictions of
your Feelings—You are so odd . . . so perfectly natural . . .
so peculiar in yourself, yet so like everybody else. (February 20,
1817; Le Faye [1995] 328–29).

While she appeared isolated, Jane Austen's large family brought
the drama of contemporary life to her: James, the eldest, after attending Oxford, became a vicar, then curate, then rector at Steventon when his father retired, widowed and remarried. His daughter,
Anna, tried to write a novel tentatively titled "Which is the Heroine," unfinished but the source of great amusement to the family.
George, the second son, was born epileptic and possibly deaf and
dumb as well, boarded out until his death at age seventy-two—and
never mentioned in Jane's letters or most biographies. Edward, the
third son, was adopted by a wealthy cousin, from whom he inherited three estates, fathered eleven children before his wife died, and
gave his widowed mother and two sisters a home at Chawton
where they could help raise the children. Henry, the fourth son,
married his widowed cousin Eliza de Feuillide, whose late husband,
a French count, had been beheaded in the Reign of Terror in 1794.
Henry joined the Oxford militia, then became a banker. After Eliza
died, Henry lost his business in the post-war depression, remarried,
became a curate, and published Jane's novels after her death. Cassandra, to whom most of Jane Austen's letters were written, was
two years older, educated with Jane briefly at the Abbey School, engaged to Tom Fowle who died of fever while serving in the West Indies, and spent the rest of her life as a companion to Jane, their sib-
lings, and many nieces and nephews. Frank, in the navy by age
fourteen, balanced his sometimes perilous service with his family of
eleven children, retiring as Admiral of the Fleet in 1863. Charles,
the youngest brother, also entered the navy and rose to the admi-
ralty before dying of cholera in 1852, leaving eight adult children,
four daughters by his first wife—whom he married in Bermuda and
who died in 1814—and three sons and one daughter by his second,
the sister of his first. All the brothers were widowed once, and Cassandra never married after losing her fiancé. In 1799, Mrs. Leigh-

Perrot, Jane's wealthy aunt with whom she had stayed in Bath, and from whom she had hoped for a legacy, was accused of stealing lace, imprisoned with her husband for eight months under the threat of public hanging or transportation to Australia, then acquitted for what many thought had been the shopkeeper's scheme for extortion.

Each of these relationships and many more friendships implicated Jane Austen in the broad world of politics, fashion, religion, law, and the endless war against which her life was played out and about which she had insightful and chilling opinions, opinions that are alien to the sheltered life of a scribbling spinster. So, in the same letter in which she finds the fashions "entertaining," "the coloured petticoats with braces over the white Spencers & enormous Bonnets," "long sleeves," high waists, "Bosoms covered," she moves on to a dinner party, then politics, and concludes with remarks on an impending war in America (which had actually started in 1812), which "will ruin us": "The Americans cannot be conquered, & we shall only be teaching them the skill in War which they may not now want. We are to make them good Sailors & Soldiers, & gain nothing ourselves. . . . I place my hope of better things on a claim to the protection of Heaven, as a Religious Nation, a Nation in spite of much Evil improving in Religion, which I cannot believe the Americans to possess" (September 2, 1814). Most of the references, however, are oblique, registering the helplessness that ordinary people feel around big events.

War was relentless: from 1771 to 1815, first in North America and then on the Continent against Napoleon. The British, defeating Napoleon repeatedly, still lived in terror of invasion, sometimes by balloon, but mostly by sea along the huge unprotected coastline. In 1797, twelve hundred armed French soldiers on three frigates invaded Fishguard, a small Welsh fishing village, where they were repelled by angry women villagers, armed with only their pitchforks and rage. This isolated incident set off a financial crisis, a run on the banks as citizens attempted to convert their paper money to gold, much of which had already been exported to France, and the Government levied the first income tax to fund the war. The country was defended by volunteers, often impoverished, lured by uniforms, parades, social approval. In the heady mix of patriotism and music, every town became a "garrison" (Colley 309), even Oxford where Jane's brother Henry rose to the rank of Captain. With three brothers engaged in the conflict against Napoleon, a sister-in-law widowed and her invalid son orphaned by the guillotine, Jane lived in a state of emotional siege through most of her life; the war was the subtext of her writing and the background noise in her letters. It makes sense, as V. S. Pritchett observes, to "think of her as a war novelist, formed very much by the Napoleonic wars, knowing directly of prize money, the shortage of men, the economic crisis and change in the value of capital."[3]

Jane Austen's life reflects the extremes and contradictions of an age that Charles Dickens called in *A Tale of Two Cities,* "the best of times and the worst of times": unprecedented extravagance and poverty, heroism and crime, altruism and greed, patriotism and alienation, elegance and squalor, invention, exploration, idealism, riots, repression, superstition, and fear, both real and imaginary. While poets and industrialists celebrated an age of individualism, to philosophers and politicians it was the start of collective life, the tyranny of the majority, and the loss of personal freedom. In the first great age of publishing, authorship, and literacy, the government taxed paper and penalized writers and publishers for speaking out, for criticizing the royal family, or simply offering alternatives to the self-destructive course of a ruling class that was out of touch with the lives of its citizens. Before the first census in 1801, a series of Defense Acts required every parish to count the eligible men between the ages of fifteen and fifty-five who would defend England should France invade. The Reverend George Austen, Jane's father, counted only thirty-five (Colley 297). Tom Paine was accused of treason; William Blake was tried as a spy; Joseph Johnson was among dozens of publishers accused of sedition and imprisoned for what they published. Being a writer with opinions, positions, or even peculiar habits was dangerous.

Music, dancing, and fashion flourished, with public displays of hats, breasts, money and emotions. Some philosophers envisioned a utopian paradise while others anticipated doom: the sexual games in which Austen's generation delighted would, as Thomas

---

[3]As quoted in Halperin (59). Following Marilyn Butler, *Jane Austen and the War of Ideas* (1975), it has become crucial to situate Jane Austen in the great events of her culture. See also Claudia Johnson, *Women, Politics, and the Novel* (1988); Warren Roberts, *Jane Austen and the French Revolution* (1979).

Malthus in his *Essay on Population* (1798) claimed, lead to over-population, and in turn, war, disease, and starvation, a balance of nature based on abundance and waste. Prostitution, illegitimacy, and birth rates soared, while babies and mothers died of diseases that could have been prevented by simply washing hands. Emotions rose and fell like tides, vacillated between good sense and passionate excess, between the sense and sensibility out of which Austen made a novel. Street culture flourished with parades, strikes, demonstrations, festivals and celebrations for royal birthdays, military victories, seasonal holidays, eclipses, even the freezing of the Thames River. Fireworks became commonplace as did poems to melancholy, dejection, despair, and suicide. John Wesley led religious revivals, built chapels and imposed mindless austerities on the already deprived, while intellectuals such as Thomas Taylor revived pagan rituals, and political theorists following Jeremy Bentham reconceived government to guarantee the greatest happiness for the greatest number—which meant not very much happiness for anyone.

The most pervasive and lasting changes, the ones closest to Jane Austen, were conceptual: in only twenty years, from 1785 to 1805, the universe was reconceived as older, larger, and more diverse than anyone had previously believed, packed with an incalculable number of invisible particles according to John Dalton, suffused with "imponderable fluids," driven by mysterious forces, "boundless" according to William Herschel, the astronomer. In 1788, Herschel, a German musician, after playing his flute in the Pump Room orchestra or his organ in the Octagonal Chapel, discovered this infinite universe by peering all night at the sky through his home-made telescopes on the pavement outside his cottage in Bath. In *The Botanic Garden* (1791), Erasmus Darwin explained a new world of process, transformation, conflict, destruction, generation, even evolution, a universe with "no sign of a beginning . . . no prospect of an end," according to James Hutton, the founder of modern geology. In 1795, from the cliffs of Lyme Regis, William Smith drew the images of fossils, which he believed were evidence of earlier creations, of eons that no one had ever known existed before, fossils that Mr. Anning (the carpenter Jane had consulted in the summer of 1804 about a "broken lid" in their rented cottage) was already harvesting and that would bring the most famous geologists in England to his daughter's shop for her perfect specimens of fossil-fish. And in Bath, in Jane Austen's neighborhood, in 1798, Smith drew the first geological map, illustrating strata, layers of rock, fossil-evidence of the catastrophic past, the ancient creations and destructions on which the new city of Bath, its ephemeral and temporary pleasures, had been built. Curiosity about secular origins led to philology and the study of myth, of sacred texts all of them conveying a sense of unity among the disparate peoples the British encountered in their explorations. Sir William Jones's study of language prompted the revival of oral traditions, myths, superstition, even religious cults.

In the new science, human beings were late creations, intruders, aliens, working out their destiny among the green and growing things on which, Joseph Priestley said, in 1793, they were dependent for life, requiring the same oxygen, the same air as their goats or pigs or house pets. Whether one liked these ideas or not, oxygen and electricity, theories of light, sound, and color changed the way human life was conceived. Progress meant power, mobility, and inventions: steam engines, tin cans, hot-air balloons, bicycles, sewing machines, cotton underwear, carbon paper, paved roads, gaslights in the streets of London, a postal service, the umbrellas in Bath, the Rumford stoves and clear glass in Northanger Abbey, and all distance, indeed all time calculated on British chronometers from the new meridian in Greenwich. Some discoveries had no practical application: electricity, for example, was first used for recreation, to animate corpses, stimulate fertility, overcome birth deformities, or manage pain, a treatment Jane Austen's brother Edward sought out when drinking and bathing in the waters at Bath had failed: "I fancy," she wrote, "we are all unanimous in expecting no advantage from it" (June 2, 1799).

Jane Austen was smart, literate, thoughtful, aware, and the new science was accessible, familiar, inescapable. It was presented in public theaters, lecture halls, even street fairs, in colloquial language with engaging visual displays, disseminated in newspapers, popular magazines, text books for children, and the *Encyclopaedia Britannica*, which reflected this expansion of knowledge in five editions during Jane Austen's lifetime. If particular sciences did not enter her life or the novels explicitly, they defined the world in which the novels were written, published and read, provided the context against which the fictional events and characters were measured—and in turn, provided the fictions against which the science was measured. Within this enlarged indeed infinite universe full of mysterious, diverse, and wonderful things, social obsessions with class, clothes, money, carriages appeared trivial, and the preoccupation with time futile.

In place of moons, seasons, and tides, the British devised instruments to predict weather, measure distance and time, regulating social activity by clocks mounted on public facades or personalized it with ornamental pocket watches. Indeed, ever since Chapman's first scholarly edition of *Northanger Abbey* (1923), even scholars have been caught up in issues of time and timing, composing precise calendars of what Catherine, Mrs. Allen, the Tilneys, and the Thorpes were doing, where and how long it took, citing references to pocket-watches, clocks, time-pieces of all sorts, even Mr. Allen's barometer to establish the calendar by the weather. Some consider the precise scheduling a sign of Austen's art, but in the new world that the novel entered, either in 1798 or in 1818, this social preoccupation with time, the control and uniformity it implied, is part of the irony: "Time," Herschel wrote, "which means everything in our schemes, is to nature endless and as nothing." Similarly, to contemporary readers, Henry Tilney's observation on Beechen Cliff, the "piece of rocky fragment with the withered oak," was natural geological evidence, the "deep time" that Smith was mapping, vestiges of a more ancient and mysterious life force than the artificial picturesque code through which he saw it.

The image of Reverend Henry Tilney standing on Beechen Cliff lecturing on the picturesque defines the pathos and humor of Jane Austen's world, another moment when she enters the conversation of her literary contemporaries. Beyond an affectation, the picturesque (see Contexts, p. 259) was a secular response to the loss of divinity that had suffused a natural world created by God, only six thousand years before, a scene of both his love and his power. In a single decade, science had turned nature into an alien, unfathomable, and giant heap of ruins in which human beings had been abandoned to work out their own destiny—or, in aesthetic terms, to discover the sublime (see Contexts, p. 224). Picturesque tours, letters, poems and novels, based on the rules of William Gilpin, the examples of Thomas Gray, paintings by Turner and Constable, domesticated nature, turned nature into art, into a social discourse, orderly, predictable, familiar. Similarly, Bath itself, although once sacred to both pagans and Christians, had become a geological wonder dominated by a decaying cathedral, devoid of spirituality and wholly devoted to worldly pleasure. Even the clergyman, Henry Tilney, knows more about novels and muslin than about God and his ministry, about which he says nothing. His religion happens when he is somewhere else.

The daughter of a rector, the sister of two clergymen, buried under a tombstone emphasizing her exemplary Christian life, Jane Austen, the novelist, lived between the two worlds of the faithful and the faithless, of piety and experience. Her fictional world has no spiritual dimension, no transcendental morality; characters worked out their lives guided by a few novels, some social models accidentally encountered in Bath, or London. Good nature replaced goodness as the ultimate virtue and it was affirmed by love, or at least marriage. As the narrator observes at the end of *Northanger Abbey*, "To begin perfect happiness at the respective ages of twenty-six and eighteen, is to do pretty well. . . ."

Jane Austen viewed her world as the picturesque tourist she parodied: a spectator, her back to the landscape, looking at its reflection in a Claude Glass, the curved and smoked mirror that composed the scene as if it were organized into a painting, the menacing, guilt-provoking, unhappy parts excluded. Along with her talents, her blessings, the familial love she cultivated, she endured the tragedies of her times, the conflict, waste, injustice, uncertainty, lost opportunities and fear of poverty, disease, abandonment, invasion. As a novelist, she excluded those things that Wordsworth said, in *Ode: Intimations of Immortality*, lie "too deep for tears," distanced and protected herself with irony and art, focused on "a little bit of ivory, two inches wide, on which I work with a brush so fine as to produce little effect after much labor" (see Postscript to Biographical Notice, p. 7).

Introduction

With its many literary, social, and political allusions, *Northanger Abbey* offers a great summing up of the British novels that preceded it, a reflection of contemporary culture at two seminal points in history, 1798 and 1818, and an anticipation of the narrative achievements that followed. From *Cupid and Psyche* to *Alice in Wonderland*, from *Don Quixote* to *Madame Bovary*, *Northanger Abbey* assimilates and contributes to the plots, themes, characters, and devices that define narrative in the West. In the first Contexts unit that follows the text of the novel, I illustrate how Austen relates to both the gothic and historical romance, to narrative tradition and contemporary novels. Here, I would like to consider some features in *Northanger Abbey* itself, unresolved issues about which critics seldom agree—the satirical form, the narrative voice, the plots, characters, diction, and settings. Though my reading is hardly conclusive, I believe that the inconsistencies, lapses and digressions, the shifts in tone, sympathy, and perspective that some critics have attributed to her youth when she first wrote it or to the long delay in publication, are, in fact, strengths reflecting the experimentalism, the mixed genre that distinguishes the Romantic style and accounts for its enduring appeal.

Satire

From William Blake's *Marriage of Heaven and Hell* to Lord Byron's *Don Juan*, James Gillray, George Cruickshank, and Thomas Rowlandson, satires, parodies, and caricatures, the voices of the counter-culture flourished during the Romantic period. Energized by the political discontent of the 1790's, writers and artists shamed, disarmed, and ridiculed texts, styles, institutions, individuals, the familiar and strange, the powerful, threatening, ineffectual, and decadent. The usual devices include imitating in another context (Henry's describing gothic horrors in the safety of his carriage on the smooth path to Northanger), inflating the trivial (turning an ordinary laundry list into a secret manuscript), trivializing the important (making the fussy father Tilney a General), simplification, exaggeration, displacement, and discrepancy between what happens and how it is perceived, between the ideals that characters profess and the realities they practice, between their commonplace lives and the heroic values the narrator measures them against. Beginning in parody, exaggerated imitation, satire is more hostile, subtle, and ranging, simultaneously attacking multiple targets: social, political, religious, literary, and public figures, especially their hypocrisy, pretension, greed, whatever is eccentric, original, unique. But satire also defends a common core of values that are worth discovering and preserving: writers as diverse as Jonathan Swift, Henry Fielding, Lord Byron, Charles Dickens, Mark Twain, and Jane Austen herself affirmed common sense, good nature, and the capacity for human beings to improve.

Northanger Abbey is partly satirical, partly an historical romance, and partly a novel about growing up. As a satire, it raises questions about education and popular literature, fashion, language, courtship rituals, the church, the military, parenting, the pursuit of happiness. Some characters such as Mrs. Allen and the Thorpes are drawn more satirically than others, as are some scenes such as the conversation on Beechen Cliff, the arrival at Northanger Abbey, or Catherine's snooping around her room. The major satirical element, however, is the narrative voice: a gossip, who filters, conveys, and invents only what interests her, a biased spectator, irreverent, self-referential, judgmental, deflating everyone's self-illusions but her own, comparable to the satiric narrator in Byron's *Don Juan*. Her fashionable preoccupation with time, for example: she keeps schedules, appointments, counts and measures, apologizes for the "compression," the rush toward "perfect felicity," and arrives late to the end of her own novel. Her solemn observation, "Where people wish to attach, they should always be ignorant," that smart women should act dumb, parodies a cliché, attributed variously to Richard Polwhele in *The Unsex'd Females* (1798), to

Mary Wollstonecraft, Frances Burney, Maria Edgeworth, an entire generation whose intelligence and achievements refute it. In the narrative voice, then, it is both bad advice and a parody of the men and women who believe it, in this case the narrator herself—if it is a she.

Even more than Catherine, the narrator loses her way, crosses the line between fiction and reality. "No one," she begins, "who had ever seen Catherine Morland in her infancy, would have supposed her born to be an heroine." But no one had ever seen her at all, at any age; she was fictional. With the first sentence, then, she draws the reader into the dizzy journey crossing arbitrarily and impulsively between history and illusion, between the documentary and the fantastic, between the real buildings and the fabricated lives. A parody of the gothic romance writer, the narrator casts the unlikely Catherine in an heroic role, then expresses contempt at her failure to fulfill it: "A heroine returning, at the close of her career, to her native village, in all the triumph of recovered reputation, and all the dignity of a countess, with a long train of noble relations in their several phaetons, and three waiting-maids in a travelling chaise-and-four, behind her, is an event on which the pen of the contriver may well delight to dwell; it gives credit to every conclusion, and the author must share in the glory she so liberally bestows.—But my affair is widely different." While her homecoming is joyful, her family loving, Catherine becomes "the humiliation of her biographer." Such is the voice that defends the novel and shapes the action, as inept at writing a gothic romance as Catherine was at living one.

Short-sighted, naïve, or sometimes completely mad, unreliable narrators who fail to recognize the point of their own story are a Romantic commonplace—and in this novel especially, the narrator's state of mind and how she views events are as important as the events themselves. Like the narrators in Wordsworth's "The Thorn," or "Peter Bell," or "We are Seven," in Byron's *Don Juan*, or even Coleridge's Ancient Mariner whose lack of understanding and mental fog reduce his entire adventure to a sermon on animal rights, the narrator of *Northanger Abbey* concludes irrelevantly: "I leave it to be settled by whomsoever it may concern, whether the tendency of this work be altogether to recommend parental tyranny, or reward filial disobedience." It may be the ultimate joke that at the very end, Jane Austen shows her narrator to have missed the point of her own story.

Characters

In *Northanger Abbey*, there are no heroes or heroines. It is the lament of the age, when the most admired person in Europe is the demonic Napoleon and all his gothic literary reflections, and the women are most noble when they are most passive and victimized. Overcoming or undermining the narrative voice, Catherine learns that, instead of heroes, the people she knew are "an unequal mixture of good and bad," for there, in "the midland counties of England," unlike the Alps or Pyranees, Italy, Switzerland, the South of France, there is "surely some security for the existence even of a wife not beloved, in the laws of the land, and the manners of the age. Murder was not tolerated, servants were not slaves, and neither poison nor sleeping potions to be procured, like rhubarb, from every druggist." Even the Thorpes, however annoying, are not murderers, and their survival skills are admirable. While John Thorpe's deceit nearly ruined Catherine's life, as his carriage-driving nearly ended it, fiction is built on deceit, and it is an odd flaw for a writer to take exception to. Thorpe provides the essential comic "intrigue," as Hugh Blair, one of Catherine's favorite authors, explained, the source of "something to wish and something to fear" (see footnote 4 on p. 87).

Henry Tilney is an accidental hero, the best one could get, like the accidental heroes in *The Arabian Nights*, in Charles Perrault's fairy tales, or Scott's Waverley: impulsive, often deluded, arbitrary, as addicted to his own false ideals as Catherine is to hers, an accidental husband as well, who gets to marry Catherine when his father allows it, whose idea of marriage is like a country dance, the "principle duties" of which are "fidelity and complaisance," and whose "affection" for Catherine, the narrator says, "originated in nothing better than gratitude, or, in other words, that a persuasion of her partiality for him had been the only cause of giving her a serious thought." Just as his father is a General without a war, he is a clergyman without a religion, as precise about language as his father is about time, as pompous about his fashionable knowledge as his father is about Northanger Abbey.

General Tilney is the contemporary man, the "improver," consumer, who, in a world where "the mere habit of learning to love is the thing," "loved a garden" and "good fruit," who provided his servants with modern stoves and protective overshoes, but a man easily deceived, victimized by both John Thorpe and by Catherine. His believing she is an heiress is no worse than her violating his hospitality by believing he is a murderer. At worst, Catherine concludes, General Tilney is "not perfectly amicable." Other "unequal mixtures," Mr. Morland and Mr. Allen, self-effacing, socially irrelevant, are the "providers," Morland with children, Allen with money. Mrs. Morland, mother of eleven, thinks her daughter Catherine a "sad little shatter-brained creature" who needs to be "contented," and together the Morlands are forgiving, well-read, but "plain matter-of-fact people, who seldom aimed at wit." In the symmetry of the novel, Mrs. Thorpe, widow with seven children, is General Tilney's impoverished counterpart, just as John Thorpe and Isabella are Henry and Eleanor Tilney's counterparts, each with secrets, deceits, delinquencies, and obsessions.

The novel is built on talk: characters are revealed by what they say, by what others say about them, their beliefs and duplicities, the contradictions and revelations. Austen's array of voices is stunning: the narrator's arch commentary, Isabella's hyperbole, Mrs. Allen's prattle, John Thorpe's slang, Henry's picturesque jargon, the brusque General Tilney, Mr. Morland "contented with a pun," the harried Mrs. Morland with her "common-place chatter," believing that some things "are not at all worth understanding." Austen captures the foolish pretension, the mock rituals of Bath-conversation, Henry's critique of women's letters, the "deficiency of subject" and of punctuation (which is a self-parody as well), and everyone's stage-French, another commonplace of the age.

While the narrator and even Catherine's mother question her intelligence, she is smart, quick, spunky, and often insightful: "I cannot speak well enough to be unintelligible," which Henry applauds as "an excellent satire on modern language." In human terms, Catherine is heroic, as most adolescents are, because she endures the dangers of growing up in public, the awkwardness and discomfort of learning her way in an unforgiving social context, dressing "to pass uncensored through the crowd," "looking at everybody and speaking to no one," "fearful of not doing exactly the right thing," as if there were a "right thing" when manners break down and the narrator judges life by novels. Catherine survives and learns because, like Austen herself, she has the gift of mimicry. She assumes the voice of the people she is talking to, adapts to conversations, and knows when to be silent. Blessed with good nature, her "mind warped by an innate principle of general integrity," as Henry says, she can, her parents conclude, "shift for herself." Catherine is capable of pleasure, of delight, prepared to be happy, as she says arriving in Bath, whether she finds a hyacinth or not.

Setting

The two major sites of the story, the historical Bath and the fictional Northanger Abbey, are both new, artificial, and built on ancient ruins. While maps, films, documentaries have reconstructed the streets, architecture, fashions and customs, they have disregarded the quality of life, the atmosphere, as Catherine and Austen herself experienced it. Of the two, Bath was the more menacing; behind the social rituals, the costumes, schedules, and events, decorum had collapsed. Bath was a resort full of temporary residents and temporary identities, a place where people escaped from their "common" lives to heal, mate, win, or die, to see and be seen, or the opposite, disguised by fashions and concealed in status symbols. Rising out of a pit, Bath resembles both an amphitheater, full of actors and illusions, and an underworld, a hell: entering Bath requires a descent into a damp and foggy valley of confusion, disease, theft, prostitution, and fraud, dominated by a cemetery. Like Catherine on Beechen Cliff, dismissing "the whole city of Bath, as unworthy to make part of a landscape," Austen herself was disappointed: "The first view of Bath in fine weather does not answer my expectations; I think I see more distinctly through rain. The sun was got behind everything, and the appearance of the place from the top of Kingsdown was all vapour, shadow, smoke, and confusion" (Letter, May 5, 1801). Northanger Abbey, however, appeared at the end of "a smooth level road of fine gravel, without obstacle, alarm or solemnity," arched windows with clear glass, carpets, wallpaper, a room "the true size for rational happiness," "so modern," "so habitable." The fictional abbey is preferable to the real Bath, limited only by the life it excludes, the poverty and pain outside its walls, and by the warped perceptions it inspires in Catherine and the narrator.

The Romantic Plot

Northanger Abbey has two well-defined plots, depending on how one reads it. First, it imitates and parodies the ancient romance plot, originating in oral traditions, captured in Apuleius's version of "Cupid and Psyche" (see Contexts, p. 202), in *The Arabian Nights*, Perrault's castle tales, in stories of Eve, Pandora, "Blue Beard," "Beauty and the Beast," the eighteenth-century sentimental as well as gothic novel. It reappears in *Alice in Wonderland,* and tales of adolescent awakening such as *The Secret Garden* and *The Wizard of Oz.* Both in the telling and in the action itself, the tale represents a female initiation rite, the awakening of sexuality. Starting with a dead parent, usually a mother, the daughter is abandoned or sent off with a stranger to find a mate, save the harvest, save the family, save her father's soul, driven by curiosity to transgress, cross a boundary, violate a rule, light a candle, open a door, a chest, a closet, and acquire forbidden knowledge, often captured, then challenged, redeemed, and ultimately married. When Henry discovers Catherine poking about his dead mother's room, he denies that "in the country and age in which we live" there is any forbidden knowledge and, by implication, a romance plot.

The second plot is characteristic of Romanticism, first appearing in Goethe's *Sorrows of Young Werther* (1774; 1787), a tale of a sensitive young man suffering from unrequited love who kills himself, setting off a wave of suicides all over Europe. The plot of disappointed expectations took a political turn in the poetry of the 1790's and in nearly all post-war writing, Byron's *Childe Harold,* Cantos III and IV especially, and the post-war gothic novels *Frankenstein, Melmouth the Wanderer,* and *Confessions of a Justified Sinner.* As much a psychological aberration as an emotional one, this plot depicts the idealizing, obsessive, and often gifted, but over-invested individual, imprisoned by his or her thinking, who awakens at some point, literally disenchanted, often dejected, even despondent, an experience Keats captures in an image drawn from the same romances that Jane Austen read: "Charmed magic casements, opening . . . on the foam / Of perilous seas, in faery lands forlorn" (*Ode to a Nightingale*, lines 69–70). With any luck, the adventure ends in reconciliation: Catherine is reconciled to the world she shared with her parents, the "common feelings of common life"; Waverley to "the romance of real life" (see the Contexts selection, p. 262), Wordsworth to "the very world," as he described it in *The Prelude*, "which is the world / Of all of us,—the place in which, in the end, / We find our happiness, or not at all" (1805, 726–28). This plot—expectation, over-investment, and disenchantment—traces not only Catherine's emotional history but also the emotional history of her generation from 1798 to 1818: "The visions of romance were over. Catherine was completely awakened."

Table of Dates

holding salons for the powerful, rich, and accomplished);
William Beckford, *The History of Caliph Vathek*

1787   Jane begins writing sketches and parodies to amuse her
family; Henry goes to Oxford and Frank to the East Indies; Mozart *Don Giovanni;* Charlotte Smith, *The Romance of Real Life,* the first of a dozen novels

1788   Mary Wollstonecraft, *Original Stories from Real Life* (illus. by Blake); Edward Gibbon, *The Decline and Fall of the Roman Empire;* Lord Byron born; George III exhibits signs of mental illness; William Herschel, *Construction of the Heavens*

1789   French Revolution; storming of the Bastille; Erasmus
Darwin, *The Loves of Plants*

1790   William Blake, *The Marriage of Heaven and Hell;* Mary
Wollstonecraft, *Vindication of the Rights of Men;* Edmund Burke, *Reflections on the Revolution in France;*
Ann Radcliffe, *A Sicilian Romance*

1791   Erasmus Darwin, *The Botanic Garden;* Tom Paine, *The Rights of Man,* Part I; Hannah More, *Cheap Repository Tracts;* Priestley's house and laboratory destroyed by mob

1792   William Gilpin, *Essays on Picturesque Beauty;* Wollstonecraft, *A Vindication of the Rights of Woman;*
Paine, *The Rights of Man,* Part II; Percy Shelley born;
Louis XVI and Marie Antoinette arrested; England prepares to invade France

1793   Henry joins Oxfordshire Militia; John Clare born; Louis
XVI executed; England declares war on France; the
Reign of Terror in Paris; trials of suspected radicals, suspension of Habeas Corpus (arrest without trial), suppression of publication; William Godwin, *An Enquiry Concerning Political Justice*

1794   JA in London with Cousin Eliza when her husband is
guillotined; Radcliffe, *The Mysteries of Udolpho;* Godwin, *Caleb Williams;* Blake, *Songs of Innocence and of Experience*

1795   "Elinor and Marianne," later to become *Sense and Sensibility;* flirtation with Tom Lefroy; John Keats and Thomas
Carlyle born; James Hutton, *Theory of the Earth;* militia
mutinies; repressive laws forbidding public meetings

1796   Matthew Gregory Lewis, *The Monk*; Beckford begins building Fonthill Abbey; Napoleon invades Austria and Italy; Spain joins France in war against England

1797   Cadell and Davies reject "First Impressions"; deaths of Edmund Burke and Mary Wollstonecraft; Mary Godwin [later Shelley] born; Radcliffe, *The Italian*; naval mutinies and victories; French land at Fishguard, Wales; JA begins *Sense and Sensibility* (based on "Elinor and Marianne")

1798   JA writes "Susan" (later named "Catherine," finally *Northanger Abbey*); William Wordsworth and Samuel Taylor Coleridge, *Lyrical Ballads*; Joanna Baillie, *Plays on the Passions, I*; Thomas Malthus, *An Essay on Population*; Maria and Thomas Edgeworth, *Practical Education*; Coleridge, *Frost at Midnight*; Charlotte Smith, *The Young Philosopher*; Godwin, *Memoirs* [of Mary Wollstonecraft]; "Monk" Lewis, "Castle Spectre"; George Colman the Younger, "Blue-Beard; or Female Curiosity" (Covent Garden); Haydn's *The Creation*; Jenner's *Essay on Inoculation*; Irish Rebellion; Napoleon invades Egypt, defeated in Battle of the Nile by Nelson; Wordsworth writes "The Ruined Cottage"

1799   JA arrives in Bath, completes "Susan"; Monk Lewis, *Tales of Terror*; Napoleon becomes first Consul; Rosetta stone discovered in Egypt; first income tax to fund war; Aunt Jane Leigh-Perrot charged with theft and jailed in Bath

1800   Father retires as Rector; *Lyrical Ballads*, 2nd ed., with Preface; Mary Robinson, *Lyrical Tales*; Maria Edgeworth, *Castle Rackrent* (the first of a dozen novels); French attempt to invade Ireland; Volta invents first electrical battery

1801   JA and family move to Bath; Henry leaves militia and becomes a banker; Union Jack adopted as flag; first census

1802   JA revises "Susan"; marriage proposal from Harris Bigg-Wither; Peace of Amiens—pause in war; Napoleon made Consul for life; Scott's *Minstrelsy of the Scottish Border*; Telford begins paving roads in Scotland; Apprentices Act restricting child labor to twelve hours a day; Baillie, *Plays of the Passions*, II

1803	JA sells "Susan" to Crosby, a London publisher, for £10; war resumes; Thomas Chatterton's *Collected Works* and Darwin's *The Temple of Nature*
1804	JA begins "The Watsons"; "Twinkle, Twinkle Little Star" in *Original Poetry for Infant Minds* by Ann and Jane Taylor; new fears of invasion, homeguards recruited; Napoleon crowned emperor; Beethoven, *Eroica* Symphony
1805	JA's father dies; Scott, *The Lay of the Last Minstrel*; Wordsworth, *The Prelude* (pub. 1850); Nelson's victory at Trafalgar; France defeats Russia and Austria at Battle of Austerlitz
1806	JA leaves Bath for Adelstrope; Castle Square, Southampton
1807	France invades Spain and Portugal; abolition of slave trade in British colonies; Byron, *Hours of Idleness*; Charles and Mary Lamb, *Tales from Shakespeare*; Charlotte Smith, *"Beachy Head" and Other Poems*; Wordsworth, *Poems in Two Volumes*
1808	The Peninsular War; Scott, *Marmion*; John Dalton's *New System of Chemical Philosophy*; Leigh Hunt founds *The Examiner*
1809	Move to Chawton; writes to Crosby to inquire about "Susan" (*Northanger Abbey*); Paine dies; Duke of Wellington in Spain; French take Vienna; *Quarterly Review* founded; gas lighting in central London; Lamarck suggests theory of evolution, Charles Darwin born; Byron, *English Bards and Scotch Reviewers*
1810	*Sense and Sensibility* completed [in 1795, "Elinor and Marianne"]; George III officially declared insane; Napoleon takes Holland; Scott, *The Lady of the Lake*
1811	*Sense and Sensibility* published anonymously; "First Impressions," 1796–97, becomes *Pride and Prejudice*; begins *Mansfield Park*; Prince of Wales becomes Regent; Shelley, *The Necessity of Atheism*; Luddite riots against machinery and price of bread in Nottingham
1812	*Pride and Prejudice* sold to Egerton; Baillie, *Plays of the Passions* (III); Barbauld, *Eighteen Hundred and Eleven*; Byron, *Childe Harold's Pilgrimage* I and II; Luddite riots, England declares war on U.S.; Napoleon invades Russia, burns Moscow, retreats with massive losses

1813   *Pride and Prejudice* appears and goes to second edition;
        Sense and Sensibility, second edition; Byron, *The Giaour*
        and *The Bride of Abydos*; Wellington victorious in
        Spain, French driven from Holland, Italy, and Switzer-
        land, defeated at Leipzig; Luddites executed

1814   Publishes *Mansfield Park* (Egerton) and begins *Emma*;
        Byron, *The Corsair* and *Lara*; Leigh Hunt, *The Feast of
        the Poets*; Scott, *Waverley*; Wordsworth, *The Excursion;*
        Allies invade France, liberate Paris; peace between
        America and England; Napoleon abdicates and exiled to
        Elba; Stephenson's steam locomotive

1815   *Emma* published; Jane Austen begins *Persuasion*; Byron,
        Hebrew Melodies; Wordsworth, *Poems*; Napoleon es-
        capes, defeated at Waterloo, and exiled to St. Helena

1816   2nd ed. of *Mansfield Park*; first signs of illness; Henry pur-
        chases "Susan" from Crosby, revised and renamed
        "Catherine"; finishes *Persuasion*; Henry's bank fails; post-
        war depression and riots; Byron, *Childe Harold's Pilgrim-
        age III*; Coleridge, *Christabel, Kubla Khan and The Pains
        of Sleep*; Scott, *The Antiquary*; Byron's scandalous separa-
        tion from wife; Shelley's wife commits suicide; Mary God-
        win, Clare Claremont, Byron, Shelley, and Polidori in
        Geneva; Thomas Love Peacock, *Headlong Hall*

1817   JA starts "Sanditon," dies on July 18; Henry arranges
        publication of *Northanger Abbey* and *Persuasion* in De-
        cember; Byron, *Manfred*; Coleridge, *Biographia Liter-
        aria*; *Blackwood's Magazine* founded; William Hazlitt,
        Characters of Shakespeare's Plays; Felicia Hemans,
        Modern Greece; Keats, *Poems*; Southey, *Wat Tyler*; Pea-
        cock, *Melincourt*

1818   *Northanger Abbey* and *Persuasion* published; Byron,
        Childe Harold's Pilgrimage IV; Beppo, writing *Don
        Juan*; Peacock, *Nightmare Abbey*; Keats, *Endymion*;
        Mary Shelley's *Frankenstein*; Bowdler, *The Family
        Shakespeare*; "Monk" Lewis dies

NORTHANGER ABBEY:

AND

PERSUASION.

BY THE AUTHOR OF " PRIDE AND PREJUDICE,"
" MANSFIELD-PARK," &c.

———◆———

WITH A BIOGRAPHICAL NOTICE OF THE
AUTHOR.

════

IN FOUR VOLUMES.

VOL. I.

════

LONDON:

JOHN MURRAY, ALBEMARLE-STREET.

1818.

BIOGRAPHICAL NOTICE
OF THE AUTHOR[1]

The following pages are the production of a pen which has already contributed in no small degree to the entertainment of the public. And when the public, which has not been insensible to the merits of "Sense and Sensibility," "Pride and Prejudice," "Mansfield Park," and "Emma," shall be informed that the hand which guided that pen is now mouldering in the grave, perhaps a brief account of Jane Austen will be read with a kindlier sentiment than simple curiosity.

Short and easy will be the task of the mere biographer. A life of usefulness, literature, and religion, was not by any means a life of event. To those who lament their irreparable loss, it is consolatory to think that, as she never deserved disapprobation, so, in the circle of her family and friends, she never met reproof; that her wishes were not only reasonable, but gratified; and that to the little disappointments incidental to human life was never added, even for a moment, an abatement of good-will from any who knew her.

Jane Austen was born on the 16th of December, 1775, at Steventon, in the county of Hants. Her father was Rector of that parish upwards of forty years. There he resided, in the conscientious and unassisted discharge of his ministerial duties, until he was turned of seventy years. Then he retired with his wife, our authoress, and her sister, to Bath, for the remainder of his life, a period of about four years. Being not only a profound scholar, but possessing a most exquisite taste in every species of literature, it is not wonderful that his daughter Jane should, at a very early age, have become sensible to the charms of style, and enthusiastic in the cultivation of her own language. On the death of her father, she removed, with her mother and sister, for a short time, to Southampton, and finally, in 1809, to the pleasant village of Chawton, in the same county. From this place she sent into the world those novels, which by many have been placed on the same shelf as the works of a D'Arblay and an

---

1. Jane Austen published all her novels anonymously, as many authors did, for example, William Wordsworth and Samuel Coleridge (*Lyrical Ballads* in 1798) and Sir Walter Scott (*Waverley* in 1814). While her authorship was common knowledge, her life was not. In this memoir, her brother Henry, who named and published the novel six months after her death, begins a process of what some biographers have called a "beatification," against which later biographers rebelled.

Edgeworth.[2] Some of these novels had been the gradual performances of her previous life. For though in composition she was equally rapid and correct, yet an invincible distrust of her own judgement induced her to withhold her works from the public, till time and many perusals had satisfied her that the charm of recent composition was dissolved. The natural constitution, the regular habits, the quiet and happy occupations of our authoress, seemed to promise a long succession of amusement to the public, and a gradual increase of reputation to herself. But the symptoms of a decay, deep and incurable, began to show themselves in the commencement of 1816. Her decline was at first deceitfully slow; and until the spring of this present year, those who knew their happiness to be involved in her existence could not endure to despair. But in the month of May, 1817, it was found advisable that she should be removed to Winchester for the benefit of constant medical aid, which none even then dared to hope would be permanently beneficial. She supported, during two months, all the varying pain, irksomeness, and tedium, attendant on decaying nature, with more than resignation, with a truly elastic cheerfulness. She retained her faculties, her memory, her fancy, her temper, and her affections, warm, clear, and unimpaired, to the last. Neither her love of God, nor of her fellow creatures flagged for a moment. She made a point of receiving the sacrament before excessive bodily weakness might have rendered her perception unequal to her wishes. She wrote whilst she could hold a pen, and with a pencil when a pen was become too laborious. The day preceding her death she composed some stanzas replete with fancy and vigour. Her last voluntary speech conveyed thanks to her medical attendant; and to the final question asked of her, purporting to know her wants, she replied, "I want nothing but death."

2. Frances ("Fanny") Burney was among the charming and intelligent London women, known as "Blue Stockings," whose conversation attracted a wide range of writers, actors, and politicians to their salons. She published her first novel, *Evelina*, in 1778, *Cecilia* in 1782, *Camilla* in 1796. Married to General D'Arblay, a French refugee, she was interned in France by Napoleon from 1802 to 1812. The three novels Austen alluded to in *Northanger Abbey* describe the adventures of innocent, beautiful, and intelligent young women as they encounter contemporary society.

Maria Edgeworth was the eldest daughter of Richard Lovell Edgeworth, a rich Irish landowner whose twenty-two children she helped to educate on the innovative schemes published in *Practical Education* (1798). In London, she enjoyed a wide circle of literary acquaintances and published a series of novels starting with the influential *Castle Rackrent* (1800), the first regional and historical novel in English to which Scott, among others, was indebted, and everyone admired.

She expired shortly after, on Friday the 18th of July, 1817, in the arms of her sister, who, as well as the relator of these events, feels too surely that they shall never look upon her like again.

Jane Austen was buried on the 24th of July, 1817, in the cathedral church of Winchester, which, in the whole catalogue of its mighty dead, does not contain the ashes of a brighter genius or a sincerer Christian.

Of personal attractions she possessed a considerable share. Her stature was that of true elegance. It could not have been increased without exceeding the middle height. Her carriage and deportment were quiet, yet graceful. Her features were separately good. Their assemblage produced an unrivalled expression of that cheerfulness, sensibility, and benevolence, which were her real characteristics. Her complexion was of the finest texure. It might with truth be said, that her eloquent blood spoke through her modest cheek. Her voice was extremely sweet. She delivered herself with fluency and precision. Indeed she was formed for elegant and rational society, excelling in conversation as much as in composition. In the present age it is hazardous to mention accomplishments. Our authoress would, probably, have been inferior to few in such acquirements, had she not been so superior to most in higher things. She had not only an excellent taste for drawing, but, in her earlier days, evinced great power of hand in the management of the pencil. Her own musical attainments she held very cheap. Twenty years ago they would have been thought more of, and twenty years hence many a parent will expect their daughters to be applauded for meaner performances. She was fond of dancing, and excelled in it. It remains now to add a few observations on that which her friends deemed more important, on those endowments which sweetened every hour of their lives.

If there be an opinion current in the world, that perfect placidity of temper is not reconcileable to the most lively imagination, and the keenest relish for wit, such an opinion will be rejected for ever by those who have had the happiness of knowing the authoress of the following works. Though the frailties, foibles, and follies of others could not escape her immediate detection, yet even on their vices did she never trust herself to comment with unkindness. The affectation of candour is not uncommon; but she had no affectation. Faultless herself, as nearly as human nature can be, she always sought, in the faults of others, something to excuse, to forgive or forget. Where extenuation was impossible, she had a sure refuge in silence. She never uttered either a hasty, a silly, or a severe expression. In short, her temper was as polished as her wit. Nor were her manners inferior to her temper. They were of the happiest kind. No one could be often in her company without feeling a strong desire of obtaining her friendship, and cherishing a hope of having obtained it. She was tranquil without reserve or stiffness; and communicative without intrusion or self-sufficiency. She became an authoress entirely from taste and inclination. Neither the hope of fame nor profit mixed with her early motives. Most of her works, as before observed, were composed many years previous to their publication. It was with extreme difficulty that her friends, whose partiality she suspected whilst she honoured their judgement, could prevail on her to publish her first work. Nay, so persuaded was she that its sale would not repay the expense of publication, that she actually made a reserve from her very moderate income to meet the expected loss. She could scarcely believe what she termed her great good fortune when "Sense and Sensibility" produced a clear profit of about £150. Few so gifted were so truly unpretending. She regarded the above sum as a prodigious recompense for that which had cost her nothing. Her readers, perhaps, will wonder that such a work produced so little at a time when some authors have received more guineas than they have written lines. The works of our authoress, however, may live as long as those which have burst on the world with more éclat. But the public has not been unjust; and our authoress was far from thinking it so. Most gratifying to her was the applause which from time to time reached her ears from those who were competent to discriminate. Still, in spite of such applause, so much did she shrink from notoriety, that no accumulation of fame would have induced her, had she lived, to affix her name to any productions of her pen. In the bosom of her own family she talked of them freely, thankful for praise, open to remark, and submissive to criticism. But in public she turned away from any allusion to the character of an authoress. She read aloud with very great taste and effect. Her own works, probably, were never heard to so much advantage as from her own mouth; for she partook largely in all the best gifts of the comic muse. She was a warm and judicious admirer of landscape, both in nature and on canvass. At a very early age she was enamoured of

Gilpin on the Picturesque,[3] and she seldom changed her opinions either on books or men.

Her reading was very extensive in history and belles lettres; and her memory extremely tenacious. Her favourite moral writers were Johnson in prose, and Cowper in verse. It is difficult to say at what age she was not intimately acquainted with the merits and defects of the best essays and novels in the English language. Richardson's power of creating, and preserving the consistency of his characters, as particularly exemplified in "Sir Charles Grandison,"[4] gratified the natural discrimination of her mind, whilst her taste secured her from the errors of his prolix style and tedious narrative. She did not rank any work of Fielding quite so high.[5] Without the slightest affectation she recoiled from every thing gross. Neither nature, wit, nor humour, could make her amends for so very low a scale of morals.

Her power of inventing characters seems to have been intuitive, and almost unlimited. She drew from nature; but, whatever may have been surmised to the contrary, never from individuals.

The style of her familiar correspondence was in all respects the same as that of her novels. Every thing came finished from her pen; for on all subjects she had ideas as clear as her expressions were well chosen. It is not hazarding too much to say that she never dispatched a note or letter unworthy of publication.

One trait only remains to be touched on. It makes all others unimportant. She was thoroughly religious and devout; fearful of giving offence to God, and incapable of feeling it towards any fellow creature. On serious subjects she was well-instructed, both by reading and meditation, and her opinions accorded strictly with those of our Established Church.

London, Dec. 13, 1817.

---

3. *Three Essays: On Picturesque Beauty; on Picturesque Travel; and on Sketching Landscape* (1792) along with Gilpin's successive tours were the main source for the picturesque mania that Austen parodies in both *Sense and Sensibility* and in *Northanger Abbey* (see Contexts, p. 270).

4. *Charles Grandison* (1754), a novel by Samuel Richardson that Catherine Morland claims her mother admires, depicts a "Good Man," comparable to the virtuous women Richardson wrote about in *Clarissa* and *Pamela*. In what reads like a parody, Jane Austen dramatized it for family performances.

5. Henry Fielding, author of *Tom Jones* (1749), considered the first modern English novelist. His comic epics both influenced and alienated subsequent writers. Jane Austen uses James Thorpe's preference for Fielding, and for Matthew Gregory Lewis's *The Monk* (see Contexts, p. 218), as an index to his low character and taste.

POSTSCRIPT

Since concluding the above remarks, the writer of them has been put in possession of some extracts from the private correspondence of the authoress. They are few and short; but are submitted to the public without apology, as being more truly descriptive of her temper, taste, feelings, and principles than any thing which the pen of a biographer can produce.

The first extract is a playful defence of herself from a mock charge of having pilfered the manuscripts of a young relation.

"What should I do, my dearest E. with your manly, vigorous sketches, so full of life and spirit? How could I possibly join them on to a little bit of ivory, two inches wide, on which I work with a brush so fine as to produce little effect after much labour?"

The remaining extracts are from various parts of a letter written a few weeks before her death.

"My attendant is encouraging, and talks of making me quite well. I live chiefly on the sofa, but am allowed to walk from one room to the other. I have been out once in a sedan-chair, and am to repeat it, and be promoted to a wheel-chair as the weather serves. On this subject I will only say further that my dearest sister, my tender, watchful, indefatigable nurse, has not been made ill by her exertions. As to what I owe to her, and to the anxious affection of all my beloved family on this occasion, I can only cry over it, and pray to God to bless them more and more."

She next touches with just and gentle animadversion on a subject of domestic disappointment. Of this the particulars do not concern the public. Yet in justice to her characteristic sweetness and resignation, the concluding observation of our authoress thereon must not be suppressed.

"But I am getting too near complaint. It has been the appointment of God, however secondary causes may have operated."

The following and final extract will prove the facility with which she could correct every impatient thought, and turn from complaint to cheerfulness.

"You will find Captain————a very respectable, well-meaning man, without much manner, his wife and sister all good humour and obligingness, and I hope (since the fashion allows it) with rather longer petticoats than last year."

London, Dec. 20, 1817.

ADVERTISEMENT,
BY THE AUTHORESS,
TO
NORTHANGER ABBEY.

This little work was finished in the year 1803, and intended for immediate publication. It was disposed of to a bookseller, it was even advertised, and why the business proceeded no farther, the author has never been able to learn. That any bookseller should think it worth while to purchase what he did not think it worth while to publish seems extraordinary. But with this, neither the author nor the public have any other concern than as some observation is necessary upon those parts of the work which thirteen years have made comparatively obsolete. The public are entreated to bear in mind that thirteen years have passed since it was finished, many more since it was begun, and that during that period, places, manners, books, and opinions have undergone considerable changes.

VOLUME I

CHAPTER I

No one who had ever seen Catherine Morland in her infancy, would have supposed her born to be an heroine. Her situation in life, the character of her father and mother, her own person and disposition, were all equally against her. Her father was a clergyman, without being neglected, or poor, and a very respectable man, though his name was Richard[1]—and he had never been handsome. He had a considerable independence, besides two good livings[2]—and he was not in the least addicted to locking up his daughters. Her mother was a woman of useful plain sense, with a good temper, and, what is more remarkable, with a good constitution. She had three sons before Catherine was born; and instead of

---

1. According to most editors, an obscure family joke but also a common name with no gothic associations.

2. A "living" is the house and income from the attached land granted to a clergyman in exchange for service during his lifetime. Given Austen's many associations with the church (her father, two brothers, cousins), clerical allusions are part of her vocabulary.

dying in bringing the latter into the world, as any body might expect, she still lived on—lived to have six children more—to see them growing up around her, and to enjoy excellent health herself. A family of ten children will be always called a fine family, where there are heads and arms and legs enough for the number; but the Morlands had little other right to the word, for they were in general very plain, and Catherine, for many years of her life, as plain as any. She had a thin awkward figure, a sallow skin without colour, dark lank hair, and strong features;—so much for her person;—and not less unpropitious for heroism seemed her mind. She was fond of all boys' plays, and greatly preferred cricket[3] not merely to dolls, but to the more heroic enjoyments of infancy, nursing a dormouse, feeding a canary-bird, or watering a rose-bush. Indeed she had no taste for a garden; and if she gathered flowers at all, it was chiefly for the pleasure of mischief—at least so it was conjectured from her always preferring those which she was forbidden to take.—Such were her propensities—her abilities were quite as extraordinary. She never could learn or understand any thing before she was taught; and sometimes not even then, for she was often inattentive, and occasionally stupid. Her mother was three months in teaching her only to repeat the "Beggar's Petition;"[4] and after all, her next sister, Sally, could say it better than she did. Not that Catherine was always stupid,—by no means; she learnt the fable of "The Hare and many Friends,"[5] as quickly as any girl in England. Her mother wished her to learn music; and Catherine was sure she should like it, for she was very fond of tinkling the keys of the old forlorn spinnet;[6] so, at eight years old she began. She learnt a year, and could not bear it;—and Mrs. Morland, who did

3. Games. Cricket is a traditional field sport originating in France in the sixteenth century, formalized into a competitive team sport comparable to American baseball.

4. A poem by Rev. Thomas Moss in *Poems on Several Occasions* (1769). The sources for the poems in this chapter as well as for Shakespeare were more likely to be from the gothic novels that Catherine read than from the originals. Gothic heroines, especially in Ann Radcliffe's novels, often quoted these authors (Pearson 101).

5. A tale in John Gay's *Fables* (1727) about a hare whose friends desert him when he is pursued by hounds.

6. Common in the eighteenth-century parlor, a spinnet was an oblong-shaped musical instrument, similar to a piano except that the mechanism plucked the strings instead of hitting them with a small hammer, such as the modern piano or the pianoforte that Jane Austen herself played.

not insist on her daughters being accomplished in spite of incapacity or distaste, allowed her to leave off. The day which dismissed the music-master was one of the happiest of Catherine's life. Her taste for drawing was not superior; though whenever she could obtain the outside of a letter from her mother, or seize upon any other odd piece of paper, she did what she could in that way, by drawing houses and trees, hens and chickens, all very much like one another.—Writing and accounts[7] she was taught by her father; French by her mother: her proficiency in either was not remarkable, and she shirked her lessons in both whenever she could. What a strange, unaccountable character!—for with all these symptoms of profligacy at ten years old, she had neither a bad heart nor a bad temper; was seldom stubborn, scarcely ever quarrelsome, and very kind to the little ones, with few interruptions of tyranny; she was moreover noisy and wild, hated confinement and cleanliness, and loved nothing so well in the world as rolling down the green slope at the back of the house.

Such was Catherine Morland at ten. At fifteen, appearances were mending; she began to curl her hair and long for balls; her complexion improved, her features were softened by plumpness and colour, her eyes gained more animation, and her figure more consequence. Her love of dirt gave way to an inclination for finery, and she grew clean as she grew smart; she had now the pleasure of sometimes hearing her father and mother remark on her personal improvement. "Catherine grows quite a good-looking girl,—she is almost pretty to day," were words which caught her ears now and then; and how welcome were the sounds! To look *almost* pretty, is an acquisition of higher delight to a girl who has been looking plain the first fifteen years of her life, than a beauty from her cradle can ever receive.

Mrs. Morland was a very good woman, and wished to see her children every thing they ought to be; but her time was so much occupied in lying-in and teaching the little ones, that her elder daughters were inevitably left to shift for themselves; and it was not very wonderful that Catherine, who had by nature nothing heroic about her, should prefer cricket, base ball, riding on horseback, and

---

7. Keeping "accounts" meant managing household money, showing that women had major financial responsibility in the financial affairs of the household.

running about the country at the age of fourteen, to books—or at least books of information—for, provided that nothing like useful knowledge could be gained from them, provided they were all story and no reflection, she had never any objection to books at all. But from fifteen to seventeen she was in training for a heroine; she read all such works as heroines must read to supply their memories with those quotations which are so serviceable and so soothing in the vicissitudes of their eventful lives.

From Pope, she learnt to censure those who

"bear about the mockery of woe."[8]

From Gray, that

"Many a flower is born to blush unseen,
"And waste its fragrance on the desert air."[9]

From Thompson, that

——"It is a delightful task
"To teach the young idea how to shoot."[10]

And from Shakspeare she gained a great store of information— amongst the rest, that

——"Trifles light as air,
"Are, to the jealous, confirmation strong,
"As proofs of Holy Writ."[11]

---

8. Alexander Pope, "Elegy to the Memory of an Unfortunate Lady" (1717), line 57.

9. Thomas Gray, "Elegy Written in a Country Churchyard" (1751), lines 55–56.

10. James Thomson, "The Seasons," adapted from "Spring" (1728), lines 1149–50. Like the other poems Catherine quotes, this one, in spite of the season, is preoccupied with death, loss, misery, deprivation, and was designed to awaken one's feelings for the landscape and for one's fellow human beings. Commonly cited in the popular novels of the day, and, out of context, the lines she learns have little to do with the pathos of the original poems.

11. Shakespeare, *Othello*, 3.2.322–24. Popular novels often quoted Shakespeare using collections of isolated quotes, or "beauties." Given Catherine's limited intellectual range, it is unlikely that she would have read or be allowed to read *Othello*.

That

> "The poor beetle, which we tread upon,
> "In corporal sufferance feels a pang as great
> "As when a giant dies."[12]

And that a young woman in love always looks

> ——"like Patience on a monument
> "Smiling at Grief."[13]

So far her improvement was sufficient—and in many other points she came on exceedingly well; for though she could not write sonnets, she brought herself to read them; and though there seemed no chance of her throwing a whole party into raptures by a prelude on the pianoforte, of her own composition, she could listen to other people's performance with very little fatigue. Her greatest deficiency was in the pencil—she had no notion of drawing—not enough even to attempt a sketch of her lover's profile, that she might be detected in the design. There she fell miserably short of the true heroic height. At present she did not know her own poverty, for she had no lover to portray. She had reached the age of seventeen, without having seen one amiable youth who could call forth her sensibility, without having excited one real passion, and without having excited even any admiration but what was very moderate and very transient. This was strange indeed! But strange things may be generally accounted for if their cause be fairly searched out. There was not one lord in the neighbourhood; no—not even a baronet. There was not one family among their acquaintance who had reared and supported a boy accidentally found at their door—not one young man whose origin was unknown. Her father had no ward, and the squire of the parish no children.

But when a young lady is to be a heroine, the perverseness of forty surrounding families cannot prevent her. Something must and will happen to throw a hero in her way.

---

12. Shakespeare, *Measure for Measure*, 3.1.78–80.
13. Shakespeare, *Twelfth Night*, 2.4.114–15.

Mr. Allen, who owned the chief of the property about Fullerton, the village in Wiltshire where the Morlands lived, was ordered to Bath for the benefit of a gouty constitution;[14]—and his lady, a good-humoured woman, fond of Miss Morland, and probably aware that if adventures will not befall a young lady in her own village, she must seek them abroad, invited her to go with them. Mr. and Mrs. Morland were all compliance, and Catherine all happiness.

CHAPTER II

In addition to what has been already said of Catherine Morland's personal and mental endowments, when about to be launched into all the difficulties and dangers of a six weeks' residence in Bath, it may be stated, for the reader's more certain information, lest the following pages should otherwise fail of giving any idea of what her character is meant to be; that her heart was affectionate, her disposition cheerful and open, without conceit or affectation of any kind—her manners just removed from the awkwardness and shyness of a girl; her person pleasing, and, when in good looks, pretty—and her mind about as ignorant and uninformed as the female mind at seventeen usually is.

When the hour of departure drew near, the maternal anxiety of Mrs. Morland will be naturally supposed to be most severe. A thousand alarming presentiments of evil to her beloved Catherine from this terrific separation must oppress her heart with sadness, and drown her in tears for the last day or two of their being together; and advice of the most important and applicable nature must of course flow from her wise lips in their parting conference in her closet. Cautions against the violence of such noblemen and baronets as delight in forcing young ladies away to some remote farm-house, must, at such a moment, relieve the fulness of her heart. Who would not think so? But Mrs. Morland knew so little of lords and baronets, that she entertained no notion of their general mischievousness, and was wholly unsuspicious of danger to her daughter from their machinations. Her cautions were confined to

14. Gout is a painful inflammation of the small joints, often starting with the big toe, associated with rich and idle men and believed to be caused by excessive eating and drinking, often depicted comically.

the following points. "I beg, Catherine, you will always wrap your-self up very warm about the throat, when you come from the Rooms at night; and I wish you would try to keep some account of the money you spend;—I will give you this little book on purpose."

Sally, or rather Sarah, (for what young lady of common gentil-ity will reach the age of sixteen without altering her name as far as she can?) must from situation be at this time the intimate friend and confidante of her sister. It is remarkable, however, that she nei-ther insisted on Catherine's writing by every post, nor exacted her promise of transmitting the character of every new acquaintance, nor a detail of every interesting conversation that Bath might pro-duce. Every thing indeed relative to this important journey was done, on the part of the Morlands, with a degree of moderation and composure, which seemed rather consistent with the common feelings of common life, than with the refined susceptibilities, the tender emotions which the first separation of a heroine from her family ought always to excite. Her father, instead of giving her an unlimited order on his banker, or even putting an hundred pounds bank-bill into her hands, gave her only ten guineas,[1] and promised her more when she wanted it.

Under these unpromising auspices, the parting took place, and the journey began. It was performed with suitable quietness and unevent-ful safety. Neither robbers nor tempests befriended them, nor one lucky overturn to introduce them to the hero. Nothing more alarming occurred than a fear on Mrs. Allen's side, of having once left her clogs behind her at an inn, and that fortunately proved to be groundless.

They arrived at Bath. Catherine was all eager delight;—her eyes were here, there, every where, as they approached its fine and strik-ing environs, and afterwards drove through those streets which conducted them to the hotel. She was come to be happy, and she felt happy already.

They were soon settled in comfortable lodgings in Pulteney-street.

---

1. A guinea is £1.1s (one pound and one shilling), a pound converting to around $1.75 in 2003, a shilling to 25 cents. In terms of value, Murray (Chapter 4), among others, suggests multiplying by fifty: Jane Austen sold her pianoforte in 1801 for eight guineas, the original manuscript of *Northanger Abbey*, then called "Susan," in 1803, for ten pounds (about $175.00 then, $9,000 now). An average novel, in multi-volumes, in the 1790's would cost about fifteen pounds ($2,525.00 in a mod-ern conversion) the same as seven cloaks or ten pair of shoes. So, Catherine's father gave her about $200 then ($10,000 now) a generous gift, a good investment if the goal was for Catherine to meet a husband.

It is now expedient to give some description of Mrs. Allen, that the reader may be able to judge, in what manner her actions will hereafter tend to promote the general distress of the work, and how she will, probably, contribute to reduce poor Catherine to all the desperate wretchedness of which a last volume is capable—whether by her imprudence, vulgarity, or jealousy—whether by intercepting her letters, ruining her character, or turning her out of doors.

Mrs. Allen was one of that numerous class of females, whose society can raise no other emotion than surprise at there being any men in the world who could like them well enough to marry them. She had neither beauty, genius, accomplishment, nor manners. The air of a gentlewoman, a great deal of quiet, inactive good temper, and a trifling turn of mind, were all that could account for her being the choice of a sensible, intelligent man, like Mr. Allen. In one respect she was admirably fitted to introduce a young lady into public, being as fond of going every where and seeing every thing herself as any young lady could be. Dress was her passion. She had a most harmless delight in being fine; and our heroine's *entrée*[2] into life could not take place till after three or four days had been spent in learning what was mostly worn, and her *chaperon*[3] was provided with a dress of the newest fashion. Catherine too made some purchases herself, and when all these matters were arranged, the important evening came which was to usher her into the Upper Rooms.[4] Her hair was cut and dressed by the best hand, her clothes put on with care, and both Mrs. Allen and her maid declared she looked quite as

2. *Entrée* means "entrance," the passage of a young person from domestic family life to a public one, the courtship and mating rituals that followed. Most French terms have common and obvious English counterparts. In popular novels and on the stage, these French phrases identify those who are pretentious rather than educated. In her letters, Austen uses French terms to parody herself, or to be secretive (alluding to letters from her brother who was in the navy). Ironically, the British middle classes, whose sons were fighting in the war against France, used French as a sign of accomplishment, even copying French fashions from the aristocratic refugees who had fled to England. Although the French were defeated on the battlefield, they conquered the English in the parlor with their language, fashions, and manners. On the stage, however, the French were often depicted as servants, comic buffoons.

3. The idea that a young single girl needed the company of an older woman or brother, a *chaperon,* to protect her was common among the upper classes before the 1780's and returned in the 1830's. But, during Jane Austen's lifetime, manners were as easy and relaxed as the revealing clothes and public sexuality of the upper classes. A *chaperon* would have been pretentious and probably served as merely an escort or, like Mrs. Allen, someone to help find eligible gentlemen.

4. The newer assembly rooms to the north on high ground.

•

she should do. With such encouragement, Catherine hoped at least to pass uncensured through the crowd. As for admiration, it was always very welcome when it came, but she did not depend on it.

Mrs. Allen was so long in dressing that they did not enter the ballroom till late. The season was full,[5] the room crowded, and the two ladies squeezed in as well as they could. As for Mr. Allen, he repaired directly to the card-room, and left them to enjoy a mob by themselves. With more care for the safety of her new gown than for the comfort of her *protegée*,[6] Mrs. Allen made her way through the throng of men by the door, as swiftly as the necessary caution would allow; Catherine, however, kept close at her side, and linked her arm too firmly within her friend's to be torn asunder by any common effort of a struggling assembly. But to her utter amazement she found that to proceed along the room was by no means the way to disengage themselves from the crowd; it seemed rather to increase as they went on, whereas she had imagined that when once fairly within the door, they should easily find seats and be able to watch the dances with perfect convenience. But this was far from being the case, and though by unwearied diligence they gained even the top of the room, their situation was just the same; they saw nothing of the dancers but the high feathers of some of the ladies. Still they moved on—something better was yet in view; and by a continued exertion of strength and ingenuity they found themselves at last in the passage behind the highest bench. Here there was something less of crowd than below; and hence Miss Morland had a comprehensive view of all the company beneath her, and of all the dangers of her late passage through them. It was a splendid sight, and she began, for the first time that evening, to feel herself at a ball: she longed to dance, but she had not an acquaintance in the room. Mrs. Allen did all that she could do in such a case by saying very placidly, every now and then, "I wish you could dance, my dear,—I wish you could get a partner." For some time her young friend felt obliged to her for these wishes; but they were repeated so often, and proved so totally ineffectual, that Catherine grew tired at last, and would thank her no more.

They were not long able, however, to enjoy the repose of the eminence they had so laboriously gained.—Every body was shortly

5. At the height of the season.

6. A *protegée* is normally a female disciple, here used ironically; Mrs. Allen as more concerned with her gown than with her pupil.

in motion for tea, and they must squeeze out like the rest. Catherine began to feel something of disappointment—she was tired of being continually pressed against by people, the generality of whose faces possessed nothing to interest, and with all of whom she was so wholly unacquainted, that she could not relieve the irksomeness of imprisonment by the exchange of a syllable with any of her fellow captives; and when at last arrived in the tea-room, she felt yet more the awkwardness of having no party to join, no acquaintance to claim, no gentleman to assist them.—They saw nothing of Mr. Allen; and after looking about them in vain for a more eligible situation, were obliged to sit down at the end of a table, at which a large party were already placed, without having any thing to do there, or any body to speak to, except each other.

Mrs. Allen congratulated herself, as soon as they were seated, on having preserved her gown from injury. "It would have been very shocking to have it torn," said she, "would not it?—It is such a delicate muslin.—For my part I have not seen any thing I like so well in the whole room, I assure you."

"How uncomfortable it is," whispered Catherine, "not to have a single acquaintance here!"

"Yes, my dear," replied Mrs. Allen, with perfect serenity, "it is very uncomfortable indeed."

"What shall we do?—The gentlemen and ladies at this table look as if they wondered why we came here—we seem forcing ourselves into their party."

"Aye, so we do.—That is very disagreeable. I wish we had a large acquaintance here."

"I wish we had *any*;—it would be somebody to go to."

"Very true, my dear; and if we knew anybody we would join them directly. The Skinners were here last year—I wish they were here now."

"Had not we better go away as it is?—Here are no tea things for us, you see."

"No more there are, indeed.—How very provoking! But I think we had better sit still, for one gets so tumbled in such a crowd! How is my head, my dear?—Somebody gave me a push that has hurt it I am afraid."

"No, indeed, it looks very nice.—But, dear Mrs. Allen, are you sure there is nobody you know in all this multitude of people? I think you *must* know somebody."

"I don't upon my word—I wish I did. I wish I had a large acquaintance here with all my heart, and then I should get you a partner.—I should be so glad to have you dance. There goes a strange-looking woman! What an odd gown she has got on!—How old-fashioned it is! Look at the back."

After some time they received an offer of tea from one of their neighbours; it was thankfully accepted, and this introduced a light conversation with the gentleman who offered it, which was the only time that any body spoke to them during the evening, till they were discovered and joined by Mr. Allen when the dance was over.

"Well, Miss Morland," said he, directly, "I hope you have had an agreeable ball."

"Very agreeable indeed," she replied, vainly endeavouring to hide a great yawn.

"I wish she had been able to dance," said his wife, "I wish we could have got a partner for her.—I have been saying how glad I should be if the Skinners were here this winter instead of last; or if the Parrys had come, as they talked of once, she might have danced with George Parry. I am so sorry she has not had a partner!"

"We shall do better another evening I hope," was Mr. Allen's consolation.

The company began to disperse when the dancing was over—enough to leave space for the remainder to walk about in some comfort; and now was the time for a heroine, who had not yet played a very distinguished part in the events of the evening, to be noticed and admired. Every five minutes, by removing some of the crowd, gave greater openings for her charms. She was now seen by many young men who had not been near her before. Not one, however, started with rapturous wonder on beholding her, no whisper of eager inquiry ran round the room, nor was she once called a divinity by any body. Yet Catherine was in very good looks, and had the company only seen her three years before, they would *now* have thought her exceedingly handsome.

She *was* looked at however, and with some admiration; for, in her own hearing, two gentlemen pronounced her to be a pretty girl. Such words had their due effect; she immediately thought the evening pleasanter than she had found it before—her humble vanity was contented—she felt more obliged to the two young men for this simple praise than a true quality heroine would have been for fifteen sonnets in celebration of her charms, and went to her chair[7] in good humour with every body, and perfectly satisfied with her share of public attention.

CHAPTER III

Every morning now brought its regular duties;—shops were to be visited; some new part of the town to be looked at; and the Pump-room to be attended, where they paraded up and down for an hour, looking at every body and speaking to no one. The wish of a numerous acquaintance in Bath was still uppermost with Mrs. Allen, and she repeated it after every fresh proof, which every morning brought, of her knowing nobody at all.

They made their appearance in the Lower Rooms;[1] and here fortune was more favourable to our heroine. The master of the ceremonies[2] introduced to her a very gentlemanlike young man as a partner;—his name was Tilney. He seemed to be about four or five and twenty, was rather tall, had a pleasing countenance, a very intelligent and lively eye, and, if not quite handsome, was very near it. His address was good, and Catherine felt herself in high luck. There was little leisure for speaking while they danced; but when they were seated at tea, she found him as agreeable as she had already given him credit for being. He talked with fluency and spirit—and there was an archness and pleasantry in his manner which interested, though it was hardly understood by her. After chatting some time on such matters as naturally arose from the objects around them, he suddenly addressed her with—"I have hitherto been very remiss, madam, in the proper attentions of a partner here; I have not yet asked you how long you have been in Bath; whether you were

---

7. A "chair" is a sedan-chair, a box large enough to seat two people carried by footmen, front and back, holding long poles attached to each side. For privacy, the occupant could close curtains on the windows. Because of the narrow slippery streets in Bath, they were preferable to horse-drawn carriages.

---

1. The smaller and older assembly rooms located close to the center of Bath.

2. Master of Ceremonies was a gentleman elected to meet every visitor and make appropriate introductions. One of the authentic historical allusions, Mr. James King was Master in the Lower Rooms from 1785 to 1805, when he was elected Master of the Upper Rooms.

ever here before; whether you have been at the Upper Rooms, the theatre, and the concert; and how you like the place altogether. I have been very negligent—but are you now at leisure to satisfy me in these particulars? If you are I will begin directly."

"You need not give yourself that trouble, sir."

"No trouble I assure you, madam." Then forming his features into a set smile, and affectedly softening his voice, he added, with a simpering air, "Have you been long in Bath, madam?"

"About a week, sir," replied Catherine, trying not to laugh.

"Really!" with affected astonishment.

"Why should you be surprized, sir?"

"Why, indeed!" said he, in his natural tone—"but some emotion must appear to be raised by your reply, and surprize is more easily assumed, and not less reasonable than any other.—Now let us go on. Were you never here before, madam?"

"Never, sir."

"Indeed! Have you yet honoured the Upper Rooms?"

"Yes, sir, I was there last Monday."

"Have you been to the theatre?"

"Yes, sir, I was at the play on Tuesday."

"To the concert?"

"Yes, sir, on Wednesday."

"And are you altogether pleased with Bath?"

"Yes—I like it very well."

"Now I must give one smirk, and then we may be rational again."

Catherine turned away her head, not knowing whether she might venture to laugh.

"I see what you think of me," said he gravely—"I shall make but a poor figure in your journal to-morrow."

"My journal!"

"Yes, I know exactly what you will say: Friday, went to the Lower Rooms; wore my sprigged muslin[3] robe with blue trimmings—plain

3. Muslins were thin fabrics, also called "gauze," originally imported from India but, with the rise of the textile industry in the north of England, they became inexpensive and common, not requiring much experience to "understand." To achieve the fashionably clinging and revealing effect, women would soak the fabric and allow it to dry on their bodies. In March 9, 1814, in spite of the weather, and having a cold, Jane wore her "gauze gown," with only the concession of long sleeves, which she hoped would be "allowable": "I have lowered the bosom, especially at the corners, and plaited black satin ribbon around the top. Such will be my costume of vine-leaves and paste" (Letter to Cassandra).

black shoes—appeared to much advantage; but was strangely harassed by a queer, half-witted man, who would make me dance with him, and distressed me by his nonsense."

"Indeed I shall say no such thing."

"Shall I tell you what you ought to say?"

"If you please."

"I danced with a very agreeable young man, introduced by Mr. King; had a great deal of conversation with him—seems a most extraordinary genius—hope I may know more of him. *That*, madam, is what I *wish* you to say."

"But, perhaps, I keep no journal."

"Perhaps you are not sitting in this room, and I am not sitting by you. These are points in which a doubt is equally possible. Not keep a journal! How are your absent cousins to understand the tenour of your life in Bath without one? How are the civilities and compliments of every day to be related as they ought to be, unless noted down every evening in a journal? How are your various dresses to be remembered, and the particular state of your complexion, and curl of your hair to be described in all their diversities, without having constant recourse to a journal?—My dear madam, I am not so ignorant of young ladies' ways as you wish to believe me; it is this delightful habit of journalizing which largely contributes to form the easy style of writing for which ladies are so generally celebrated. Every body allows that the talent of writing agreeable letters is peculiarly female. Nature may have done something, but I am sure it must be essentially assisted by the practice of keeping a journal."

"I have sometimes thought," said Catherine, doubtingly, "whether ladies do write so much better letters than gentlemen! That is—I should not think the superiority was always on our side."

"As far as I have had opportunity of judging, it appears to me that the usual style of letter-writing among women is faultless, except in three particulars."

"And what are they?"

"A general deficiency of subject, a total inattention to stops,[4] and a very frequent ignorance of grammar."

---

4. "Stops" refer to punctuation. This discussion is a self-parody: Austen wrote voluminous letters and framed her early works in the popular epistolary form, as a collection of letters.

"Upon my word! I need not have been afraid of disclaiming the compliment. You do not think too highly of us in that way."

"I should no more lay it down as a general rule that women write better letters than men, than that they sing better duets, or draw better landscapes. In every power, of which taste is the foundation, excellence is pretty fairly divided between the sexes."

They were interrupted by Mrs. Allen:—"My dear Catherine," said she, "do take this pin out of my sleeve; I am afraid it has torn a hole already; I shall be quite sorry if it has, for this is a favourite gown, though it cost but nine shillings a yard."

"That is exactly what I should have guessed it, madam," said Mr. Tilney, looking at the muslin.

"Do you understand muslins, sir?"

"Particularly well; I always buy my own cravats,[5] and am allowed to be an excellent judge; and my sister has often trusted me in the choice of a gown. I bought one for her the other day, and it was pronounced to be a prodigious bargain by every lady who saw it. I gave but five shillings a yard for it, and a true Indian muslin."

Mrs. Allen was quite struck by his genius. "Men commonly take so little notice of those things," said she: "I can never get Mr. Allen to know one of my gowns from another. You must be a great comfort to your sister, sir."

"I hope I am, madam."

"And pray, sir, what do you think of Miss Morland's gown?"

"It is very pretty, madam," said he, gravely examining it; "but I do not think it will wash well; I am afraid it will fray."

"How can you," said Catherine, laughing, "be so——" she had almost said, strange.

"I am quite of your opinion, sir," replied Mrs. Allen; "and so I told Miss Morland when she bought it."

"But then you know, madam, muslin always turns to some account or other; Miss Morland will get enough out of it for a handkerchief, or a cap, or a cloak.—Muslin can never be said to be wasted. I have heard my sister say so forty times, when she has

5. A long white muslin or linen scarf intricately tied around the neck, in 1798, part of the costume of the young, but by 1817, associated with the decadent Beau Brummel and the Prince Regent whose followers were called *dandies*. Their look consisted of leggings, a buff-colored waistcoat, a black frock coat cut high to the waist in front, a voluminous cravat that wound high on their necks, a tall stove-pipe hat, gloves, shiny boots during the day, buckled pumps at night. (See illustration, p. 236.)

been extravagant in buying more than she wanted, or careless in cutting it to pieces."

"Bath is a charming place, sir; there are so many good shops here.—We are sadly off in the country; not but what we have very good shops in Salisbury, but it is so far to go;—eight miles is a long way; Mr. Allen says it is nine, measured nine; but I am sure it cannot be more than eight; and it is such a fag[6]—I come back tired to death. Now here one can step out of doors and get a thing in five minutes."

Mr. Tilney was polite enough to seem interested in what she said; and she kept him on the subject of muslins till the dancing recommenced. Catherine feared, as she listened to their discourse, that he indulged himself a little too much with the foibles of others.—"What are you thinking of so earnestly?" said he, as they walked back to the ball-room;—"not of your partner, I hope, for, by that shake of the head, your meditations are not satisfactory."

Catherine coloured, and said, "I was not thinking of any thing."

"That is artful and deep, to be sure; but I had rather be told at once that you will not tell me."

"Well then, I will not."

"Thank you; for now we shall soon be acquainted, as I am authorized to tease you on this subject whenever we meet, and nothing in the world advances intimacy so much."

They danced again; and, when the assembly closed, parted, on the lady's side at least, with a strong inclination for continuing the acquaintance. Whether she thought of him so much, while she drank her warm wine and water, and prepared herself for bed, as to dream of him when there, cannot be ascertained; but I hope it was no more than in a slight slumber or a morning doze at most; for if it be true, as a celebrated writer has maintained, that no young lady can be justified in falling in love before the gentleman's love is declared,[7] it

---

6. Bath was famous for its shops, which grew up instantly to serve the large transient population and sold notoriously shabby merchandise. "Fag" is contemporary slang for hard work, drudgery, toil, or the person who engages in it. Mrs. Allen is exhausted from riding nine miles in a carriage. The combination of slang, literary language, and French was both fashionable and affected.

7. According to Austen's note, the source is Samuel Richardson, *The Rambler* (1751): "That a young lady should be in love, and the love of a young gentleman undeclared, is an heterodoxy which prudence, and even policy, must not allow." [Vide a letter from Mr. Richardson, No. 97, Vol. ii. Rambler.]

must be very improper that a young lady should dream of a gentleman before the gentleman is first known to have dreamt of her. How proper Mr. Tilney might be as a dreamer or a lover, had not yet perhaps entered Mr. Allen's head, but that he was not objectionable as a common acquaintance for his young charge he was on inquiry satisfied; for he had early in the evening taken pains to know who her partner was, and had been assured of Mr. Tilney's being a clergyman, and of a very respectable family in Gloucestershire.

CHAPTER IV

With more than usual eagerness did Catherine hasten to the Pump-room[1] the next day, secure within herself of seeing Mr. Tilney there before the morning were over, and ready to meet him with a smile:—but no smile was demanded—Mr. Tilney did not appear. Every creature in Bath, except himself, was to be seen in the room at different periods of the fashionable hours; crowds of people were every moment passing in and out, up the steps and down; people whom nobody cared about, and nobody wanted to see; and he only was absent. "What a delightful place Bath is," said Mrs. Allen, as they sat down near the great clock, after parading the room till they were tired; "and how pleasant it would be if we had any acquaintance here."

This sentiment had been uttered so often in vain, that Mrs. Allen had no particular reason to hope it would be followed with more advantage now; but we are told to "despair of nothing we would attain," as "unwearied diligence our point would gain;"[2] and the unwearied diligence with which she had every day wished for the same thing was at length to have its just reward, for hardly had she been seated ten minutes before a lady of about her own

1. The social heart of Bath, the Pump Room was a large, elegant new building, finished in 1795 in the Palladian style, with a covered walkway, next to the ancient Abbey courtyard. Drawing on the same thermal springs as the ancient baths, both invalids and socialites visited often, drinking several cups a day. Here, from early morning, an orchestra played for dancing, while card games and billiards were always available.

2. "Despair of nothing . . . our point would gain" is a familiar rhyme for teaching pronunciation, spelling, and morals (Fergus [1991] 37) and probably one of the adages Austen embroidered in a sampler (Le Faye [2004] 60).

age, who was sitting by her, and had been looking at her attentively for several minutes, addressed her with great complaisance in these words:—"I think, madam, I cannot be mistaken; it is a long time since I had the pleasure of seeing you, but is not your name Allen?" This question answered, as it readily was, the stranger pronounced her's to be Thorpe; and Mrs. Allen immediately recognized the features of a former school-fellow and intimate, whom she had seen only once since their respective marriages, and that many years ago. Their joy on this meeting was very great, as well it might, since they had been contented to know nothing of each other for the last fifteen years. Compliments on good looks now passed; and, after observing how time had slipped away since they were last together, how little they had thought of meeting in Bath, and what a pleasure it was to see an old friend, they proceeded to make inquiries and give intelligence as to their families, sisters, and cousins, talking both together, far more ready to give than to receive information, and each hearing very little of what the other said. Mrs. Thorpe, however, had one great advantage as a talker, over Mrs. Allen, in a family of children; and when she expatiated on the talents of her sons, and the beauty of her daughters,—when she related their different situation and views,—that John was at Oxford, Edward at Merchant-Taylors,[3] and William at sea,—and all of them more beloved and respected in their different station than any other three beings ever were, Mrs. Allen had no similar information to give, no similar triumphs to press on the unwilling and unbelieving ear of her friend, and was forced to sit and appear to listen to all these maternal effusions, consoling herself, however, with the discovery, which her keen eye soon made, that the lace on Mrs. Thorpe's *pelisse*[4] was not half so handsome as that on her own.

"Here come my dear girls," cried Mrs. Thorpe, pointing at three smart looking females, who, arm in arm, were then moving towards her. "My dear Mrs. Allen, I long to introduce them; they will be so delighted to see you: the tallest is Isabella, my eldest; is

---

3. Merchant-Taylors was a school in London established by the guild-members, which led to a fellowship at Oxford.

4. A tunic or outer garment often of decorated silk or velvet worn over a longer diaphanous muslin gown. Austen wrote to her niece, Anna, "Mrs. Clement walks about in a new black velvet pelisse lined with yellow, and a white bobbin net veil, and looks remarkably well in them" (November 21, 1814).

•

not she a fine young woman? The others are very much admired too, but I believe Isabella is the handsomest."

The Miss Thorpes were introduced; and Miss Morland, who had been for a short time forgotten, was introduced likewise. The name seemed to strike them all; and, after speaking to her with great civility, the eldest young lady observed aloud to the rest, "How excessively like her brother Miss Morland is!"

"The very picture of him indeed!" cried the mother—and "I should have known her any where for his sister!" was repeated by them all, two or three times over. For a moment Catherine was surprized; but Mrs. Thorpe and her daughters had scarcely begun the history of their acquaintance with Mr. James Morland, before she remembered that her eldest brother had lately formed an intimacy with a young man of his own college, of the name of Thorpe; and that he had spent the last week of the Christmas vacation with his family, near London.

The whole being explained, many obliging things were said by the Miss Thorpes of their wish of being better acquainted with her; of being considered as already friends, through the friendship of their brothers, &c. which Catherine heard with pleasure, and answered with all the pretty expressions she could command; and, as the first proof of amity, she was soon invited to accept an arm of the eldest Miss Thorpe, and take a turn with her about the room. Catherine was delighted with this extension of her Bath acquaintance, and almost forgot Mr. Tilney while she talked to Miss Thorpe. Friendship is certainly the finest balm for the pangs of disappointed love.

Their conversation turned upon those subjects, of which the free discussion has generally much to do in perfecting a sudden intimacy between two young ladies, such as dress, balls, flirtations, and quizzes.[5] Miss Thorpe, however, being four years older than Miss Morland, and at least four years better informed, had a very decided advantage in discussing such points; she could compare the balls of Bath with those of Tunbridge; its fashions with the fashions of London; could rectify the opinions of her new friend in many articles of tasteful attire; could discover a flirtation between any gentleman and lady who only smiled on each other; and point out a

---

5. Contemporary slang for a practical joke, riddle, or oddity.

quiz through the thickness of a crowd. These powers received due admiration from Catherine, to whom they were entirely new; and the respect which they naturally inspired might have been too great for familiarity, had not the easy gaiety of Miss Thorpe's manners, and her frequent expressions of delight on this acquaintance with her, softened down every feeling of awe, and left nothing but tender affection. Their increasing attachment was not to be satisfied with half a dozen turns in the Pump-room, but required, when they all quitted it together, that Miss Thorpe should accompany Miss Morland to the very door of Mr. Allen's house; and that they should there part with a most affectionate and lengthened shake of hands, after learning, to their mutual relief, that they should see each other across the theatre at night, and say their prayers in the same chapel the next morning. Catherine then ran directly up stairs, and watched Miss Thorpe's progress down the street from the drawing-room window; admired the graceful spirit of her walk, the fashionable air of her figure and dress, and felt grateful, as well she might, for the chance which had procured her such a friend.

Mrs. Thorpe was a widow, and not a very rich one; she was a good-humoured, well-meaning woman, and a very indulgent mother. Her eldest daughter had great personal beauty, and the younger ones, by pretending to be as handsome as their sister, imitating her air, and dressing in the same style, did very well.

This brief account of the family is intended to supersede the necessity of a long and minute detail from Mrs. Thorpe herself, of her past adventures and sufferings, which might otherwise be expected to occupy the three or four following chapters; in which the worthlessness of lords and attournies might be set forth, and conversations, which had passed twenty years before, be minutely repeated.

CHAPTER V

Catherine was not so much engaged at the theatre that evening, in returning the nods and smiles of Miss Thorpe, though they certainly claimed much of her leisure, as to forget to look with an inquiring eye for Mr. Tilney in every box which her eye could reach; but she looked in vain. Mr. Tilney was no fonder of the play than the Pump-room. She hoped to be more fortunate the next day; and when her wishes for fine weather were answered by seeing a beautiful morning, she hardly felt a doubt of it; for a fine Sunday in Bath empties every house of its inhabitants, and all the world appears on such an occasion to walk about and tell their acquaintance what a charming day it is.

As soon as divine service was over, the Thorpes and Allens eagerly joined each other; and after staying long enough in the Pump-room to discover that the crowd was insupportable, and that there was not a genteel face to be seen, which every body discovers every Sunday throughout the season, they hastened away to the Crescent,[1] to breathe the fresh air of better company. Here Catherine and Isabella, arm in arm, again tasted the sweets of friendship in an unreserved conversation;—they talked much, and with much enjoyment; but again was Catherine disappointed in her hope of re-seeing her partner. He was no where to be met with; every search for him was equally unsuccessful, in morning lounges or evening assemblies; neither at the Upper nor Lower Rooms, at dressed or undressed balls, was he perceivable; nor among the walkers, the horsemen, or the curricle-drivers of the morning. His name was not in the Pump-room book, and curiosity could do no more. He must be gone from Bath. Yet he had not mentioned that his stay would be so short! This sort of mysteriousness, which is always so becoming in a hero, threw a fresh grace in Catherine's imagination around his person and manners, and increased her anxiety to know more of him. From the Thorpes she could learn nothing, for they had been only two days in Bath before they met with Mrs. Allen. It was a subject, however, in which she often indulged with her fair friend, from whom she received every possible encouragement to continue to think of him; and his impression on her fancy was not suffered therefore to weaken. Isabella was very sure that he must be a charming young man; and was equally sure that he must have been delighted with her dear Catherine, and would therefore shortly return. She liked him the better for being a clergyman, "for she must confess herself very partial to the profession;" and something like a sigh escaped her as she said it. Perhaps Catherine was wrong in not

1. The most beautiful of all the new Bath neighborhoods, the Crescent was lined with a curved façade of Palladian style town houses at the very top of the hills with a view of both the country and the city below in the valley. Here lived the wealthiest visitors, usually political figures, and the others paraded around the center gardens.

demanding the cause of that gentle emotion—but she was not experienced enough in the finesse of love, or the duties of friendship, to know when delicate raillery was properly called for, or when a confidence should be forced.

Mrs. Allen was now quite happy—quite satisfied with Bath. She had found some acquaintance, had been so lucky too as to find in them the family of a most worthy old friend; and, as the completion of good fortune, had found these friends by no means so expensively dressed as herself. Her daily expressions were no longer, "I wish we had some acquaintance in Bath!" They were changed into—"How glad I am we have met with Mrs. Thorpe!"—and she was as eager in promoting the intercourse of the two families, as her young charge and Isabella themselves could be; never satisfied with the day unless she spent the chief of it by the side of Mrs. Thorpe, in what they called conversation, but in which there was scarcely ever any exchange of opinion, and not often any resemblance of subject, for Mrs. Thorpe talked chiefly of her children, and Mrs. Allen of her gowns.

The progress of the friendship between Catherine and Isabella was quick as its beginning had been warm, and they passed so rapidly through every gradation of increasing tenderness, that there was shortly no fresh proof of it to be given to their friends or themselves. They called each other by their Christian name, were always arm in arm when they walked, pinned up each other's train for the dance, and were not to be divided in the set; and if a rainy morning deprived them of other enjoyments, they were still resolute in meeting in defiance of wet and dirt, and shut themselves up, to read novels together. Yes, novels;—for I will not adopt that ungenerous and impolitic custom so common with novel writers, of degrading by their contemptuous censure the very performances, to the number of which they are themselves adding—joining with their greatest enemies in bestowing the harshest epithets on such works, and scarcely ever permitting them to be read by their own heroine, who, if she accidentally take up a novel, is sure to turn over its insipid pages with disgust. Alas! if the heroine of one novel be not patronized by the heroine of another, from whom can she expect protection and regard? I cannot approve of it. Let us leave it to the Reviewers to abuse such effusions of fancy at their leisure, and over every new novel to talk in threadbare strains of the trash with which the press now groans. Let us not desert one another; we are an injured body. Although our productions have afforded more extensive and unaffected pleasure than those of any other literary corporation in the world, no species of composition has been so much decried. From pride, ignorance, or fashion, our foes are almost as many as our readers. And while the abilities of the nine-hundredth abridger of the History of England, or of the man who collects and publishes in a volume some dozen lines of Milton, Pope, and Prior, with a paper from the Spectator, and a chapter from Sterne, are eulogized by a thousand pens,—there seems almost a general wish of decrying the capacity and under-valuing the labour of the novelist, and of slighting the perfor-mances which have only genius, wit, and taste to recommend them. "I am no novel reader—I seldom look into novels—Do not imagine that *I* often read novels—It is really very well for a novel."—Such is the common cant.—"And what are you reading, Miss——?" "Oh! it is only a novel!" replies the young lady; while she lays down her book with affected indifference, or momentary shame.—"It is only Cecilia, or Camilla, or Belinda;[2] or, in short, only some work in which the greatest powers of the mind are dis-played, in which the most thorough rough knowledge of human nature, the happiest delineation of its varieties, the liveliest effusions of wit and humour are conveyed to the world in the best chosen language. Now, had the same young lady been engaged with a vol-ume of the Spectator, instead of such a work, how proudly would she have produced the book, and told its name; though the chances must be against her being occupied by any part of that voluminous publication, of which either the matter or manner would not dis-gust a young person of taste: the substance of its papers so often consisting in the statement of improbable circumstances, unnatural

---

2. Heroines of Fanny Burney's *Cecelia* (1782) and *Camilla* (1796), and Maria Edge-worth's *Belinda* (1801). Although, out of context, many critics quote this passage as Austen's defending her art, in fact it is part of the parody, one of the mock-gothic devices. Authorial defenses were common in gothic romances such as those she al-ludes to in the text (Lewis, *The Monk*; Clara Reeve, *The Progress of Romance*; Eleanor Sleath, *The Orphan of the Rhine*) and other parodies (Charlotte Lennox, *The Female Quixote*; Eaton Stannard Barrett, *The Heroine*). Here, ironically, the narrator defends real novels as part of a fiction, and Austen presents fictional char-acters who read them. Moreover, the defense is offered by the fictional narrative voice, who may not be Austen, a character who has demonstrated the limits of her (or his) insight.

characters, and topics of conversation, which no longer concern any one living; and their language, too, frequently so coarse as to give no very favourable idea of the age that could endure it.

CHAPTER VI

The following conversation, which took place between the two friends in the Pump-room one morning, after an acquaintance of eight or nine days, is given as a specimen of their very warm attachment, and of the delicacy, discretion, originality of thought, and literary taste which marked the reasonableness of that attachment.

They met by appointment; and as Isabella had arrived nearly five minutes before her friend, her first address naturally was— "My dearest creature, what can have made you so late? I have been waiting for you at least this age!"

"Have you, indeed!—I am very sorry for it; but really I thought I was in very good time. It is but just one. I hope you have not been here long?"

"Oh! these ten ages at least. I am sure I have been here this half hour. But now, let us go and sit down at the other end of the room, and enjoy ourselves. I have a hundred things to say to you. In the first place, I was so afraid it would rain this morning, just as I wanted to set off; it looked very showery, and that would have thrown me into agonies! Do you know, I saw the prettiest hat you can imagine, in a shop window in Milsom-street just now—very like yours, only with *coquelicot*[1] ribbons instead of green; I quite longed for it. But, my dearest Catherine, what have you been doing with yourself all this morning?—Have you gone on with *Udolpho*?"[2]

"Yes, I have been reading it ever since I woke; and I am got to the black veil."

"Are you, indeed? How delightful! Oh! I would not tell you what is behind the black veil for the world! Are not you wild to know?"

---

1. "Coquelicot is to be all the fashion this winter," Jane Austen wrote in a letter to Cassandra, December 18, 1798. This brilliant red-orange color was a great achievement for the native textile industry, ironically identified by a French term.

2. Ann Radcliffe, *The Mysteries of Udolpho* (1794), which Coleridge called "the most interesting novel in the English language" (*Critical Review*, 1794).

"Oh! yes, quite; what can it be?—But do not tell me—I would not be told upon any account. I know it must be a skeleton, I am sure it is Laurentina's skeleton. Oh! I am delighted with the book! I should like to spend my whole life in reading it. I assure you, if it had not been to meet you, I would not have come away from it for all the world."

"Dear creature! how much I am obliged to you; and when you have finished *Udolpho*, we will read *The Italian*[3] together; and I have made out a list of ten or twelve more of the same kind for you."

"Have you, indeed! How glad I am!—What are they all?"

"I will read you their names directly; here they are, in my pocketbook. '*Castle of Wolfenback, Clermont, Mysterious Warnings, Necromancer of the Black Forest, Midnight Bell, Orphan of the Rhine,* and *Horrid Mysteries.*'[4] Those will last us some time."

"Yes, pretty well; but are they all horrid, are you sure they are all horrid?"

"Yes, quite sure; for a particular friend of mine, a Miss Andrews, a sweet girl, one of the sweetest creatures in the world, has read every one of them. I wish you knew Miss Andrews, you would be delighted with her. She is netting herself the sweetest cloak you can conceive. I think her as beautiful as an angel, and I am so vexed with the men for not admiring her!—I scold them all amazingly about it."

"Scold them! Do you scold them for not admiring her?"

"Yes, that I do. There is nothing I would not do for those who are really my friends. I have no notion of loving people by halves, it is not my nature. My attachments are always excessively strong. I told Capt. Hunt at one of our assemblies this winter, that if he was

3. Ann Radcliffe, *The Italian* (1797): Ellena, the perfect heroine, is imprisoned in a convent where she meets her real mother among the nuns.

4. Eliza Parsons, *Castle of Wolfenbach* (1793) and *Mysterious Warnings* (1796), two of Mrs. Parsons' sixty novels written to support her children after their father died. Her plots depend on the improbable, on supernatural intervention, and on depravity including incest. Regina Maria Roche's *Clermont* (1798) describes a heroine looking for her noble origins, and Francis Lathom's *Midnight Bell* (1798) presents a hero in search of his origins, complicated by a debauched monk. Tales of German origin include Peter Teuthold's *Necromancer of the Black Forest* (1794) and Eleanor Sleuth's *Orphan of the Rhine: A Romance* (1798). Peter Will's *Horrid Mysteries* (1797) presents an aristocratic hero unwillingly inducted into a secret society called the Illuminati and his attempts to disentangle himself from them and the many crimes they commit.

to tease me all night, I would not dance with him, unless he would allow Miss Andrews to be as beautiful as an angel. The men think us incapable of real friendship you know, and I am determined to show them the difference. Now, if I were to hear any body speak slightingly of you, I should fire up in a moment:—but that is not at all likely, for *you* are just the kind of girl to be a great favourite with the men."

"Oh! dear," cried Catherine, colouring, "how can you say so?"

"I know you very well; you have so much animation, which is exactly what Miss Andrews wants, for I must confess there is something amazingly insipid about her. Oh! I must tell you, that just after we parted yesterday, I saw a young man looking at you so earnestly—I am sure he is in love with you." Catherine coloured, and disclaimed again. Isabella laughed. "It is very true, upon my honour, but I see how it is; you are indifferent to every body's admiration, except that of one gentleman, who shall be nameless. Nay, I cannot blame you—"(speaking more seriously) "—your feelings are easily understood. Where the heart is really attached, I know very well how little one can be pleased with the attention of any body else. Every thing is so insipid, so uninteresting, that does not relate to the beloved object! I can perfectly comprehend your feelings."

"But you should not persuade me that I think so very much about Mr. Tilney, for perhaps I may never see him again."

"Not see him again! My dearest creature, do not talk of it. I am sure you would be miserable if you thought so."

"No, indeed, I should not. I do not pretend to say that I was not very much pleased with him; but while I have *Udolpho* to read, I feel as if nobody could make me miserable. Oh! the dreadful black veil! My dear Isabella, I am sure there must be Laurentina's skeleton behind it."

"It is so odd to me, that you should never have read *Udolpho* before; but I suppose Mrs. Morland objects to novels."

"No, she does not. She very often reads *Sir Charles Grandison*[5] herself; but new books do not fall in our way."

5. Samuel Richardson's *Sir Charles Grandison* in seven volumes (1753–54) was not horrid at all, but the sentimental novel Austen dramatized for her family to enact. Like *Pamela* and *Clarissa*, *Sir Charles Grandison* was an epistolary novel (composed of letters) depicting a good man confronting evil, challenging temptation, offering advice, a man whose wisdom and virtue save two women from bad marriages and reconcile them to their parents.

"*Sir Charles Grandison!* That is an amazing horrid book, is it not?—I remember Miss Andrews could not get through the first volume."

"It is not like *Udolpho* at all; but yet I think it is very entertaining."

"Do you indeed!—you surprize me; I thought it had not been readable. But, my dearest Catherine, have you settled what to wear on your head tonight? I am determined at all events to be dressed exactly like you. The men take notice of *that* sometimes you know."

"But it does not signify if they do;" said Catherine, very innocently.

"Signify! Oh, heavens! I make it a rule never to mind what they say. They are very often amazingly impertinent if you do not treat them with spirit, and make them keep their distance."

"Are they?—Well, I never observed *that*. They always behave very well to me."

"Oh! they give themselves such airs. They are the most conceited creatures in the world, and think themselves of so much importance!—By the bye, though I have thought of it a hundred times, I have always forgot to ask you what is your favourite complexion in a man. Do you like them best dark or fair?"

"I hardly know. I never much thought about it. Something between both, I think. Brown—not fair, and not very dark."

"Very well, Catherine. That is exactly he. I have not forgot your description of Mr. Tilney;—'a brown skin, with dark eyes, and rather dark hair.'—Well, my taste is different. I prefer light eyes, and as to complexion—do you know—I like a sallow better than any other. You must not betray me, if you should ever meet with one of your acquaintance answering that description."

"Betray you!—What do you mean?"

"Nay, do not distress me. I believe I have said too much. Let us drop the subject."

Catherine, in some amazement, complied; and after remaining a few moments silent, was on the point of reverting to what interested her at that time rather more than any thing else in the world, Laurentina's skeleton; when her friend prevented her, by saying,—"For Heaven's sake! let us move away from this end of the room. Do you know, there are two odious young men who have been staring at me this half hour. They really put me quite out of countenance. Let us go and look at the arrivals. They will hardly follow us there."

Away they walked to the book; and while Isabella examined the names, it was Catherine's employment to watch the proceedings of these alarming young men.

"They are not coming this way, are they? I hope they are not so impertinent as to follow us. Pray let me know if they are coming. I am determined I will not look up."

In a few moments Catherine, with unaffected pleasure, assured her that she need not be longer uneasy, as the gentlemen had just left the Pump-room.

"And which way are they gone?" said Isabella, turning hastily round. "One was a very good-looking young man."

"They went towards the church-yard."

"Well, I am amazingly glad I have got rid of them! And now, what say you to going to Edgar's Buildings[6] with me, and looking at my new hat? You said you should like to see it."

Catherine readily agreed. "Only," she added, "perhaps we may overtake the two young men."

"Oh! never mind that. If we make haste, we shall pass by them presently, and I am dying to show you my hat."

"But if we only wait a few minutes, there will be no danger of our seeing them at all."

"I shall not pay them any such compliment, I assure you. I have no notion of treating men with such respect. *That* is the way to spoil them."

Catherine had nothing to oppose against such reasoning; and therefore, to show the independence of Miss Thorpe, and her resolution of humbling the sex, they set off immediately as fast as they could walk, in pursuit of the two young men.

CHAPTER VII

Half a minute conducted them through the Pump-yard to the archway, opposite Union-passage; but here they were stopped. Every body acquainted with Bath may remember the difficulties of crossing Cheap-street at this point; it is indeed a street of so impertinent a

6. The Thorpes lived in Edgar's Buildings, up the hill in a newer, more crowded, and less fashionable district than the Allens on Pulteney Street or the Tilneys on Milsom Street.

nature, so unfortunately connected with the great London and Oxford roads, and the principal inn of the city, that a day never passes in which parties of ladies, however important their business, whether in quest of pastry, millinery, or even (as in the present case) of young men, are not detained on one side or other by carriages, horsemen, or carts. This evil had been felt and lamented, at least three times a day, by Isabella since her residence in Bath; and she was now fated to feel and lament it once more, for at the very moment of coming opposite to Union-passage, and within view of the two gentlemen who were proceeding through the crowds, and threading the gutters of that interesting alley, they were prevented crossing by the approach of a gig,[1] driven along on bad pavement by a most knowing-looking coachman with all the vehemence that could most fitly endanger the lives of himself, his companion, and his horse.

"Oh, these odious gigs!" said Isabella, looking up, "how I detest them." But this detestation, though so just, was of short duration, for she looked again and exclaimed, "Delightful! Mr. Morland and my brother!"

"Good heaven! 'tis James!" was uttered at the same moment by Catherine; and, on catching the young men's eyes, the horse was immediately checked with a violence which almost threw him on his haunches, and the servant having now scampered up, the gentlemen jumped out, and the equipage was delivered to his care.

Catherine, by whom this meeting was wholly unexpected, received her brother with the liveliest pleasure; and he, being of a very amiable disposition, and sincerely attached to her, gave every proof on his side of equal satisfaction, which he could have leisure to do, while the bright eyes of Miss Thorpe were incessantly challenging his notice; and to her his *devoirs*[2] were speedily paid, with a mixture of joy and embarrassment which might have informed Catherine, had she been more expert in the developement of other people's feelings, and less simply engrossed by her own, that her brother thought her friend quite as pretty as she could do herself.

John Thorpe, who in the mean time had been giving orders about the horses, soon joined them, and from him she directly

1. A gig was a two-wheeled carriage with one horse, youthful and sporty, unlike the larger curricle, which required two horses. Both were unstable and dangerous especially at high speeds on the rutted and unpaved roads.
2. Obligatory or dutiful greetings.

received the amends which were her due; for while he slightly and carelessly touched the hand of Isabella, on her he bestowed a whole scrape and half a short bow.[3] He was a stout young man of middling height, who, with a plain face and ungraceful form, seemed fearful of being too handsome unless he wore the dress of a groom, and too much like a gentleman unless he were easy where he ought to be civil, and impudent where he might be allowed to be easy. He took out his watch: "How long do you think we have been running it from Tetbury, Miss Morland?"

"I do not know the distance." Her brother had told her that it was twenty-three miles.

"*Three*-and-twenty!" cried Thorpe; "five-and-twenty if it is an inch." Morland remonstrated, pleaded the authority of road-books, innkeepers, and milestones; but his friend disregarded them all; he had a surer test of distance. "I know it must be five-and-twenty," said he, "by the time we have been doing it. It is now half after one; we drove out of the inn-yard at Tetbury as the town-clock struck eleven; and I defy any man in England to make my horse go less than ten miles an hour in harness; that makes it exactly twenty-five."

"You have lost an hour," said Morland; "it was only ten o'-clock when we came from Tetbury."

"Ten o'clock! It was eleven, upon my soul! I counted every stroke. This brother of yours would persuade me out of my senses, Miss Morland; do but look at my horse; did you ever see an animal so made for speed in your life?" (The servant had just mounted the carriage and was driving off.) "Such true blood! Three hours and a half indeed coming only three-and-twenty miles! look at that creature, and suppose it possible if you can."

"He *does* look very hot to be sure."

"Hot! he had not turned a hair till we came to Walcot Church: but look at his forehand; look at his loins; only see how he moves; that horse *cannot* go less than ten miles an hour: tie his legs and he will get on. What do you think of my gig, Miss Morland? a neat one, is not it? Well hung; town built; I have not had it a month. It was built for a Christchurch man,[4] a friend of mine, a very good

3. A return to the social rituals of Bath, measuring status and relationship by the degree of a bow.

4. A Christchurch man is a student at Christ Church College, Oxford.

sort of fellow; he ran it a few weeks, till, I believe, it was convenient to have done with it. I happened just then to be looking out for some light thing of the kind, though I had pretty well determined on a curricle too; but I chanced to meet him on Magdalen Bridge, as he was driving into Oxford, last term: 'Ah! Thorpe,' said he, 'do you happen to want such a little thing as this? it is a capital one of the kind, but I am cursed tired of it.' 'Oh! d——,' said I, 'I am your man; what do you ask?' And how much do you think he did, Miss Morland?"

"I am sure I cannot guess at all."

"Curricle-hung⁵ you see; seat, trunk, sword-case, splashing-board, lamps, silver moulding, all you see complete; the iron-work as good as new, or better. He asked fifty guineas; I closed with him directly, threw down the money, and the carriage was mine."

"And I am sure," said Catherine, "I know so little of such things that I cannot judge whether it was cheap or dear."

"Neither one nor t'other; I might have got it for less I dare say; but I hate haggling, and poor Freeman wanted cash."

"That was very good-natured of you," said Catherine, quite pleased.

"Oh! d—— it, when one has the means of doing a kind thing by a friend, I hate to be pitiful."

An inquiry now took place into the intended movements of the young ladies; and, on finding whither they were going, it was decided that the gentlemen should accompany them to Edgar's Buildings, and pay their respects to Mrs. Thorpe. James and Isabella led the way; and so well satisfied was the latter with her lot, so contentedly was she endeavouring to ensure a pleasant walk to him who brought the double recommendation of being her brother's friend, and her friend's brother, so pure and uncoquettish were her feelings, that, though they overtook and passed the two offending young men in Milsom-street, she was so far from seeking to attract their notice, that she looked back at them only three times.

John Thorpe kept of course with Catherine, and, after a few minutes' silence, renewed the conversation about his gig—"You will find, however, Miss Morland, it would be reckoned a cheap

---

5. Thorpe's pride in his gig is comparable to an adolescent with his first car, not much to look at, but trimmed with the accessories of an elaborate curricle.

thing by some people, for I might have sold it for ten guineas more the next day; Jackson, of Oriel, bid me sixty at once; Morland was with me at the time."

"Yes," said Morland, who overheard this; "but you forget that your horse was included."

"My horse! oh, d—— it! I would not sell my horse for a hundred. Are you fond of an open carriage, Miss Morland?"

"Yes, very; I have hardly ever an opportunity of being in one; but I am particularly fond of it."

"I am glad of it; I will drive you out in mine every day."

"Thank you," said Catherine, in some distress, from a doubt of the propriety of accepting such an offer.

"I will drive you up Lansdown Hill to-morrow."

"Thank you; but will not your horse want rest?"

"Rest! he has only come three-and-twenty miles to-day; all nonsense; nothing ruins horses so much as rest; nothing knocks them up so soon. No, no; I shall exercise mine at the average of four hours every day while I am here."

"Shall you indeed!" said Catherine very seriously, "that will be forty miles a day."

"Forty! aye fifty, for what I care. Well, I will drive you up Lansdown to-morrow; mind, I am engaged."

"How delightful that will be!" cried Isabella, turning round; "my dearest Catherine, I quite envy you; but I am afraid, brother, you will not have room for a third."

"A third indeed! no, no; I did not come to Bath to drive my sisters about; that would be a good joke, faith! Morland must take care of you."

This brought on a dialogue of civilities between the other two; but Catherine heard neither the particulars nor the result. Her companion's discourse now sunk from its hitherto animated pitch, to nothing more than a short decisive sentence of praise or condemnation on the face of every woman they met; and Catherine, after listening and agreeing as long as she could, with all the civility and deference of the youthful female mind, fearful of hazarding an opinion of its own in opposition to that of a self-assured man, especially where the beauty of her own sex is concerned, ventured at length to vary the subject by a question which had been long uppermost in her thoughts; it was, "Have you ever read *Udolpho*, Mr. Thorpe?"

"*Udolpho*! Oh, Lord! not I; I never read novels; I have something else to do."

Catherine, humbled and ashamed, was going to apologize for her question, but he prevented her by saying, "Novels are all so full of nonsense and stuff; there has not been a tolerably decent one come out since *Tom Jones*, except *The Monk*; I read that t'other day; but as for all the others, they are the stupidest things in creation."[6]

"I think you must like *Udolpho*, if you were to read it; it is so very interesting."

"Not I, faith! No, if I read any, it shall be Mrs. Radcliffe's; her novels are amusing enough; they are worth reading; some fun and nature in *them*."

"*Udolpho* was written by Mrs. Radcliffe," said Catherine, with some hesitation, from the fear of mortifying him.

"No sure; was it? Aye, I remember, so it was; I was thinking of that other stupid book, written by that woman they make such a fuss about, she who married the French emigrant."

"I suppose you mean *Camilla*?"[7]

"Yes, that's the book; such unnatural stuff!—An old man playing at see-saw! I took up the first volume once and looked it over, but I soon found it would not do; indeed I guessed what sort of stuff it must be before I saw it: as soon as I heard she had married an emigrant, I was sure I should never be able to get through it."

"I have never read it."

"You had no loss I assure; it is the horridest nonsense you can imagine; there is nothing in the world in it but an old man's playing at see-saw and learning Latin; upon my soul there is not."

This critique, the justness of which was unfortunately lost on poor Catherine, brought them to the door of Mrs. Thorpe's lodgings, and the feelings of the discerning and unprejudiced reader of *Camilla* gave way to the feelings of the dutiful and affectionate son, as they met Mrs. Thorpe, who had descried them from above, in the passage. "Ah, mother! how do you do?" said he, giving her a

---

6. Henry Fielding, *Tom Jones* (1748), and Matthew Gregory Lewis, *The Monk* (1795).

7. Burney's *Camilla, or a Picture of Youth* (1796), five volumes, relates the adventures of the Tyrold sisters, including Camilla, their selfish cousin Indiana Lynmere, Camilla's cool but worthy suitor Edgar Mandlebert, and her uncle, Sir Hugh Tyrold, a well-intentioned but inept man, who dropped his niece, Eugenia, from a see-saw and crippled her for life.

hearty shake of the hand: "where did you get that quiz of a hat,[8] it makes you look like an old witch? Here is Morland and I come to stay a few days with you, so you must look out for a couple of good beds some where near." And this address seemed to satisfy all the fondest wishes of the mother's heart, for she received him with the most delighted and exulting affection. On his two younger sisters he then bestowed an equal portion of his fraternal tenderness, for he asked each of them how they did, and observed that they both looked very ugly.

These manners did not please Catherine; but he was James's friend and Isabella's brother; and her judgment was further bought off by Isabella's assuring her, when they withdrew to see the new hat, that John thought her the most charming girl in the world, and by John's engaging her before they parted to dance with him that evening. Had she been older or vainer, such attacks might have done little; but, where youth and diffidence are united, it requires uncommon steadiness of reason to resist the attraction of being called the most charming girl in the world, and of being so very early engaged as a partner; and the consequence was, that, when the two Morlands, after sitting an hour with the Thorpes, set off to walk together to Mr. Allen's, and James, as the door was closed on them, said, "Well, Catherine, how do you like my friend Thorpe?" instead of answering, as she probably would have done, had there been no friendship and no flattery in the case, "I do not like him at all;" she directly replied, "I like him very much; he seems very agreeable."

"He is as good-natured a fellow as ever lived; a little of a rattle;[9] but that will recommend him to your sex I believe: and how do you like the rest of the family?"

"Very, very much indeed: Isabella particularly."

"I am very glad to hear you say so; she is just the kind of young woman I could wish to see you attached to; she has so much good sense, and is so thoroughly unaffected and amiable; I always wanted you to know her; and she seems very fond of you. She said the highest things in your praise that could possibly be; and the praise of such a girl as Miss Thorpe even you, Catherine," taking her hand with affection, "may be proud of."

8. Eccentric.
9. A cockscomb, a fop, silly and vain, or someone who chatters.

"Indeed I am," she replied; "I love her exceedingly, and am delighted to find that you like her too. You hardly mentioned any thing of her, when you wrote to me after your visit there."

"Because I thought I should soon see you myself. I hope you will be a great deal together while you are in Bath. She is a most amiable girl; such a superior understanding! How fond all the family are of her; she is evidently the general favourite; and how much she must be admired in such a place as this—is not she?"

"Yes, very much indeed, I fancy; Mr. Allen thinks her the prettiest girl in Bath."

"I dare say he does; and I do not know any man who is a better judge of beauty than Mr. Allen. I need not ask you whether you are happy here, my dear Catherine; with such a companion and friend as Isabella Thorpe, it would be impossible for you to be otherwise; and the Allens I am sure are very kind to you?"

"Yes, very kind; I never was so happy before; and now you are come it will be more delightful than ever; how good it is of you to come so far on purpose to see *me*."

James accepted this tribute of gratitude, and qualified his conscience for accepting it too, by saying with perfect sincerity, "Indeed, Catherine, I love you dearly."

Inquiries and communications concerning brothers and sisters, the situation of some, the growth of the rest, and other family matters, now passed between them, and continued, with only one small digression on James's part, in praise of Miss Thorpe, till they reached Pulteney-street, where he was welcomed with great kindness by Mr. and Mrs. Allen, invited by the former to dine with them, and summoned by the latter to guess the price and weigh the merits of a new muff and tippet. A pre-engagement in Edgar's Buildings prevented his accepting the invitation of one friend, and obliged him to hurry away as soon as he had satisfied the demands of the other. The time of the two parties uniting in the Octagon Room being correctly adjusted, Catherine was then left to the luxury of a raised, restless, and frightened imagination over the pages of *Udolpho*, lost from all worldly concerns of dressing and dinner, incapable of soothing Mrs. Allen's fears on the delay of an expected dress-maker, and having only one minute in sixty to bestow even on the reflection of her own felicity, in being already engaged for the evening.

CHAPTER VIII

In spite of *Udolpho* and the dress-maker, however, the party from Pulteney-street reached the Upper Rooms in very good time. The Thorpes and James Morland were there only two minutes before them; and Isabella having gone through the usual ceremonial of meeting her friend with the most smiling and affectionate haste, of admiring the set of her gown, and envying the curl of her hair, they followed their chaperons, arm in arm, into the ball-room, whispering to each other whenever a thought occurred, and supplying the place of many ideas by a squeeze of the hand or a smile of affection.

The dancing began within a few minutes after they were seated; and James, who had been engaged quite as long as his sister, was very importunate with Isabella to stand up; but John was gone into the card-room to speak to a friend, and nothing, she declared, should induce her to join the set before her dear Catherine could join it too: "I assure you," said she, "I would not stand up without your dear sister for all the world; for if I did we should certainly be separated the whole evening." Catherine accepted this kindness with gratitude, and they continued as they were for three minutes longer, when Isabella, who had been talking to James on the other side of her, turned again to his sister and whispered, "My dear creature, I am afraid I must leave you, your brother is so amazingly impatient to begin; I know you will not mind my going away, and I dare say John will be back in a moment, and then you may easily find me out." Catherine, though a little disappointed, had too much good-nature to make any opposition, and the others rising up, Isabella had only time to press her friend's hand and say, "Good bye, my dear love," before they hurried off. The younger Miss Thorpes being also dancing, Catherine was left to the mercy of Mrs. Thorpe and Mrs. Allen, between whom she now remained. She could not help being vexed at the non-appearance of Mr. Thorpe, for she not only longed to be dancing, but was likewise aware that, as the real dignity of her situation could not be known, she was sharing with the scores of other young ladies still sitting down all the discredit of wanting a partner. To be disgraced in the eye of the world, to wear the appearance of infamy while her heart is all purity, her actions all innocence, and the misconduct of another the true source of her debasement, is one of those circumstances which peculiarly belong to the heroine's life, and her fortitude under it what particularly dignifies her character. Catherine had fortitude too; she suffered, but no murmur passed her lips.

From this state of humiliation, she was roused, at the end of ten minutes, to a pleasanter feeling, by seeing, not Mr. Thorpe, but Mr. Tilney, within three yards of the place where they sat; he seemed to be moving that way, but he did not see her, and therefore the smile and the blush, which his sudden reappearance raised in Catherine, passed away without sullying her heroic importance. He looked as handsome and as lively as ever, and was talking with interest to a fashionable and pleasing-looking young woman, who leant on his arm, and whom Catherine immediately guessed to be his sister; thus unthinkingly throwing away a fair opportunity of considering him lost to her for ever, by being married already. But guided only by what was simple and probable, it had never entered her head that Mr. Tilney could be married; he had not behaved, he had not talked, like the married men to whom she had been used; he had never mentioned a wife, and he had acknowledged a sister. From these circumstances sprang the instant conclusion of his sister's now being by his side; and therefore, instead of turning of a deathlike paleness, and falling in a fit on Mrs. Allen's bosom, Catherine sat erect, in the perfect use of her senses, and with cheeks only a little redder than usual.

Mr. Tilney and his companion, who continued, though slowly, to approach, were immediately preceded by a lady, an acquaintance of Mrs. Thorpe; and this lady stopping to speak to her, they, as belonging to her, stopped likewise, and Catherine, catching Mr. Tilney's eye, instantly received from him the smiling tribute of recognition. She returned it with pleasure, and then advancing still nearer, he spoke both to her and Mrs. Allen, by whom he was very civilly acknowledged. "I am very happy to see you again, sir, indeed; I was afraid you had left Bath." He thanked her for her fears, and said that he had quitted it for a week, on the very morning after his having had the pleasure of seeing her.

"Well, sir, and I dare say you are not sorry to be back again, for it is just the place for young people—and indeed for every body else too. I tell Mr. Allen, when he talks of being sick of it, that I am sure he should not complain, for it is so very agreeable a place, that it is much better to be here than at home at this dull time of year. I tell him he is quite in luck to be sent here for his health."

"And I hope, madam, that Mr. Allen will be obliged to like the place, from finding it of service to him."

"Thank you, sir. I have no doubt that he will.—A neighbour of ours, Dr. Skinner, was here for his health last winter, and came away quite stout."

"That circumstance must give great encouragement."

"Yes, sir—and Dr. Skinner and his family were here three months; so I tell Mr. Allen he must not be in a hurry to get away."

Here they were interrupted by a request from Mrs. Thorpe to Mrs. Allen, that she would move a little to accommodate Mrs. Hughes and Miss Tilney with seats, as they had agreed to join their party. This was accordingly done, Mr. Tilney still continuing standing before them; and after a few minutes consideration, he asked Catherine to dance with him. This compliment, delightful as it was, produced severe mortification to the lady; and in giving her denial, she expressed her sorrow on the occasion so very much as if she really felt it, that had Thorpe, who joined her just afterwards, been half a minute earlier, he might have thought her sufferings rather too acute. The very easy manner in which he then told her that he had kept her waiting, did not by any means reconcile her more to her lot; nor did the particulars which he entered into while they were standing up, of the horses and dogs of the friend whom he had just left, and of a proposed exchange of terriers between them, interest her so much as to prevent her looking very often towards that part of the room where she had left Mr. Tilney. Of her dear Isabella, to whom she particularly longed to point out that gentleman, she could see nothing. They were in different sets. She was separated from all her party, and away from all her acquaintance;—one mortification succeeded another, and from the whole she deduced this useful lesson, that to go previously engaged to a ball, does not necessarily increase either the dignity or enjoyment of a young lady. From such a moralizing strain as this, she was suddenly roused by a touch on the shoulder, and turning round, perceived Mrs. Hughes directly behind her, attended by Miss Tilney and a gentleman. "I beg your pardon, Miss Morland," said she, "for this liberty,—but I cannot any how get to Miss Thorpe, and Mrs. Thorpe said she was sure you would not have the least objection to letting in this young lady by you." Mrs. Hughes could not have applied to any creature in the room more happy to oblige her than Catherine. The young ladies were introduced to each other,

Miss Tilney expressing a proper sense of such goodness, Miss Morland with the real delicacy of a generous mind making light of the obligation; and Mrs. Hughes, satisfied with having so respectably settled her young charge, returned to her party.

Miss Tilney had a good figure, a pretty face, and a very agreeable countenance; and her air, though it had not all the decided pretension, the resolute stylishness of Miss Thorpe's, had more real elegance. Her manners showed good sense and good breeding; they were neither shy, nor affectedly open; and she seemed capable of being young, attractive, and at a ball, without wanting to fix the attention of every man near her, and without exaggerated feelings of extatic delight or inconceivable vexation on every little trifling occurrence. Catherine, interested at once by her appearance and her relationship to Mr. Tilney, was desirous of being acquainted with her, and readily talked therefore whenever she could think of any thing to say, and had courage and leisure for saying it. But the hindrance thrown in the way of a very speedy intimacy, by the frequent want of one or more of these requisites, prevented their doing more than going through the first rudiments of an acquaintance, by informing themselves how well the other liked Bath, how much she admired its buildings and surrounding country, whether she drew, or played or sang, and whether she was fond of riding on horseback.

The two dances were scarcely concluded before Catherine found her arm gently seized by her faithful Isabella, who in great spirits exclaimed—"At last I have got you. My dearest creature, I have been looking for you this hour. What could induce you to come into this set, when you knew I was in the other? I have been quite wretched without you."

"My dear Isabella, how was it possible for me to get at you? I could not even see where you were."

"So I told your brother all the time—but he would not believe me. Do go and see for her, Mr. Morland, said I—but all in vain—he would not stir an inch. Was not it so, Mr. Morland? But you men are all so immoderately lazy! I have been scolding him to such a degree, my dear Catherine, you would be quite amazed.—You know I never stand upon ceremony with such people."

"Look at that young lady with the white beads round her head," whispered Catherine, detaching her friend from James—"It is Mr. Tilney's sister."

"Oh! heavens! You don't say so! Let me look at her this moment. What a delightful girl! I never saw any thing half so beautiful! But where is her all-conquering brother? Is he in the room? Point him out to me this instant, if he is. I die to see him. Mr. Morland, you are not to listen. We are not talking about you."

"But what is all this whispering about? What is going on?"

"There now, I knew how it would be. You men have such restless curiosity! Talk of the curiosity of women, indeed!—'tis nothing. But be satisfied, for you are not to know any thing at all of the matter."

"And is that likely to satisfy me, do you think?"

"Well, I declare I never knew any thing like you. What can it signify to you, what we are talking of? Perhaps we are talking about you, therefore I would advise you not to listen, or you may happen to hear something not very agreeable."

In this common-place chatter, which lasted some time, the original subject seemed entirely forgotten; and though Catherine was very well pleased to have it dropped for a while, she could not avoid a little suspicion at the total suspension of all Isabella's impatient desire to see Mr. Tilney. When the orchestra struck up a fresh dance, James would have led his fair partner away, but she resisted. "I tell you, Mr. Morland," she cried, "I would not do such a thing for all the world. How can you be so teasing; only conceive, my dear Catherine, what your brother wants me to do. He wants me to dance with him again, though I tell him that it is a most improper thing, and entirely against the rules. It would make us the talk of the place, if we were not to change partners."

"Upon my honour," said James, "in these public assemblies, it is as often done as not."

"Nonsense, how can you say so? But when you men have a point to carry, you never stick at any thing. My sweet Catherine, do support me, persuade your brother how impossible it is. Tell him, that it would quite shock you to see me do such a thing; now would not it?"

"No, not at all; but if you think it wrong, you had much better change."

"There," cried Isabella, "you hear what your sister says, and yet you will not mind her. Well, remember that it is not my fault, if we set all the old ladies in Bath in a bustle. Come along, my dearest

Catherine, for heaven's sake, and stand by me." And off they went, to regain their former place. John Thorpe, in the meanwhile, had walked away; and Catherine, ever willing to give Mr. Tilney an opportunity of repeating the agreeable request which had already flattered her once, made her way to Mrs. Allen and Mrs. Thorpe as fast as she could, in the hope of finding him still with them—a hope which, when it proved to be fruitless, she felt to have been highly unreasonable. "Well, my dear," said Mrs. Thorpe, impatient for praise of her son, "I hope you have had an agreeable partner."

"Very agreeable, madam."

"I am glad of it. John has charming spirits, has not he?"

"Did you meet Mr. Tilney, my dear?" said Mrs. Allen.

"No, where is he?"

"He was with us just now, and said he was so tired of lounging about, that he was resolved to go and dance; so I thought perhaps he would ask you, if he met with you."

"Where can he be?" said Cathreine, looking round; but she had not looked round long before she saw him leading a young lady to the dance.

"Ah! he has got a partner, I wish he had asked *you*," said Mrs. Allen; and after a short silence, she added, "he is a very agreeable young man."

"Indeed he is, Mrs. Allen," said Mrs. Thorpe, smiling complacently; "I must say it, though I *am* his mother, that there is not a more agreeable young man in the world."

This inapplicable answer might have been too much for the comprehension of many; but it did not puzzle Mrs. Allen, for after only a moment's consideration, she said, in a whisper to Catherine, "I dare say she thought I was speaking of her son."

Catherine was disappointed and vexed. She seemed to have missed by so little the very object she had had in view; and this persuasion did not incline her to a very gracious reply, when John Thorpe came up to her soon afterwards, and said, "Well, Miss Morland, I suppose you and I are to stand up and jig it together again."

"Oh, no; I am much obliged to you, our two dances are over; and, besides, I am tired, and do not mean to dance any more."

"Do not you?—then let us walk about and quiz people. Come along with me, and I will show you the four greatest quizzers in the room; my two younger sisters and their partners. I have been laughing at them this half hour."

Again Catherine excused herself; and at last he walked off to quiz his sisters by himself. The rest of the evening she found very dull; Mr. Tilney was drawn away from their party at tea, to attend that of his partner; Miss Tilney, though belonging to it, did not sit near her, and James and Isabella were so much engaged in conversing together, that the latter had no leisure to bestow more on her friend than one smile, one squeeze, and one "dearest Catherine."

CHAPTER IX

The progress of Catherine's unhappiness from the events of the evening, was as follows. It appeared first in a general dissatisfaction with every body about her, while she remained in the rooms, which speedily brought on considerable weariness and a violent desire to go home. This, on arriving in Pulteney-street, took the direction of extraordinary hunger, and when that was appeased, changed into an earnest longing to be in bed; such was the extreme point of her distress; for when there she immediately fell into a sound sleep which lasted nine hours, and from which she awoke perfectly revived, in excellent spirits, with fresh hopes and fresh schemes. The first wish of her heart was to improve her acquaintance with Miss Tilney, and almost her first resolution, to seek her for that purpose, in the Pump-room at noon. In the Pump-room, one so newly arrived in Bath must be met with, and that building she had already found so favourable for the discovery of female excellence, and the completion of female intimacy, so admirably adapted for secret discourses and unlimited confidence, that she was most reasonably encouraged to expect another friend from within its walls. Her plan for the morning thus settled, she sat quietly down to her book after breakfast, resolving to remain in the same place and the same employment till the clock struck one; and from habitude very little incommoded by the remarks and ejaculations of Mrs. Allen, whose vacancy of mind and incapacity for thinking were such, that as she never talked a great deal, so she could never be entirely silent; and, therefore, while she sat at her work, if she lost her needle or broke her thread, if she heard a carriage in the street, or saw a speck upon her gown, she must observe it aloud, whether there were any one at leisure to answer her or not. At about half past twelve, a remarkably loud rap drew her in haste to the window, and scarcely had she time to inform Catherine of there being two open carriages at the door, in the first only a servant, her brother driving Miss Thorpe in the second, before John Thorpe came running up stairs, calling out, "Well, Miss Morland, here I am. Have you been waiting long? We could not come before; the old devil of a coachmaker was such an eternity finding out a thing fit to be got into, and now it is ten thousand to one, but they break down before we are out of the street. How do you do, Mrs. Allen? a famous ball last night, was not it? Come, Miss Morland, be quick, for the others are in a confounded hurry to be off. They want to get their tumble over."

"What do you mean?" said Catherine, "where are you all going to?"

"Going to? why, you have not forgot our engagement! Did not we agree together to take a drive this morning? What a head you have! We are going up Claverton Down."

"Something was said about it, I remember," said Catherine, looking at Mrs. Allen for her opinion; "but really I did not expect you."

"Not expect me! that's a good one! And what a dust you would have made, if I had not come."

Catherine's silent appeal to her friend, meanwhile, was entirely thrown away, for Mrs. Allen, not being at all in the habit of conveying any expression herself by a look, was not aware of its being ever intended by any body else; and Catherine, whose desire of seeing Miss Tilney again could at that moment bear a short delay in favour of a drive, and who thought there could be no impropriety in her going with Mr. Thorpe, as Isabella was going at the same time with James, was therefore obliged to speak plainer. "Well, ma'am, what do you say to it? Can you spare me for an hour or two? shall I go?"

"Do just as you please, my dear," replied Mrs. Allen, with the most placid indifference. Catherine took the advice, and ran off to get ready. In a very few minutes she re-appeared, having scarcely allowed the two others time enough to get through a few short sentences in her praise, after Thorpe had procured Mrs. Allen's admiration of his gig; and then receiving her friend's parting good wishes, they both hurried down stairs. "My dearest creature," cried Isabella, to whom the duty of friendship immediately called her before she could get into the carriage, "you have been at least three hours getting ready. I was afraid you were ill. What a delightful ball we had last night. I have a thousand things to say to you; but make haste and get in, for I long to be off."

Catherine followed her orders and turned away, but not too soon to hear her friend exclaim aloud to James, "What a sweet girl she is! I quite dote on her."

"You will not be frightened, Miss Morland," said Thorpe, as he handed her in, "if my horse should dance about a little at first setting off. He will, most likely, give a plunge or two, and perhaps take the rest for a minute; but he will soon know his master. He is full of spirits, playful as can be, but there is no vice in him."

Catherine did not think the portrait a very inviting one, but it was too late to retreat, and she was too young to own herself frightened; so, resigning herself to her fate, and trusting to the animal's boasted knowledge of its owner, she sat peaceably down, and saw Thorpe sit down by her. Every thing being then arranged, the servant who stood at the horse's head was bid in an important voice "to let him go," and off they went in the quietest manner imaginable, without a plunge or a caper, or any thing like one. Catherine, delighted at so happy an escape, spoke her pleasure aloud with grateful surprize; and her companion immediately made the matter perfectly simple by assuring her that it was entirely owing to the peculiarly judicious manner in which he had then held the reins, and the singular discernment and dexterity with which he had directed his whip. Catherine, though she could not help wondering that with such perfect command of his horse, he should think it necessary to alarm her with a relation of its tricks, congratulated herself sincerely on being under the care of so excellent a coachman; and perceiving that the animal continued to go on in the same quiet manner, without showing the smallest propensity towards any unpleasant vivacity, and (considering its inevitable pace was ten miles an hour) by no means alarmingly fast, gave herself up to all the enjoyment of air and exercise of the most invigorating kind, in a fine mild day of February, with the consciousness of safety. A silence of several minutes succeeded their first short dialogue;—it was broken by Thorpe's saying very abruptly, "Old Allen is as rich as a Jew—is not he?"

Catherine did not understand him—and he repeated his question, adding in explanation, "Old Allen, the man you are with."

"Oh! Mr. Allen, you mean. Yes, I believe, he is very rich."

"And no children at all?"

"No—not any."

"A famous thing for his next heirs. He is *your* godfather, is not he?"

"My godfather!—no."

"But you are always very much with them."

"Yes, very much."

"Aye, that is what I meant. He seems a good kind of old fellow enough, and has lived very well in his time, I dare say; he is not gouty for nothing. Does he drink his bottle a-day now?"

"His bottle a-day!—no. Why should you think of such a thing? He is a very temperate man, and you could not fancy him in liquor last night?"

"Lord help you!—You women are always thinking of men's being in liquor. Why you do not suppose a man is overset by a bottle? I am sure of *this*—that if every body was to drink their bottle a-day, there would not be half the disorders in the world there are now. It would be a famous good thing for us all."

"I cannot believe it."

"Oh! lord, it would be the saving of thousands. There is not the hundredth part of the wine consumed in this kingdom, that there ought to be. Our foggy climate wants help."

"And yet I have heard that there is a great deal of wine drank in Oxford."

"Oxford! There is no drinking at Oxford now, I assure you. Nobody drinks there. You would hardly meet with a man who goes beyond his four pints at the utmost. Now, for instance, it was reckoned a remarkable thing at the last party in my rooms, that upon an average we cleared about five pints a head. It was looked upon as something out of the common way. *Mine* is famous good stuff to be sure. You would not often meet with anything like it in Oxford—and that may account for it. But this will just give you a notion of the general rate of drinking there."

"Yes, it does give a notion," said Catherine, warmly, "and that is, that you all drink a great deal more wine than I thought you did. However, I am sure James does not drink so much."

This declaration brought on a loud and overpowering reply, of which no part was very distinct, except the frequent exclamations, amounting almost to oaths, which adorned it, and Catherine was left, when it ended, with rather a strengthened belief of their being a great deal of wine drank in Oxford, and the same happy conviction of her brother's comparative sobriety.

Thorpe's ideas then all reverted to the merits of his own equipage, and she was called on to admire the spirit and freedom with which his horse moved along, and the ease which his paces, as well as the excellence of the springs, gave the motion of the carriage. She followed him in all his admiration as well as she could. To go before, or beyond him was impossible. His knowledge and her ignorance of the subject, his rapidity of expression, and her diffidence of herself put that out of her power; she could strike out nothing new in commendation, but she readily echoed whatever he chose to assert, and it was finally settled between them without any difficulty, that his equipage was altogether the most complete of its kind in England, his carriage the neatest, his horse the best goer, and himself the best coachman.—"You do not really think, Mr. Thorpe," said Catherine, venturing after some time to consider the matter as entirely decided, and to offer some little variation on the subject, "that James's gig will break down?"

"Break down! Oh! lord! Did you ever see such a little tittuppy[1] thing in your life? There is not a sound piece of iron about it. The wheels have been fairly worn out these ten years at least—and as for the body! Upon my soul, you might shake it to pieces yourself with a touch. It is the most devilish little ricketty business I ever beheld!—Thank God! we have got a better. I would not be bound to go two miles in it for fifty thousand pounds."

"Good heavens!" cried Catherine, quite frightened, "then pray let us turn back; they will certainly meet with an accident if we go on. Do let us turn back, Mr. Thorpe; stop and speak to my brother, and tell him how very unsafe it is."

"Unsafe! Oh, lord! what is there in that? they will only get a roll if it does break down; and there is plenty of dirt, it will be excellent falling. Oh, curse it! the carriage is safe enough, if a man knows how to drive it; a thing of that sort in good hands will last

1. Shaky.

above twenty years after it is fairly worn out. Lord bless you! I would undertake for five pounds to drive it to York and back again, without losing a nail."

Catherine listened with astonishment; she knew not how to reconcile two such very different accounts of the same thing; for she had not been brought up to understand the propensities of a rattle, nor to know to how many idle assertions and impudent falsehoods the excess of vanity will lead. Her own family were plain matter-of-fact people, who seldom aimed at wit of any kind; her father, at the utmost, being contented with a pun, and her mother with a proverb; they were not in the habit therefore of telling lies to increase their importance, or of asserting at one moment what they would contradict the next. She reflected on the affair for some time in much perplexity, and was more than once on the point of requesting from Mr. Thorpe a clearer insight into his real opinion on the subject; but she checked herself, because it appeared to her that he did not excel in giving those clearer insights, in making those things plain which he had before made ambiguous; and, joining to this, the consideration, that he would not really suffer his sister and his friend to be exposed to a danger from which he might easily preserve them, she concluded at last, that he must know the carriage to be in fact perfectly safe, and therefore would alarm herself no longer. By him the whole matter seemed entirely forgotten; and all the rest of his conversation, or rather talk, began and ended with himself and his own concerns. He told her of horses which he had bought for a trifle and sold for incredible sums; of racing matches, in which his judgment had infallibly foretold the winner; of shooting parties, in which he had killed more birds (though without having one good shot) than all his companions together; and described to her some famous day's sport, with the fox-hounds, in which his foresight and skill in directing the dogs had repaired the mistakes of the most experienced huntsman, and in which the boldness of his riding, though it had never endangered his own life for a moment, had been constantly leading others into difficulties, which he calmly concluded had broken the necks of many.

Little as Catherine was in the habit of judging for herself, and unfixed as were her general notions of what men ought to be, she could not entirely repress a doubt, while she bore with the effusions of his endless conceit, of his being altogether completely agreeable. It was a bold surmise, for he was Isabella's brother; and she had been assured by James, that his manners would recommend him to all her sex; but in spite of this, the extreme weariness of his company, which crept over her before they had been out an hour, and which continued unceasingly to increase till they stopped in Pulteney-street again, induced her, in some small degree, to resist such high authority, and to distrust his powers of giving universal pleasure.

When they arrived at Mrs. Allen's door, the astonishment of Isabella was hardly to be expressed, on finding that it was too late in the day for them to attend her friend into the house:—"Past three o'clock!" it was inconceivable, incredible, impossible! and she would neither believe her own watch, nor her brother's, nor the servant's; she would believe no assurance of it founded on reason or reality, till Morland produced his watch, and ascertained the fact; to have doubted a moment longer *then*, would have been equally inconceivable, incredible, and impossible; and she could only protest, over and over again, that no two hours and a half had ever gone off so swiftly before, as Catherine was called on to confirm; Catherine could not tell a falsehood even to please Isabella; but the latter was spared the misery of her friend's dissenting voice, by not waiting for her answer. Her own feelings entirely engrossed her; her wretchedness was most acute on finding herself obliged to go directly home.—It was ages since she had had a moment's conversation with her dearest Catherine; and, though she had such thousands of things to say to her, it appeared as if they were never to be together again; so, with smiles of most exquisite misery, and the laughing eye of utter despondency, she bade her friend adieu and went on.

Catherine found Mrs. Allen just returned from all the busy idleness of the morning, and was immediately greeted with, "Well, my dear, here you are;" a truth which she had no greater inclination than power to dispute; "and I hope you have had a pleasant airing?"

"Yes, ma'am, I thank you; we could not have had a nicer day."

"So Mrs. Thorpe said; she was vastly pleased at your all going."

"You have seen Mrs. Thorpe then?"

"Yes, I went to the Pump-room as soon as you were gone, and there I met her, and we had a great deal of talk together. She says there was hardly any veal to be got at market this morning, it so uncommonly scarce."

"Did you see any body else of our acquaintance?"

"Yes, we agreed to take a turn in the Crescent, and there we met Mrs. Hughes, and Mr. and Miss Tilney walking with her."

"Did you indeed? and did they speak to you?"

"Yes, we walked along the Crescent together for half an hour. They seem very agreeable people. Miss Tilney was in a very pretty spotted muslin, and I fancy, by what I can learn, that she always dresses very handsomely. Mrs. Hughes talked to me a great deal about the family."

"And what did she tell you of them?"

"Oh! a vast deal indeed; she hardly talked of any thing else."

"Did she tell you what part of Gloucestershire they come from?"

"Yes, she did; but I cannot recollect now. But they are very good kind of people, and very rich. Mrs. Tilney was a Miss Drummond, and she and Mrs. Hughes were school-fellows; and Miss Drummond had a very large fortune; and, when she married, her father gave her twenty thousand pounds, and five hundred to buy wedding-clothes. Mrs. Hughes saw all the clothes after they came from the warehouse."

"And are Mr. and Mrs. Tilney in Bath?"

"Yes, I fancy they are, but I am not quite certain. Upon recollection, however, I have a notion they are both dead; at least the mother is; yes, I am sure Mrs. Tilney is dead, because Mrs. Hughes told me there was a very beautiful set of pearls that Mr. Drummond gave his daughter on her wedding-day and that Miss Tilney has got now, for they were put by for her when her mother died."

"And is Mr. Tilney, my partner, the only son?"

"I cannot be quite positive about that, my dear; I have some idea he is; but, however, he is a very fine young man Mrs. Hughes says, and likely to do very well."

Catherine inquired no further; she had heard enough to feel that Mrs. Allen had no real intelligence to give, and that she was most particularly unfortunate herself in having missed such a meeting with both brother and sister. Could she have foreseen such a circumstance, nothing should have persuaded her to go out with the others; and, as it was, she could only lament her ill-luck, and think over what she had lost, till it was clear to her, that the drive had by no means been very pleasant and that John Thorpe himself was quite disagreeable.

CHAPTER X

The Allens, Thorpes, and Morlands, all met in the evening at the
theatre; and, as Catherine and Isabella sat together, there was then
an opportunity for the latter to utter some few of the many thousand things which had been collecting within her for communication, in the immeasurable length of time which had divided them.—
"Oh, heavens! my beloved Catherine, have I got you at last?" was
her address on Catherine's entering the box and sitting by her.
"Now, Mr. Morland," for he was close to her on the other side, "I
shall not speak another word to you all the rest of the evening; so I
charge you not to expect it. My sweetest Catherine, how have you
been this long age? but I need not ask you, for you look delightfully. You really have done your hair in a more heavenly style than
ever: you mischievous creature, do you want to attract every body?
I assure you, my brother is quite in love with you already; and as
for Mr. Tilney—but *that* is a settled thing—even *your* modesty cannot doubt his attachment now; his coming back to Bath makes it
too plain. Oh! what would not I give to see him! I really am quite
wild with impatience. My mother says he is the most delightful
young man in the world; she saw him this morning you know: you
must introduce him to me. Is he in the house now?—Look about
for heaven's sake! I assure you, I can hardly exist till I see him."

"No," said Catherine, "he is not here; I cannot see him any
where."

"Oh, horrid! am I never to be acquainted with him? How do
you like my gown? I think it does not look amiss; the sleeves were
entirely my own thought. Do you know I get so immoderately sick
of Bath; your brother and I were agreeing this morning that,
though it is vastly well to be here for a few weeks, we would not
live here for millions. We soon found out that our tastes were exactly alike in preferring the country to every other place; really, our
opinions were so exactly the same, it was quite ridiculous! There
was not a single point in which we differed; I would not have had
you by for the world; you are such a sly thing, I am sure you would
have made some droll remark or other about it."

"No, indeed I should not."

"Oh, yes you would indeed; I know you better than you know
yourself. You would have told us that we seemed born for each

other, or some nonsense of that kind, which would have distressed me beyond conception; my cheeks would have been as red as your roses; I would not have had you by for the world."

"Indeed you do me injustice; I would not have made so improper a remark upon any account; and besides, I am sure it would never have entered my head."

Isabella smiled incredulously, and talked the rest of the evening to James.

Catherine's resolution of endeavouring to meet Miss Tilney again continued in full force the next morning; and till the usual moment of going to the Pump-room, she felt some alarm from the dread of a second prevention. But nothing of that kind occurred, no visitors appeared to delay them, and they all three set off in good time for the Pump-room, where the ordinary course of events and conversation took place; Mr. Allen, after drinking his glass of water, joined some gentlemen to talk over the politics of the day and compare the accounts of their newspapers; and the ladies walked about together, noticing every new face, and almost every new bonnet in the room. The female part of the Thorpe family, attended by James Morland, appeared among the crowd in less than a quarter of an hour, and Catherine immediately took her usual place by the side of her friend. James, who was now in constant attendance, maintained a similar position, and separating themselves from the rest of their party, they walked in that manner for some time, till Catherine began to doubt the happiness of a situation which confining her entirely to her friend and brother, gave her very little share in the notice of either. They were always engaged in some sentimental discussion or lively dispute, but their sentiment was conveyed in such whispering voices, and their vivacity attended with so much laughter, that though Catherine's supporting opinion was not unfrequently called for by one or the other, she was never able to give any, from not having heard a word of the subject. At length however she was empowered to disengage herself from her friend, by the avowed necessity of speaking to Miss Tilney, whom she most joyfully saw just entering the room with Mrs. Hughes, and whom she instantly joined, with a firmer determination to be acquainted, than she might have had courage to command, had she not been urged by the disappointment of the day before. Miss Tilney met her with great civility, returned her advances with equal good will, and they continued talking together as long as both parties remained in the room; and though in all probability not an observation was made, nor an expression used by either which had not been made and used some thousands of times before, under that roof, in every Bath season, yet the merit of their being spoken with simplicity and truth, and without personal conceit, might be something uncommon.—

"How well your brother dances!" was an artless exclamation of Catherine's towards the close of their conversation, which at once surprized and amused her companion.

"Henry!" she replied with a smile. "Yes, he does dance very well."

"He must have thought it very odd to hear me say I was engaged the other evening, when he saw me sitting down. But I really had been engaged the whole day to Mr. Thorpe." Miss Tilney could only bow. "You cannot think," added Catherine after a moment's silence, "how surprized I was to see him again. I felt so sure of his being quite gone away."

"When Henry had the pleasure of seeing you before, he was in Bath but for a couple of days. He came only to engage lodgings for us."

"*That* never occurred to me; and of course, not seeing him any where, I thought he must be gone. Was not the young lady he danced with on Monday a Miss Smith?"

"Yes, an acquaintance of Mrs. Hughes."

"I dare say she was very glad to dance. Do you think her pretty?"

"Not very."

"He never comes to the Pump-room, I suppose?"

"Yes, sometimes; but he has rid out this morning with my father."

Mrs. Hughes now joined them, and asked Miss Tilney if she was ready to go. "I hope I shall have the pleasure of seeing you again soon," said Catherine. "Shall you be at the cotillion ball to-morrow?"

"Perhaps we——yes, I think we certainly shall."

"I am glad of it, for we shall all be there."—This civility was duly returned; and they parted—on Miss Tilney's side with some knowledge of her new acquaintance's feelings, and on Catherine's, without the smallest consciousness of having explained them.

She went home very happy. The morning had answered all her hopes, and the evening of the following day was now the object of expectation, the future good. What gown and what head-dress she should wear on the occasion became her chief concern. She cannot be justified in it. Dress is at all times a frivolous distinction, and excessive solicitude about it often destroys its own aim. Catherine knew all this very well; her great aunt had read her a lecture on the subject only the Christmas before; and yet she lay awake ten minutes on Wednesday night debating between her spotted and her tamboured[1] muslin, and nothing but the shortness of the time prevented her buying a new one for the evening. This would have been an error in judgment, great though not uncommon, from which one of the other sex rather than her own, a brother rather than a great aunt might have warned her, for man only can be aware of the insensibility of man towards a new gown. It would be mortifying to the feelings of many ladies, could they be made to understand how little the heart of man is affected by what is costly or new in their attire; how little it is biassed by the texture of their muslin, and how unsusceptible of peculiar tenderness towards the spotted, the sprigged, the *mull* or the *jackonet*.[2] Woman is fine for her own satisfaction alone. No man will admire her the more, no woman will like her the better for it. Neatness and fashion are enough for the former, and a something of shabbiness or impropriety will be most endearing to the latter.—But not one of these grave reflections troubled the tranquillity of Catherine.

She entered the rooms on Thursday evening with feelings very different from what had attended her thither the Monday before. She had then been exulting in her engagement to Thorpe, and was now chiefly anxious to avoid his sight, lest he should engage her again; for though she could not, dared not expect that Mr. Tilney should ask her a third time to dance, her wishes, hopes and plans all centered in nothing less. Every young lady may feel for my heroine in this critical moment, for every young lady has at some time or other known the same agitation. All have been, or at least all have believed themselves to be, in danger from the pursuit of some one whom they wished to avoid; and all have been anxious for the attentions of some one whom they wished to please. As

1. Embroidered.
2. Mull and jackonet are thin imported cottons from India, embossed or with polka dots.

soon as they were joined by the Thorpes, Catherine's agony began; she fidgetted about if John Thorpe came towards her, hid herself as much as possible from his view, and when he spoke to her pretended not to hear him. The cotillions were over, the country-dancing beginning, and she saw nothing of the Tilneys. "Do not be frightened, my dear Catherine," whispered Isabella, "but I am really going to dance with your brother again. I declare positively it is quite shocking. I tell him he ought to be ashamed of himself, but you and John must keep us in countenance. Make haste, my dear creature, and come to us. John is just walked off, but he will be back in a moment."

Catherine had neither time nor inclination to answer. The others walked away, John Thorpe was still in view, and she gave herself up for lost. That she might not appear, however, to observe or expect him, she kept her eyes intently fixed on her fan; and a self-condemnation for her folly, in supposing that among such a crowd they should even meet with the Tilneys in any reasonable time, had just passed through her mind, when she suddenly found herself addressed and again solicited to dance, by Mr. Tilney himself. With what sparkling eyes and ready motion she granted his request, and with how pleasing a flutter of heart she went with him to the set, may be easily imagined. To escape, and, as she believed, so narrowly escape John Thorpe, and to be asked, so immediately on his joining her, asked by Mr. Tilney, as if he had sought her on purpose!—it did not appear to her that life could supply any greater felicity.

Scarcely had they worked themselves into the quiet possession of a place, however, when her attention was claimed by John Thorpe, who stood behind her. "Heyday, Miss Morland!" said he, "what is the meaning of this?—I thought you and I were to dance together."

"I wonder you should think so, for you never asked me."

"That is a good one, by Jove!—I asked you as soon as I came into the room, and I was just going to ask you again, but when I turned round, you were gone!—this is a cursed shabby trick! I only came for the sake of dancing with *you*, and I firmly believe you were engaged to me ever since Monday. Yes; I remember, I asked you while you were waiting in the lobby for your cloak. And here have I been telling all my acquaintance that I was going to dance with the prettiest girl in the room; and when they see you standing up with somebody else, they will quiz me famously."

"Oh, no; they will never think of *me*, after such a description as that."

"By heavens, if they do not, I will kick them out of the room for blockheads. What chap have you there?" Catherine satisfied his curiosity. "Tilney," he repeated, "Hum—I do not know him. A good figure of a man; well put together.—Does he want a horse?—Here is a friend of mine, Sam Fletcher, has got one to sell that would suit any body. A famous clever animal for the road—only forty guineas. I had fifty minds to buy it myself, for it is one of my maxims always to buy a good horse when I meet with one; but it would not answer my purpose, it would not do for the field. I would give any money for a real good hunter. I have three now, the best that ever were back'd. I would not take eight hundred guineas for them. Fletcher and I mean to get a house in Leicestershire, against the next season. It is so d—— uncomfortable, living at an inn."

This was the last sentence by which he could weary Catherine's attention, for he was just then born off by the resistless pressure of a long string of passing ladies. Her partner now drew near, and said, "That gentleman would have put me out of patience, had he staid with you half a minute longer. He has no business to withdraw the attention of my partner from me. We have entered into a contract of mutual agreeableness for the space of an evening, and all our agreeableness belongs solely to each other for that time. Nobody can fasten themselves on the notice of one, without injuring the rights of the other. I consider a country-dance as an emblem of marriage. Fidelity and complaisance are the principal duties of both; and those men who do not chuse to dance or marry themselves, have no business with the partners or wives of their neighbours."

"But they are such very different things!—"

"—That you think they cannot be compared together."

"To be sure not. People that marry can never part, but must go and keep house together. People that dance, only stand opposite each other in a long room for half an hour."

"And such is your definition of matrimony and dancing. Taken in that light certainly, their resemblance is not striking; but I think I could place them in such a view.—You will allow, that in both, man has the advantage of choice, woman only the power of refusal; that in both, it is an engagement between man and woman, formed for the advantgage of each; and that when once entered into, they belong exclusively to each other till the moment of its dissolution; that it is their duty, each to endeavour to give the other no cause for wishing that he or she had bestowed themselves elsewhere, and their best interest to keep their own imaginations from wandering towards the perfections of their neighbours, or fancying that they should have been better off with any one else. You will allow all this?"

"Yes, to be sure, as you state it, all this sounds very well; but still they are so very different.—I cannot look upon them at all in the same light, nor think the same duties belong to them."

"In one respect, there certainly is a difference. In marriage, the man is supposed to provide for the support of the woman; the woman to make the home agreeable to the man; he is to purvey, and she is to smile. But in dancing, their duties are exactly changed; the agreeableness, the compliance are expected from him, while she furnishes the fan and lavender water. *That*, I suppose, was the difference of duties which struck you, as rendering the conditions incapable of comparison."

"No, indeed, I never thought of that."

"Then I am quite at a loss. One thing, however, I must observe. This disposition on your side is rather alarming. You totally disallow any similarity in the obligations; and may I not thence infer, that your notions of the duties of the dancing state are not so strict as your partner might wish? Have I not reason to fear, that if the gentleman who spoke to you just now were to return, or if any other gentleman were to address you, there would be nothing to restrain you from conversing with him as long as you chose?"

"Mr. Thorpe is such a very particular friend of my brother's, that if he talks to me, I must talk to him again; but there are hardly three young men in the room besides him, that I have any acquaintance with."

"And is that to be my only security? alas, alas!"

"Nay, I am sure you cannot have a better; for if I do not know any body, it is impossible for me to talk to them; and, besides, I do not *want* to talk to any body."

"Now you have given me a security worth having; and I shall proceed with courage. Do you find Bath as agreeable as when I had the honour of making the inquiry before?"

"Yes, quite—more so, indeed."

"More so!—Take care, or you will forget to be tired of it at the proper time.—You ought to be tired at the end of six weeks."

"I do not think I should be tired, if I were to stay here six months."

"Bath, compared with London, has little variety, and so every body finds out every year. 'For six weeks, I allow Bath is pleasant enough; but beyond *that*, it is the most tiresome place in the world.' You would be told so by people of all descriptions, who come regularly every winter, lengthen their six weeks into ten or twelve, and go away at last because they can afford to stay no longer."

"Well, other people must judge for themselves, and those who go to London may think nothing of Bath. But I, who live in a small retired village in the country, can never find greater sameness in such a place as this, than in my own home; for here are a variety of amusements, a variety of things to be seen and done all day long, which I can know nothing of there."

"You are not fond of the country."

"Yes, I am. I have always lived there, and always been very happy. But certainly there is much more sameness in a country life than in a Bath life. One day in the country is exactly like another."

"But then you spend your time so much more rationally in the country."

"Do I?"

"Do you not?"

"I do not believe there is much difference."

"Here you are in pursuit only of amusement all day long."

"And so I am at home—only I do not find so much of it. I walk about here, and so I do there;—but here I see a variety of people in every street, and there I can only go and call on Mrs. Allen."

Mr. Tilney was very much amused. "Only go and call on Mrs. Allen!" he repeated. "What a picture of intellectual poverty! However, when you sink into this abyss again, you will have more to say. You will be able to talk of Bath, and of all that you did here."

"Oh! yes. I shall never be in want of something to talk of again to Mrs. Allen, or any body else. I really believe I shall always be talking of Bath, when I am at home again—I *do* like it so very much. If I could but have papa and mamma, and the rest of them here, I suppose I should be too happy! James's coming (my eldest brother) is quite delightful—and especially as it turns out, that the very family we are just got so intimate with, are his intimate friends already. Oh! who can ever be tired of Bath?"

"Not those who bring such fresh feelings of every sort to it, as you do. But papas and mammas, and brothers and intimate friends are a good deal gone by, to most of the frequenters of Bath—and the honest relish of balls and plays, and every-day sights, is past with them."

Here their conversation closed; the demands of the dance becoming now too importunate for a divided attention.

Soon after their reaching the bottom of the set, Catherine perceived herself to be earnestly regarded by a gentleman who stood among the lookers-on, immediately behind her partner. He was a very handsome man, of a commanding aspect, past the bloom, but not past the vigour of life; and with his eye still directed towards her, she saw him presently address Mr. Tilney in a familiar whisper. Confused by his notice, and blushing from the fear of its being excited by something wrong in her appearance, she turned away her head. But while she did so, the gentleman retreated, and her partner coming nearer, said, "I see that you guess what I have just been asked. That gentleman knows your name, and you have a right to know his. It is General Tilney, my father."

Catherine's answer was only "Oh!"—but it was an "Oh!" expressing every thing needful; attention to his words, and perfect reliance on their truth. With real interest and strong admiration did her eye now follow the General, as he moved through the crowd, and "How handsome a family they are!" was her secret remark.

In chatting with Miss Tilney before the evening concluded, a new source of felicity arose to her. She had never taken a country walk since her arrival in Bath. Miss Tilney, to whom all the commonly-frequented environs were familiar, spoke of them in terms which made her all eagerness to know them too; and on her openly fearing that she might find nobody to go with her, it was proposed by the brother and sister that they should join in a walk, some morning or other. "I shall like it," she cried, "beyond any thing in the world; and do not let us put it off—let us go tomorrow." This was readily agreed to, with only a proviso of Miss Tilney's, that it did not rain, which Catherine was sure it would not. At twelve o'clock, they were to call for her in Pulteney-street—and "remember—twelve o'clock," was her parting speech to her new friend. Of her other, her older, her more established friend, Isabella, of whose fidelity and worth she had enjoyed a fortnight's experience, she scarcely saw any thing during the evening. Yet, though longing to make her acquainted with her happiness, she cheerfully submitted to the wish of Mr. Allen, which took them rather early away, and her spirits danced within her, as she danced in her chair all the way home.

CHAPTER XI

The morrow brought a very sober looking morning; the sun making only a few efforts to appear; and Catherine augured from it, every thing most favourable to her wishes. A bright morning so early in the year, she allowed would generally turn to rain, but a cloudy one foretold improvement as the day advanced. She applied to Mr. Allen for confirmation of her hopes, but Mr. Allen not having his own skies and barometer about him, declined giving any absolute promise of sunshine. She applied to Mrs. Allen, and Mrs. Allen's opinion was more positive. She had no doubt in the world of its being a very fine day, if the clouds would only go off, and the sun keep out.

At about eleven o'clock however, a few specks of small rain upon the windows caught Catherine's watchful eye, and "Oh! dear, I do believe it will be wet," broke from her in a most desponding tone.

"I thought how it would be," said Mrs. Allen.

"No walk for me to-day," sighed Catherine;—"but perhaps it may come to nothing, or it may hold up before twelve."

"Perhaps it may, but then, my dear, it will be so dirty."

"Oh! that will not signify; I never mind dirt."

"No," replied her friend very placidly, "I know you never mind dirt."

After a short pause, "It comes on faster and faster!" said Catherine, as she stood watching at a window.

"So it does indeed. If it keeps raining, the streets will be very wet."

"There are four umbrellas up already. How I hate the sight of an umbrella!"

"They are disagreeable things to carry. I would much rather take a chair at any time."

"It was such a nice looking morning! I felt so convinced it would be dry!"

"Any body would have thought so indeed. There will be very few people in the Pump-room, if it rains all the morning. I hope Mr. Allen will put on his great coat when he goes, but I dare say he will not, for he had rather do any thing in the world than walk out in a great coat; I wonder he should dislike it, it must be so comfortable."

The rain continued—fast, though not heavy. Catherine went every five minutes to the clock, threatening on each return that, if it still kept on raining another five minutes, she would give up the matter as hopeless. The clock struck twelve, and it still rained.—"You will not be able to go, my dear."

"I do not quite despair yet. I shall not give it up till a quarter after twelve. This is just the time of day for it to clear up, and I do think it looks a little lighter. There, it is twenty minutes after twelve, and now I *shall* give it up entirely. Oh! that we had such weather here as they had at Udolpho, or at least in Tuscany and the South of France!—the night that poor St. Aubin[1] died!—such beautiful weather!"

At half past twelve, when Catherine's anxious attention to the weather was over, and she could no longer claim any merit from its amendment, the sky began voluntarily to clear. A gleam of sunshine took her quite by surprize; she looked round; the clouds were parting, and she instantly returned to the window to watch over and encourage the happy appearance. Ten minutes more made it certain that a bright afternoon would succeed, and justified the opinion of Mrs. Allen, who had "always thought it would clear up." But whether Catherine might still expect her friends, whether there had not been too much rain for Miss Tilney to venture, must yet be a question.

It was too dirty for Mrs. Allen to accompany her husband to the Pump-room; he accordingly set off by himself, and Catherine had barely watched him down the street, when her notice was claimed by the approach of the same two open carriages, containing the same three people that had surprised her so much a few mornings back.

1. St. Aubin (actually St. Aubert) is the heroine's father in *The Mysteries of Udolpho.*

"Isabella, my brother, and Mr. Thorpe, I declare! They are coming for me perhaps—but I shall not go—I cannot go indeed, for you
know Miss Tilney may still call." Mrs. Allen agreed to it. John
Thorpe was soon with them, and his voice was with them yet
sooner, for on the stairs he was calling out to Miss Morland to be
quick. "Make haste! make haste!" as he threw open the door—
"put on your hat this moment—there is no time to be lost—we are
going to Bristol.—How d'ye do, Mrs. Allen?"

"To Bristol! Is not that a great way off?—But, however, I cannot go with you to-day, because I am engaged; I expect some
friends every moment." This was of course vehemently talked
down as no reason at all; Mrs. Allen was called on to second him,
and the two others walked in, to give their assistance. "My sweetest Catherine, is not this delightful? We shall have a most heavenly
drive. You are to thank your brother and me for the scheme; it
darted into our heads at breakfast-time, I verily believe at the same
instant; and we should have been off two hours ago if it had not
been for this detestable rain. But it does not signify, the nights are
moonlight, and we shall do delightfully. Oh! I am in such extasies
at the thoughts of a little country air and quiet!—so much better
than going to the Lower Rooms. We shall drive directly to Clifton
and dine there; and, as soon as dinner is over, if there is time for it,
go on to Kingsweston."

"I doubt our being able to do so much," said Morland.

"You croaking fellow!" cried Thorpe, "we shall be able to do
ten times more. Kingsweston! aye, and Blaize Castle too;[2] and
any thing else we can hear of; but here is your sister says she will
not go."

"Blaize Castle!" cried Catherine; "what is that?"

"The finest place in England—worth going fifty miles at any
time to see."

"What, is it really a castle, an old castle?"

"The oldest in the kingdom."

"But is it like what one reads of?"

"Exactly—the very same."

---

2. Bristol, eleven miles north of Bath, a full day's journey, and Kingsweston, four
miles beyond. Blaize Castle is a gothic folly built in 1766.

"But now really—are there towers and long galleries?"

"By dozens."

"Then I should like to see it; but I cannot——I cannot go."

"Not go!—my beloved creature, what do you mean?"

"I cannot go, because"——(looking down as she spoke, fearful of Isabella's smile) "I expect Miss Tilney and her brother to call on me to take a country walk. They promised to come at twelve, only it rained; but now, as it is so fine, I dare say they will be here soon."

"Not they indeed," cried Thorpe; "for, as we turned into Broadstreet, I saw them—does he not drive a phaeton with bright chestnuts?"

"I do not know indeed."

"Yes, I know he does; I saw him. You are talking of the man you danced with last nght, are not you?"

"Yes."

"Well, I saw him at that moment turn up the Lansdown-road,—driving a smart-looking girl."

"Did you indeed?"

"Did upon my soul; knew him again directly, and he seemed to have got some very pretty cattle too."

"It is very odd! but I suppose they thought it would be too dirty for a walk."

"And well they might, for I never saw so much dirt in my life. Walk! you could no more walk than you could fly! it has not been so dirty the whole winter; it is ankle-deep every where."

Isabella corroborated it:—"My dearest Catherine, you cannot form an idea of the dirt; come, you must go; you cannot refuse going now."

"I should like to see the castle; but may we go all over it? may we go up every staircase, and into every suite of rooms?"

"Yes, yes, every hole and corner."

"But then,—if they should only be gone out for an hour till it is drier, and call by and bye?"

"Make yourself easy, there is no danger of that, for I heard Tilney hallooing to a man who was just passing by on horseback, that they were going as far as Wick Rocks."

"Then I will. Shall I go, Mrs. Allen?"

"Just as you please, my dear."

"Mrs. Allen, you must persuade her to go," was the general cry. Mrs. Allen was not inattentive to it:—"Well, my dear," said she, "suppose you go."—And in two minutes they were off.

Catherine's feelings, as she got into the carriage, were in a very unsettled state; divided between regret for the loss of one great pleasure, and the hope of soon enjoying another, almost its equal in degree, however unlike in kind. She could not think the Tilneys had acted quite well by her, in so readily giving up their engagement, without sending her any message of excuse. It was now but an hour later than the time fixed on for the beginning of their walk; and, in spite of what she had heard of the prodigious accumulation of dirt in the course of that hour, she could not from her own observation help thinking, that they might have gone with very little inconvenience. To feel herself slighted by them was very painful. On the other hand, the delight of exploring an edifice like Udolpho, as her fancy represented Blaize Castle to be, was such a counterpoise of good, as might console her for almost any thing.

They passed briskly down Pulteney-street, and through Laura-place, without the exchange of many words. Thorpe talked to his horse, and she meditated, by turns, on broken promises and broken arches, phaetons and false hangings, Tilneys and trap-doors. As they entered Argyle-buildings, however, she was roused by this address from her companion, "Who is that girl who looked at you so hard as she went by?"

"Who?—where?"

"On the right-hand pavement—she must be almost out of sight now." Catherine looked round and saw Miss Tilney leaning on her brother's arm, walking slowly down the street. She saw them both looking back at her. "Stop, stop, Mr. Thorpe," she impatiently cried, "it is Miss Tilney; it is indeed.—How could you tell me they were gone?—Stop, stop, I will get out this moment and go to them." But to what purpose did she speak?—Thorpe only lashed his horse into a brisker trot; the Tilneys, who had soon ceased to look after her, were in a moment out of sight round the corner of Laura-place, and in another moment she was herself whisked into the Market-place. Still, however, and during the length of another street, she entreated him to stop. "Pray, pray stop, Mr. Thorpe.—I cannot go on.—I will not go on.—I must go back to Miss Tilney." But Mr. Thorpe only laughed, smacked his whip, encouraged his horse, made odd noises, and drove on; and Catherine, angry and vexed as she was, having no power of getting away, was obliged to give up the point and submit. Her reproaches, however, were not spared. "How could you deceive me so, Mr. Thorpe?—How could you say, that you saw them driving up the Lansdown-road?—I would not have had it happen so for the world.—They must think it so strange; so rude of me! to go by them, too, without saying a word! You do not know how vexed I am—I shall have no pleasure at Clifton, nor in any thing else. I had rather, ten thousand times rather get out now, and walk back to them. How could you say, you saw them driving out in a phaeton?" Thorpe defended himself very stoutly, declared he had never seen two men so much alike in his life, and would hardly give up the point of its having been Tilney himself.

Their drive, even when this subject was over, was not likely to be very agreeable. Catherine's complaisance was no longer what it had been in their former airing. She listened reluctantly, and her replies were short. Blaize Castle remained her only comfort; towards *that*, she still looked at intervals with pleasure; though rather than be disappointed of the promised walk, and especially rather than be thought ill of by the Tilneys, she would willingly have given up all the happiness which its walls could supply—the happiness of a progress through a long suite of lofty rooms, exhibiting the remains of magnificent furniture, though now for many years deserted—the happiness of being stopped in their way along narrow, winding vaults, by a low, grated door; or even of having their lamp, their only lamp, extinguished by a sudden gust of wind, and of being left in total darkness. In the meanwhile, they proceeded on their journey without any mischance; and were within view of the town of Keynsham, when a halloo from Morland, who was behind them, made his friend pull up, to know what was the matter. The others then came close enough for conversation, and Morland said, "We had better go back, Thorpe; it is too late to go on to-day; your sister thinks so as well as I. We have been exactly an hour coming from Pulteney-street, very little more than seven miles; and, I suppose, we have at least eight more to go. It will never do. We set out a great deal too late. We had much better put it off till another day, and turn round."

"It is all one to me," replied Thorpe rather angrily; and instantly turning his horse, they were on their way back to Bath.

"If your brother had not got such a d—— beast to drive," said he soon afterwards, "we might have done it very well. My horse would have trotted to Clifton within the hour, if left to himself, and I have almost broke my arm with pulling him in to that cursed broken-winded jade's pace. Morland is a fool for not keeping a horse and gig of his own."

"No, he is not," said Catherine warmly, "for I am sure he could not afford it."

"And why cannot he afford it?"

"Because he has not money enough."

"And whose fault is that?"

"Nobody's, that I know of." Thorpe then said something in the loud, incoherent way to which he had often recourse, about its being a d—— thing to be miserly; and that if people who rolled in money could not afford things, he did not know who could; which Catherine did not even endeavour to understand. Disappointed of what was to have been the consolation for her first disappointment, she was less and less disposed either to be agreeable herself, or to find her companion so; and then returned to Pulteney-street without her speaking twenty words.

As she entered the house, the footman told her, that a gentleman and lady had called and inquired for her a few minutes after her setting off; that, when he told them she was gone out with Mr. Thorpe, the lady had asked whether any message had been left for her; and on his saying no, had felt for a card, but said she had none about her, and went away. Pondering over these heart-rending tidings, Catherine walked slowly up stairs. At the head of them she was met by Mr. Allen, who, on hearing the reason of their speedy return, said, "I am glad your brother had so much sense; I am glad you are come back. It was a strange, wild scheme."

They all spent the evening together at Thorpe's. Catherine was disturbed and out of spirits; but Isabella seemed to find a pool of commerce,[3] in the fate of which she shared, by private partnership with Morland, a very good equivalent for the quiet and country air of an inn at Clifton. Her satisfaction, too, in not being at the Lower Rooms, was spoken more than once. "How I pity the poor creatures

---

3. A card game in which cards are traded among players, another expression of the commodification of life.

that are going there! How glad I am that I am not amongst them! I wonder whether it will be a full ball or not! They have not begun dancing yet. I would not be there for all the world. It is so delightful to have an evening now and then to oneself. I dare say it will not be a very good ball. I know the Mitchells will not be there. I am sure I pity every body that is. But I dare say, Mr. Morland, you long to be at it, do not you? I am sure you do. Well, pray do not let any body here be a restraint on you. I dare say we could do very well without you; but you men think yourselves of such consequence."

Catherine could almost have accused Isabella of being wanting in tenderness towards herself and her sorrows; so very little did they appear to dwell on her mind, and so very inadequate was the comfort she offered. "Do not be so dull, my dearest creature," she whispered. "You will quite break my heart. It was amazingly shocking to be sure; but the Tilneys were entirely to blame. Why were not they more punctual? It was dirty, indeed, but what did that signify? I am sure John and I should not have minded it. I never mind going through anything, where a friend is concerned; that is my disposition, and John is just the same; he has amazing strong feelings. Good heavens! what a delightful hand you have got! Kings, I vow! I never was so happy in my life! I would fifty times rather you should have them than myself."

And now I may dismiss my heroine to the sleepless couch, which is the true heroine's portion; to a pillow strewed with thorns and wet with tears. And lucky may she think herself, if she get another good night's rest in the course of the next three months.

CHAPTER XII

"Mrs. Allen," said Catherine the next morning, "will there be any harm in my calling on Miss Tilney to-day? I shall not be easy till I have explained every thing."

"Go by all means, my dear; only put on a white gown; Miss Tilney always wears white."

Catherine cheerfully complied; and being properly equipped, was more impatient than ever to be at the Pump-room, that she might inform herself of General Tilney's lodgings, for though she believed they were in Milsom-street, she was not certain of the house, and Mrs. Allen's wavering convictions only made it more doubtful. To Milsom-street she was directed; and having made herself perfect in the number, hastened away with eager steps and a beating heart to pay her visit, explain her conduct, and be forgiven; tripping lightly through the church-yard, and resolutely turning away her eyes, that she might not be obliged to see her beloved Isabella and her dear family, who, she had reason to believe, were in a shop hard by. She reached the house without any impediment, looked at the number, knocked at the door, and inquired for Miss Tilney. The man believed Miss Tilney to be at home, but was not quite certain. Would she be pleased to send up her name? She gave her card. In a few minutes the servant returned, and with a look which did not quite confirm his words, said he had been mistaken, for that Miss Tilney was walked out. Catherine, with a blush of mortification, left the house. She felt almost persuaded that Miss Tilney *was* at home, and too much offended to admit her; and as she retired down the street, could not withhold one glance at the drawing-room windows, in expectation of seeing her there, but no one appeared at them. At the bottom of the street, however, she looked back again, and then, not at a window, but issuing from the door, she saw Miss Tilney herself. She was followed by a gentleman, whom Catherine believed to be her father, and they turned up towards Edgar's Buildings. Catherine, in deep mortification, proceeded on her way. She could almost be angry herself at such angry incivility; but she checked the resentful sensation; she remembered her own ignorance. She knew not how such an offence as her's might be classed by the laws of worldly politeness, to what a degree of unforgivingness it might with propriety lead, nor to what rigours of rudeness in return it might justly make her amenable.

Dejected and humbled, she had even some thoughts of not going with the others to the theatre that night; but it must be confessed that they were not of long continuance: for she soon recollected, in the first place, that she was without any excuse for staying at home; and, in the second, that it was a play she wanted very much to see. To the theatre accordingly they all went; no Tilneys appeared to plague or please her; she feared that, amongst the many perfections of the family, a fondness for plays was not to be ranked; but perhaps it was because they were habituated to the finer performances of the London stage, which she knew, on Isabella's authority, rendered everything else of the kind "quite horrid." She was not deceived in her own expectation of pleasure; the comedy so well suspended her care, that no one observing her during the first four acts, would have supposed she had any wretchedness about her. On the beginning of the fifth, however, the sudden view of Mr. Henry Tilney and his father, joining a party in the opposite box, recalled her to anxiety and distress. The stage could no longer excite genuine merriment—no longer keep her whole attention. Every other look upon an average was directed towards the opposite box; and, for the space of two entire scenes, did she thus watch Henry Tilney, without being once able to catch his eye. No longer could he be suspected of indifference for a play; his notice was never withdrawn from the stage during two whole scenes. At length, however, he did look towards her, and he bowed—but such a bow! no smile, no continued observance attended it; his eyes were immediately returned to their former direction. Catherine was restlessly miserable; she could almost have run round to the box in which he sat, and forced him to hear her explanation. Feelings rather natural than heroic possessed her; instead of considering her own dignity injured by this ready condemnation—instead of proudly resolving, in conscious innocence, to show her resentment towards him who could harbour a doubt of it, to leave to him all the trouble of seeking an explanation, and to enlighten him on the past only by avoiding his sight, or flirting with somebody else, she took to herself all the shame of misconduct, or at least of its appearance, and was only eager for an opportunity of explaining its cause.

The play concluded—the curtain fell—Henry Tilney was no longer to be seen where he had hitherto sat, but his father remained, and perhaps he might be now coming round to their box. She was right; in a few minutes he appeared, and, making his way through the then thinning rows, spoke with like calm politeness to Mrs. Allen and her friend.—Not with such calmness was he answered by the latter: "Oh! Mr. Tilney, I have been quite wild to speak to you, and make my apologies. You must have thought me so rude; but indeed it was not my own fault,—was it, Mrs. Allen? Did not they tell me that Mr. Tilney and his sister were gone out in a phaeton together? and then what could I do? But I had ten thousand times rather have been with you; now had not I, Mrs. Allen?"

"My dear, you tumble my gown," was Mrs. Allen's reply.

Her assurance, however, standing sole as it did, was not thrown away; it brought a more cordial, more natural smile into his countenance, and he replied in a tone which retained only a little affected reserve:—"We were much obliged to you at any rate for wishing us a pleasant walk after our passing you in Argyle-street: you were so kind as to look back on purpose."

"But indeed I did not wish you a pleasant walk; I never thought of such a thing; but I begged Mr. Thorpe so earnestly to stop; I called out to him as soon as ever I saw you; now, Mrs. Allen, did not——Oh! you were not there; but indeed I did; and, if Mr. Thorpe would only have stopped, I would have jumped out and run after you."

Is there a Henry in the world who could be insensible to such a declaration? Henry Tilney at least was not. With a yet sweeter smile, he said every thing that need be said of his sister's concern, regret, and dependence on Catherine's honour.—"Oh! do not say Miss Tilney was not angry," cried Catherine, "because I know she was; for she would not see me this morning when I called; I saw her walk out of the house the next minute after my leaving it; I was hurt, but I was not affronted. Perhaps you did not know I had been there."

"I was not within at the time; but I heard of it from Eleanor, and she has been wishing ever since to see you, to explain the reason of such incivility; but perhaps I can do it as well. It was nothing more than that my father——they were just preparing to walk out, and he being hurried for time, and not caring to have it put off, made a point of her being denied. That was all, I do assure you. She was very much vexed, and meant to make her apology as soon as possible."

Catherine's mind was greatly eased by this information, yet a something of solicitude remained, from which sprang the following question, thoroughly artless in itself, though rather distressing to the gentleman:—"But, Mr. Tilney, why were *you* less generous than your sister? If she felt such confidence in my good intentions, and could suppose it to be only a mistake, why should *you* be so ready to take offence?"

"Me!—I take offence!"

"Nay, I am sure by your look, when you came into the box, you were angry."

"I angry! I could have no right."

"Well, nobody would have thought you had no right who saw your face." He replied by asking her to make room for him, and talking of the play.

He remained with them some time, and was only too agreeable for Catherine to be contented when he went away. Before they parted, however, it was agreed that the projected walk should be taken as soon as possible; and, setting aside the misery of his quitting their box, she was, upon the whole, left one of the happiest creatures in the world.

While talking to each other, she had observed with some surprize, that John Thorpe, who was never in the same part of the house for ten minutes together, was engaged in conversation with General Tilney; and she felt something more than surprize, when she thought she could perceive herself the object of their attention and discourse. What could they have to say of her? She feared General Tilney did not like her appearance: she found it was implied in his preventing her admittance to his daughter, rather than postpone his own walk a few minutes. "How came Mr. Thorpe to know your father?" was her anxious inquiry, as she pointed them out to her companion. He knew nothing about it; but his father, like every military man, had a very large acquaintance.

When the entertainment was over, Thorpe came to assist them in getting out. Catherine was the immediate object of his gallantry; and, while they waited in the lobby for a chair, he prevented the inquiry which had travelled from her heart almost to the tip of her tongue, by asking, in a consequential manner, whether she had seen him talking with General Tilney:—"He is a fine old fellow, upon my soul!—stout, active—looks as young as his son. I have a great regard for him, I assure you: a gentleman-like, good sort of fellow as ever lived."

"But how came you to know him?"

"Know him!—There are few people much about town that I do not know. I have met him for ever at the Bedford;[1] and I knew his face again to-day the moment he came into the billiard-room. One of the best players we have, by the bye; and we had a little touch together, though I was almost afraid of him at first: the odds were five to four against me; and, if I had not made one of the cleanest strokes that perhaps ever was made in this world——I took his ball exactly——but I could not make you understand it without a

1. A coffee house in Covent Garden, London.

\

table;—however I *did* beat him. A very fine fellow; as rich as a Jew. I should like to dine with him; I dare say he gives famous dinners. But what do you think we have been talking of?—You. Yes, by heavens!—and the General thinks you the finest girl in Bath."

"Oh! nonsense! how can you say so?"

"And what do you think I said?" (lowering his voice) "Well done, General, said I, I am quite of your mind."

Here Catherine, who was much less gratified by his admiration than by General Tilney's, was not sorry to be called away by Mr. Allen. Thorpe, however, would see her to her chair, and, till she entered it, continued the same kind of delicate flattery, in spite of her entreating him to have done.

That General Tilney, instead of disliking, should admire her, was very delightful; and she joyfully thought, that there was not one of the family whom she need now fear to meet.—The evening had done more, much more, for her, than could have been expected.

CHAPTER XIII

Monday, Tuesday, Wednesday, Thursday, Friday and Saturday have now passed in review before the reader; the events of each day, its hopes and fears, mortifications and pleasures have been separately stated, and the pangs of Sunday only now remain to be described, and close the week. The Clifton scheme had been deferred, not relinquished, and on the afternoon's Crescent of this day, it was brought forward again. In a private consultation between Isabella and James, the former of whom had particularly set her heart upon going, and the latter no less anxiously placed his upon pleasing her, it was agreed that, provided the weather were fair, the party should take place on the following morning; and they were to set off very early, in order to be at home in good time. The affair thus determined, and Thorpe's approbation secured, Catherine only remained to be apprized of it. She had left them for a few minutes to speak to Miss Tilney. In that interval the plan was completed, and as soon as she came again, her agreement was demanded; but instead of the gay acquiescence expected by Isabella, Catherine looked grave, was very sorry, but could not go. The engagement which ought to have kept her from joining in the former attempt, would make it impossible for her to accompany them now. She had that moment settled with Miss Tilney to take their promised walk tomorrow; it was quite determined, and she would not, upon any account, retract. But that she *must* and *should* retract, was instantly the eager cry of both the Thorpes; they must go to Clifton to-morrow, they would not go without her, it would be nothing to put off a mere walk for one day longer, and they would not hear of a refusal. Catherine was distressed, but not subdued. "Do not urge me, Isabella. I am engaged to Miss Tilney. I cannot go." This availed nothing. The same arguments assailed her again; she must go, she should go, and they would not hear of a refusal. "It would be so easy to tell Miss Tilney that you had just been reminded of a prior engagement, and must only beg to put off the walk till Tuesday."

"No, it would not be easy. I could not do it. There has been no prior engagement." But Isabella became only more and more urgent; calling on her in the most affectionate manner; addressing her by the most endearing names. She was sure her dearest, sweetest Catherine would not seriously refuse such a trifling request to a friend who loved her so dearly. She knew her beloved Catherine to have so feeling a heart, so sweet a temper, to be so easily persuaded by those she loved. But all in vain; Catherine felt herself to be in the right, and though pained by such tender, such flattering supplication, could not allow it to influence her. Isabella then tried another method. She reproached her with having more affection for Miss Tilney, though she had known her so little a while, than for her best and oldest friends; with being grown cold and indifferent, in short, towards herself. "I cannot help being jealous, Catherine, when I see myself slighted for strangers, I, who love you so excessively! When once my affections are placed, it is not in the power of any thing to change them. But I believe my feelings are stronger than any body's; I am sure they are too strong for my own peace; and to see myself supplanted in your friendship by strangers, does cut me to the quick, I own. These Tilneys seem to swallow up every thing else."

Catherine thought this reproach equally strange and unkind. Was it the part of a friend thus to expose her feelings to the notice of others? Isabella appeared to her ungenerous and selfish, regardless of every thing but her own gratification. These painful ideas crossed her mind, though she said nothing. Isabella, in the meanwhile, had applied her handkerchief to her eyes; and Morland, miserable at such a sight, could not help saying, "Nay, Catherine. I think you cannot stand out any longer now. The sacrifice is not much; and to oblige such a friend—I shall think you quite unkind, if you still refuse."

This was the first time of her brother's openly siding against her, and anxious to avoid his displeasure, she proposed a compromise. If they would only put off their scheme till Tuesday, which they might easily do, as it depended only on themselves, she could go with them, and every body might then be satisfied. But "No, no, no!" was the immediate answer; "that could not be, for Thorpe did not know that he might not go to town on Tuesday." Catherine was sorry, but could do no more; and a short silence ensued, which was broken by Isabella; who in a voice of cold resentment said, "Very well, then there is an end of the party. If Catherine does not go, I cannot. I cannot be the only woman. I would not, upon any account in the world, do so improper a thing."

"Catherine, you must go," said James.

"But why cannot Mr. Thorpe drive one of his other sisters? I dare say either of them would like to go."

"Thank ye," cried Thorpe, "but I did not come to Bath to drive my sisters about, and look like a fool. No, if you do not go, d—— me if I do. I only go for the sake of driving you."

"That is a compliment which gives me no pleasure." But her words were lost on Thorpe, who had turned abruptly away.

The three others still continued together, walking in a most uncomfortable manner to poor Catherine; sometimes not a word was said, sometimes she was again attacked with supplications or reproaches, and her arm was still linked within Isabella's, though their hearts were at war. At one moment she was softened, at another irritated; always distressed, but always steady.

"I did not think you had been so obstinate, Catherine," said James; "you were not used to be so hard to persuade; you once were the kindest, best-tempered of my sisters."

"I hope I am not less so now," she replied, very feelingly; "but indeed I cannot go. If I am wrong, I am doing what I believe to be right."

"I suspect," said Isabella, in a low voice, "there is no great struggle."

Catherine's heart swelled; she drew away her arm, and Isabella made no opposition. Thus passed a long ten minutes, till they were again joined by Thorpe, who coming to them with a gayer look, said, "Well, I have settled the matter, and now we may all go to-morrow with a safe conscience. I have been to Miss Tilney, and made your excuses."

"You have not!" cried Catherine.

"I have, upon my soul. Left her this moment. Told her you had sent me to say, that having just recollected a prior engagement of going to Clifton with us to-morrow, you could not have the pleasure of walking with her till Tuesday. She said very well, Tuesday was just as convenient to her; so there is an end of all our difficulties.—A pretty good thought of mine—hey?"

Isabella's countenance was once more all smiles and good humour, and James too looked happy again.

"A most heavenly thought indeed! Now, my sweet Catherine, all our distresses are over; you are honourably acquitted, and we shall have a most delightful party."

"This will not do," said Catherine; "I cannot submit to this. I must run after Miss Tilney directly and set her right."

Isabella, however, caught hold of one hand; Thorpe of the other; and remonstrances poured in from all three. Even James was quite angry. When every thing was settled, when Miss Tilney herself said that Tuesday would suit her as well, it was quite ridiculous, quite absurd to make any further objection.

"I do not care. Mr. Thorpe had no business to invent any such message. If I had thought it right to put it off, I could have spoken to Miss Tilney myself. This is only doing it in a ruder way; and how do I know that Mr. Thorpe has——he may be mistaken again perhaps; he led me into one act of rudeness by his mistake on Friday. Let me go, Mr. Thorpe; Isabella, do not hold me."

Thorpe told her it would be in vain to go after the Tilneys; they were turning the corner into Brock-street, when he had overtaken them, and were at home by this time.

"Then I will go after them," said Catherine; "wherever they are I will go after them. It does not signify[1] talking. If I could not be persuaded into doing what I thought wrong, I never will be tricked into it." And with these words she broke away and hurried off.

1. A term Austen uses often in her letters, meaning that talking will make no difference, comparable to contemporary American slang "whatever," dismissive with a little attitude.

Thorpe would have darted after her, but Morland withheld him. "Let her go, let her go, if she will go. She is as obstinate as ——"

Thorpe never finished the simile, for it could hardly have been a proper one.

Away walked Catherine in great agitation, as fast as the crowd would permit her, fearful of being pursued, yet determined to persevere. As she walked, she reflected on what had passed. It was painful to her to disappoint and displease them, particularly to displease her brother; but she could not repent her resistance. Setting her own inclination apart, to have failed a second time in her engagement to Miss Tilney, to have retracted a promise voluntarily made only five minutes before, and on a false pretence too, must have been wrong. She had not been withstanding them on selfish principles alone, she had not consulted merely her own gratification; *that* might have been ensured in some degree by the excursion itself, by seeing Blaize Castle; no, she had attended to what was due to others, and to her own character in their opinion. Her conviction of being right however was not enough to restore her composure, till she had spoken to Miss Tilney she could not be at ease; and quickening her pace when she got clear of the Crescent, she almost ran over the remaining ground till she gained the top of Milsom-street. So rapid had been her movements, that in spite of the Tilneys' advantage in the outset, they were but just turning into their lodgings as she came within view of them; and the servant still remaining at the open door, she used only the ceremony of saying that she must speak with Miss Tilney that moment, and hurrying by him proceeded up stairs. Then, opening the first door before her, which happened to be the right, she immediately found herself in the drawing-room with General Tilney, his son and daughter. Her explanation, defective only in being—from her irritation of nerves and shortness of breath—no explanation at all, was instantly given. "I am come in a great hurry—It was all a mistake—I never promised to go—I told them from the first I could not go.—I ran away in a great hurry to explain it.—I did not care what you thought of me.—I would not stay for the servant."

The business however, though not perfectly elucidated by this speech, soon ceased to be a puzzle. Catherine found that John Thorpe *had* given the message; and Miss Tilney had no scruple in owning herself greatly surprised by it. But whether her brother had still exceeded her in resentment, Catherine, though she instinctively addressed herself as much to one as to the other in her vindication, had no means of knowing. Whatever might have been felt before her arrival, her eager declarations immediately made every look and sentence as friendly as she could desire.

The affair thus happily settled, she was introduced by Miss Tilney to her father, and received by him with such ready, such solicitous politeness as recalled Thorpe's information to her mind, and made her think with pleasure that he might be sometimes depended on. To such anxious attention was the General's civility carried, that not aware of her extraordinary swiftness in entering the house, he was quite angry with the servant whose neglect had reduced her to open the door of the apartment herself. What did William mean by it? He should make a point of inquiring into the matter. And if Catherine had not most warmly asserted his innocence, it seemed likely that William would lose the favour of his master for ever, if not his place, by her rapidity.

After sitting with them a quarter of an hour, she rose to take leave, and was then most agreeably surprized by General Tilney's asking her if she would do his daughter the honour of dining and spending the rest of the day with her. Miss Tilney added her own wishes. Catherine was greatly obliged; but it was quite out of her power. Mr. and Mrs. Allen would expect her back every moment. The General declared he could say no more; the claims of Mr. and Mrs. Allen were not to be superseded; but on some other day he trusted, when longer notice could be given, they would not refuse to spare her to her friend. Oh, no; Catherine was sure they would not have the least objection, and she should have great pleasure in coming. The General attended her himself to the street-door, saying every thing gallant as they went down stairs, admiring the elasticity of her walk, which corresponded exactly with the spirit of her dancing, and making her one of the most graceful bows she had ever beheld, when they parted.

Catherine, delighted by all that had passed, proceeded gaily to Pulteney-street; walking, as she concluded, with great elasticity,[2] though she had never thought of it before. She reached home without seeing any thing more of the offended party; and now that she had been triumphant throughout, had carried her point and was secure of her walk, she began (as the flutter of her spirits subsided) to

2. Catherine is walking alone in the streets of Bath with lively and unaffected spring, sprightliness, and energy.

doubt whether she had been perfectly right. A sacrifice was always noble; and if she had given way to their entreaties, she should have been spared the distressing idea of a friend displeased, a brother angry, and a scheme of great happiness to both destroyed, perhaps through her means. To ease her mind, and ascertain by the opinion of an unprejudiced person what her own conduct had really been, she took occasion to mention before Mr. Allen the half-settled scheme of her brother and the Thorpes for the following day. Mr. Allen caught at it directly. "Well," said he, "and do you think of going too?"

"No; I had just engaged myself to walk with Miss Tilney before they told me of it; and therefore you know I could not go with them, could I?"

"No, certainly not; and I am glad you do not think of it. These schemes are not at all the thing. Young men and women driving about the country in open carriages! Now and then it is very well; but going to inns and public places together! It is not right; and I wonder Mrs. Thorpe should allow it. I am glad you do not think of going; I am sure Mrs. Morland would not be pleased. Mrs. Allen, are not you of my way of thinking? Do not you think these kind of projects objectionable?'

"Yes, very much so indeed. Open carriages are nasty things. A clean gown is not five minutes wear in them. You are splashed getting in and getting out; and the wind takes your hair and your bonnet in every direction. I hate an open carriage myself."

"I know you do; but that is not the question. Do not you think it has an odd appearance, if young ladies are frequently driven about in them by young men, to whom they are not even related?"

"Yes, my dear, a very odd appearance indeed. I cannot bear to see it."

"Dear madam," cried Catherine, "then why did not you tell me so before? I am sure if I had known it to be improper, I would not have gone with Mr. Thorpe at all; but I always hoped you would tell me, if you thought I was doing wrong."

"And so I should, my dear, you may depend on it; for as I told Mrs. Morland at parting, I would always do the best for you in my power. But one must not be over particular. Young people *will* be young people, as your good mother says herself. You know I wanted you, when we first came, not to buy that sprigged muslin, but you would. Young people do not like to be always thwarted."

"But this was something of real consequence; and I do not think you would have found me hard to persuade."

"As far as it has gone hitherto, there is no harm done," said Mr. Allen; "and I would only advise you, my dear, not to go out with Mr. Thorpe any more."

"That is just what I was going to say," added his wife.

Catherine, relieved for herself, felt uneasy for Isabella; and after a moment's thought, asked Mr. Allen whether it would not be both proper and kind in her to write to Miss Thorpe, and explain the indecorum of which she must be as insensible as herself; for she considered that Isabella might otherwise perhaps be going to Clifton the next day, in spite of what had passed. Mr. Allen however discouraged her from doing any such thing. "You had better leave her alone, my dear, she is old enough to know what she is about; and if not, has a mother to advise her. Mrs. Thorpe is too indulgent beyond a doubt; but however you had better not interfere. She and your brother chuse to go, and you will be only getting ill-will."

Catherine submitted; and though sorry to think that Isabella should be doing wrong, felt greatly relieved by Mr. Allen's approbation of her own conduct, and truly rejoiced to be preserved by his advice from the danger of falling into such an error herself. Her escape from being one of the party to Clifton was now an escape indeed; for what would the Tilneys have thought of her, if she had broken her promise to them in order to do what was wrong in itself? if she had been guilty of one breach of propriety, only to enable her to be guilty of another?

CHAPTER XIV

The next morning was fair, and Catherine almost expected another attack from the assembled party. With Mr. Allen to support her, she felt no dread of the event: but she would gladly be spared a contest, where victory itself was painful; and was heartily rejoiced therefore at neither seeing nor hearing any thing of them. The Tilneys called for her at the appointed time; and no new difficulty arising, no sudden recollection, no unexpected summons, no impertinent intrusion to disconcert their measures, my heroine was most unnaturally able to fulfil her engagement, though it was made with the hero himself. They determined on walking round Beechen Cliff,[1] that noble hill, whose beautiful verdure and hanging coppice render it so striking an object from almost every opening in Bath.

"I never look at it," said Catherine, as they walked along the side of the river, "without thinking of the South of France."

"You have been abroad then?" said Henry, a little surprized.

"Oh! no, I only mean what I have read about. It always puts me in mind of the country that Emily and her father travelled through, in *The Mysteries of Udolpho*. But you never read novels, I dare say?"

"Why not?"

"Because they are not clever enough for you—gentlemen read better books."

"The person, be it gentleman or lady, who has not pleasure in a good novel, must be intolerably stupid. I have read all Mrs. Radcliffe's works, and most of them with great pleasure. *The Mysteries of Udolpho*, when I had once begun it, I could not lay down again;—I remember finishing it in two days—my hair standing on end the whole time."

"Yes," added Miss Tilney, "and I remember that you undertook to read it aloud to me, and that when I was called away for only five minutes to answer a note, instead of waiting for me, you took the volume into the Hermitage-walk, and I was obliged to stay till you had finished it."

"Thank you, Eleanor;—a most honourable testimony. You see, Miss Morland, the injustice of your suspicions. Here was I, in my eagerness to get on, refusing to wait only five minutes for my sister; breaking the promise I had made of reading it aloud, and keeping her in suspense at a most interesting part, by running away with the volume, which, you are to observe, was her own, particularly her own. I am proud when I reflect on it, and I think it must establish me in your good opinion."

"I am very glad to hear it indeed, and now I shall never be ashamed of liking *Udolpho* myself. But I really thought before, young men despised novels amazingly."

"It is *amazingly*; it may well suggest *amazement* if they do—for they read nearly as many as women. I myself have read hundreds and hundreds. Do not imagine that you can cope with me in a

---

1. A cliff to the south of Bath, a genuine hike, especially in a long skirt and slippers, but offering a view of the entire city.

knowledge of Julias and Louisas. If we proceed to particulars, and engage in the never-ceasing inquiry of 'Have you read this?' and 'Have you read that?' I shall soon leave you as far behind me as—what shall I say?—I want an appropriate simile;—as far as your friend Emily herself left poor Valancourt when she went with her aunt into Italy.[2] Consider how many years I have had the start of you. I had entered on my studies at Oxford, while you were a good little girl working your sampler at home!"

"Not very good I am afraid. But now really, do not you think *Udolpho* the nicest book in the world?"

"The nicest;—by which I suppose you mean the neatest.[3] That must depend upon the binding."

"Henry," said Miss Tilney, "you are very impertinent. Miss Morland, he is treating you exactly as he does his sister. He is for ever finding fault with me, for some incorrectness of language, and now he is taking the same liberty with you. The word 'nicest,' as you used it, did not suit him; and you had better change it as soon as you can, or we shall be overpowered with Johnson and Blair[4] all the rest of the way."

"I am sure," cried Catherine, "I did not mean to say any thing wrong; but it *is* a nice book, and why should not I call it so?"

"Very true," said Henry, "and this is a very nice day, and we are taking a very nice walk, and you are two very nice young ladies. Oh! it is a very nice word indeed!—it does for every thing. Originally perhaps it was applied only to express neatness, propriety, delicacy, or refinement;—people were nice in their dress, in their sentiments, or their choice. But now every commendation on every subject is comprised in that one word."

2. Emily, the heroine of *The Mysteries of Udolpho*, is sent away when her father dies and is separated from her true love, Valancourt.

3. Most editors agree that Tilney's objection to using "nice" and "good" instead of the conventional "particular" is a sign of his pedantry.

4. Samuel Johnson's *Dictionary of the English Language* (1755) was the first, with over 40,000 words illustrated by quotations, "a dictionary," he wrote, "by which the pronunciation of our language may be fixed, and its attainment facilitated; by which its purity may be preserved, its use ascertained, and its duration guaranteed." Appearing in a novel that represents the fashionable, ephemeral, and eclectic use of language, it provides an ironic point of reference. Hugh Blair's immensely influential *Lectures on Rhetoric and Belles Lettres* (1783) represented the Scottish school of Rhetoric, concerned with both public speaking and writing. Blair's comments on comedy [for which I am grateful to John Guillory] help explain Austen's narrative technique: "Without some interesting and well-conducted story, mere conversation is apt to become insipid. There should be always as much intrigue as to give us something to wish, and something to fear" (Lecture XLVII).

"While, in fact," cried his sister, "it ought only to be applied to you, without any commendation at all. You are more nice than wise. Come, Miss Morland, let us leave him to meditate over our faults in the utmost propriety of diction, while we praise *Udolpho* in whatever terms we like best. It is a most interesting work. You are fond of that kind of reading?"

"To say the truth, I do not much like any other."

"Indeed!"

"That is, I can read poetry and plays, and things of that sort, and do not dislike travels. But history, real solemn history, I cannot be interested in. Can you?"

"Yes, I am fond of history."

"I wish I were too. I read it a little as a duty, but it tells me nothing that does not either vex or weary me. The quarrels of popes and kings, with wars or pestilences, in every page; the men all so good for nothing, and hardly any women at all—it is very tiresome: and yet I often think it odd that it should be so dull, for a great deal of it must be invention. The speeches that are put into the heroes' mouths, their thoughts and designs—the chief of all this must be invention, and invention is what delights me in other books."

"Historians, you think," said Miss Tilney, "are not happy in their flights of fancy. They display imagination without raising interest. I am fond of history—and am very well contented to take the false with the true. In the principal facts they have sources of intelligence in former histories and records, which may be as much depended on, I conclude, as any thing that does not actually pass under one's own observation; and as for the little embellishments you speak of, they are embellishments, and I like them as such. If a speech be well drawn up, I read it with pleasure, by whomsoever it may be made—and probably with much greater, if the production of Mr. Hume or Mr. Robertson, than if the genuine words of Caractacus, Agricola, or Alfred the Great."[5]

---

5. David Hume and William Robertson wrote dramatic and sentimental histories shifting the emphasis from politics to social behavior and the lower classes, influenced, according to Phillips in *Society and Sentiment*, by the contemporary sentimental novel. Heroines reading history is a common device in the gothic novels, according to Pearson in *Women's Reading in Britain*. From a literary point of view, authors such as Edgeworth, Scott, and Austen had to decide how much history belonged in the novel, if any at all.

"You are fond of history!—and so are Mr. Allen and my father; and I have two brothers who do not dislike it. So many instances within my small circle of friends is remarkable! At this rate, I shall not pity the writers of history any longer. If people like to read their books, it is all very well, but to be at so much trouble in filling great volumes, which, as I used to think, nobody would willingly ever look into, to be labouring only for the torment of little boys and girls, always struck me as a hard fate; and though I know it is all very right and necessary, I have often wondered at the person's courage that could sit down on purpose to do it."

"That little boys and girls should be tormented," said Henry, "is what no one at all acquainted with human nature in a civilized state can deny; but in behalf of our most distinguished historians, I must observe, that they might well be offended at being supposed to have no higher aim; and that by their method and style, they are perfectly well qualified to torment readers of the most advanced reason and mature time of life. I use the verb 'to torment,' as I oberved to be your own method, instead of 'to instruct,' supposing them to be now admitted as synonymous."

"You think me foolish to call instruction a torment, but if you had been as much used as myself to hear poor little children first learning their letters and then learning to spell, if you had ever seen how stupid they can be for a whole morning together, and how tired my poor mother is at the end of it, as I am in the habit of seeing almost every day of my life at home, you would allow that to *torment* and to *instruct* might sometimes be used as synonymous words."

"Very probably. But historians are not accountable for the difficulty of learning to read; and even you yourself, who do not altogether seem particularly friendly to very severe, very intense application, may perhaps be brought to acknowledge that it is very well worth while to be tormented for two or three years of one's life, for the sake of being able to read all the rest of it. Consider—if reading had not been taught, Mrs. Radcliffe would have written in vain— or perhaps might not have written at all."

Catherine assented—and a very warm panegyric from her on that lady's merits, closed the subject.—The Tilneys were soon engaged in another on which she had nothing to say. They were viewing the country with the eyes of persons accustomed to drawing, and decided on its capability of being formed into pictures, with all the eagerness of real taste.[6] Here Catherine was quite lost. She knew nothing of drawing—nothing of taste:—and she listened to them with an attention which brought her little profit, for they talked in phrases which conveyed scarcely any idea to her. The little which she could understand however appeared to contradict the very few notions she had entertained on the matter before. It seemed as if a good view were no longer to be taken from the top of an high hill, and that a clear blue sky was no longer a proof of a fine day. She was heartily ashamed of her ignorance. A misplaced shame. Where people wish to attach, they should always be ignorant. To come with a well-informed mind, is to come with an inability of administering to the vanity of others, which a sensible person would always wish to avoid. A woman especially, if she have the misfortune of knowing any thing, should conceal it as well as she can.

The advantages of natural folly in a beautiful girl have been already set forth by the capital pen of a sister author;[7]—and to her treatment of the subject I will only add in justice to men, that though to the larger and more trifling part of the sex, imbecility in females is a great enhancement of their personal charms, there is a portion of them too reasonable and too well informed themselves to desire anything more in woman than ignorance. But Catherine did not know her own advantages—did not know that a good-looking girl, with an affectionate heart and a very ignorant mind, cannot fail of attracting a clever young man, unless circumstances are particularly untoward. In the present instance, she confessed and lamented her want of knowledge; declared that she would give any thing in the world to be able to draw; and a lecture on the picturesque immediately followed, in which his instructions were so clear that she soon began to see beauty in every thing admired by him, and her attention was so earnest, that he became perfectly satisfied of her having a great deal of natural taste. He talked of fore-grounds, distances, and second distances—side-screens and perspectives— lights and shades;—and Catherine was so hopeful a scholar, that when they gained the top of Beechen Cliff, she voluntarily rejected

6. They are describing "the picturesque" (see Contexts, p. 259).

7. In the 1790's many women authors, most notably, Burney and Wollstonecraft, parodied or openly protested depicting beautiful women whose success depended on their acting as if they were ignorant and helpless.

the whole city of Bath, as unworthy to make part of a landscape. Delighted with her progress, and fearful of wearying her with too much wisdom at once, Henry suffered the subject to decline, and by an easy transition from a piece of rocky fragment and the withered oak which he had placed near its summit, to oaks in general, to forests, the inclosure of them, waste lands, crown lands and government, he shortly found himself arrived at politics; and from politics, it was an easy step to silence. The general pause which succeeded his short disquisition on the state of the nation, was put an end to by Catherine, who, in rather a solemn tone of voice, uttered these words, "I have heard that something very shocking indeed, will soon come out in London."

Miss Tilney, to whom this was chiefly addressed, was startled, and hastily replied, "Indeed!—and of what nature?"

"That I do not know; nor who is the author. I have only heard that it is to be more horrible than anything we have met with yet."

"Good heaven!—Where could you hear of such a thing?"

"A particular friend of mine had an account of it in a letter from London yesterday. It is to be uncommonly dreadful. I shall expect murder and every thing of the kind."

"You speak with astonishing composure! But I hope your friend's accounts have been exaggerated;—and if such a design is known beforehand, proper measures will undoubtedly be taken by government to prevent its coming to effect."

"Government," said Henry, endeavouring not to smile, "neither desires nor dares to interefere in such matters. There must be murder; and government cares not how much."

The ladies stared. He laughed, and added, "Come, shall I make you understand each other, or leave you to puzzle out an explanation as you can? No—I will be noble. I will prove myself a man, no less by the generosity of my soul than the clearness of my head. I have no patience with such of my sex as disdain to let themselves sometimes down to the comprehension of yours. Perhaps the abilities of women are neither sound nor acute—neither vigorous nor keen. Perhaps they may want observation, discernment, judgment, fire, genius, and wit."

"Miss Morland, do not mind what he says;—but have the goodness to satisfy me as to this dreadful riot."

"Riot!—what riot?"

"My dear Eleanor, the riot is only in your own brain. The confusion there is scandalous. Miss Morland has been talking of nothing more dreadful than a new publication which is shortly to come out, in three duodecimo volumes, two hundred and seventy-six pages in each, with a frontispiece to the first, of two tombstones and a lantern—do you understand?[8]—And you, Miss Morland— my stupid sister has mistaken all your clearest expressions. You talked of expected horrors in London—and instead of instantly conceiving, as any rational creature would have done, that such words could relate only to a circulating library, she immediately pictured to herself a mob of three thousand men assembling in St. George's Fields; the Bank attacked, the Tower threatened, the streets of London flowing with blood, a detachment of the 12th Light Dragoons, (the hopes of the nation,) called up from Northampton to quell the insurgents,[9] and the gallant Capt. Frederick Tilney, in the moment of charging at the head of his troop, knocked off his horse by a brickbat from an upper window. Forgive her stupidity. The fears of the sister have added to the weakness of the woman; but she is by no means a simpleton in general."

Catherine looked grave. "And now, Henry," said Miss Tilney, "that you have made us understand each other, you may as well make Miss Morland understand yourself—unless you mean to have her think you intolerably rude to your sister, and a great brute in your opinion of women in general. Miss Morland is not used to your odd ways."

"I shall be most happy to make her better acquainted with them."

"No doubt;—but that is no explanation of the present."

"What am I to do?"

"You know what you ought to do. Clear your character handsomely before her. Tell her that you think very highly of the understanding of women."

---

8. Most editors believe this reference to rioting in London refers to the Gordon Riots of 1780, but there were frequent riots in London in the 1790's over the cost of food and political repression and again in 1816–18, when post-war depression led many laborers called Luddites to destroy the machines they thought were replacing them. Because the repression included arresting publishers and destroying publications, even a writer such as Austen and her publishers were endangered.

9. Citizen rebels, *cf.* Sir W. Scott's *Waverley*, 1814, Ch. 38.

"Miss Morland, I think very highly of the understanding of all the women in the world—especially of those—whoever they may be—with whom I happen to be in company."

"That is not enough. Be more serious."

"Miss Morland, no one can think more highly of the understanding of women than I do. In my opinion, nature has given them so much, that they never find it necessary to use more than half."

"We shall get nothing more serious from him now, Miss Morland. He is not in a sober mood. But I do assure you that he must be entirely misunderstood, if he can ever appear to say an unjust thing of any woman at all, or an unkind one of me."

It was no effort to Catherine to believe that Henry Tilney could never be wrong. His manner might sometimes surprize, but his meaning must always be just:—and what she did not understand, she was almost as ready to admire, as what she did. The whole walk was delightful, and though it ended too soon, its conclusion was delightful too;—her friends attended her into the house, and Miss Tilney, before they parted, addressing herself with respectful form, as much to Mrs. Allen as to Catherine, petitioned for the pleasure of her company to dinner on the day after the next. No difficulty was made on Mrs. Allen's side—and the only difficulty on Catherine's was in concealing the excess of her pleasure.

The morning had passed away so charmingly as to banish all her friendship and natural affection; for no thought of Isabella or James had crossed her during their walk. When the Tilneys were gone, she became amiable again, but she was amiable for some time to little effect; Mrs. Allen had no intelligence to give that could relieve her anxiety, she had heard nothing of any of them. Towards the end of the morning however, Catherine having occasion for some indispensable yard of ribbon which must be bought without a moment's delay, walked out into the town, and in Bond-street overtook the second Miss Thorpe, as she was loitering towards Edgar's buildings between two of the sweetest girls in the world, who had been her dear friends all the morning. From her, she soon learned that the party to Clifton had taken place. "They set off at eight this morning," said Miss Anne, "and I am sure I do not envy them their drive. I think you and I are very well off to be out of the scrape.—It must be the dullest thing in the world, for there is not a soul at Clifton at this time of year. Belle went with your brother, and John drove Maria."

Catherine spoke the pleasure she really felt on hearing this part of the arrangement.

"Oh! yes," rejoined the other, "Maria is gone. She was quite wild to go. She thought it would be something very fine. I cannot say I admire her taste; and for my part I was determined from the first not to go, if they pressed me ever so much."

Catherine, a little doubtful of this, could not help answering, "I wish you could have gone too. It is a pity you could not all go."

"Thank you; but it is quite a matter of indifference to me. Indeed, I would not have gone on any account. I was saying so to Emily and Sophia when you overtook us."

Catherine was still unconvinced; but glad that Anne should have the friendship of an Emily and a Sophia to console her, she bade her adieu without much uneasiness, and returned home, pleased that the party had not been prevented by her refusing to join it, and very heartily wishing that it might be too pleasant to allow either James or Isabella to resent her resistance any longer.

CHAPTER XV

Early the next day, a note from Isabella, speaking peace and tenderness in every line, and entreating the immediate presence of her friend on a matter of the utmost importance, hastened Catherine, in the happiest state of confidence and curiosity, to Edgar's Buildings.—The two youngest Miss Thorpes were by themselves in the parlour; and, on Anne's quitting it to call her sister, Catherine took the opportunity of asking the other for some particulars of their yesterday's party. Maria desired no greater pleasure than to speak of it; and Catherine immediately learnt that it had been altogether the most delightful scheme in the world; that nobody could imagine how charming it had been, and that it had been more delightful than any body could conceive. Such was the information of the first five minutes; the second unfolded thus much in detail,—that they had driven directly to the York Hotel, ate some soup, and bespoke an early dinner, walked down to the Pump-room, tasted the water, and laid out some shillings in purses and spars;[1] thence adjourned

---

1. Spent money on purses and ornaments or shiny gem-stones.

to eat ice at a pastry-cook's, and hurrying back to the Hotel, swallowed their dinner in haste, to prevent being in the dark; and then had a delightful drive back, only the moon was not up, and it rained a little, and Mr. Morland's horse was so tired he could hardly get it along.

Catherine listened with heartfelt satisfaction. It appeared that Blaize Castle had never been thought of; and, as for all the rest, there was nothing to regret for half an instant.—Maria's intelligence concluded with a tender effusion of pity for her sister Anne, whom she represented as insupportably cross, from being excluded the party.

"She will never forgive me, I am sure; but, you know, how could I help it? John would have me go, for he vowed he would not drive her, because she had such thick ankles. I dare say she will not be in good humour again this month; but I am determined I will not be cross; it is not a little matter that puts me out of temper."

Isabella now entered the room with so eager a step, and a look of such happy importance, as engaged all her friend's notice. Maria was without ceremony sent away, and Isabella, embracing Catherine, thus began:—"Yes, my dear Catherine, it is so indeed; your penetration has not deceived you.—Oh! that arch eye of yours!—It sees through every thing."

Catherine replied only by a look of wondering ignorance.

"Nay, my beloved, sweetest friend," continued the other, "compose yourself.—I am amazingly agitated, as you perceive. Let us sit down and talk in comfort. Well, and so you guessed it the moment you had my note?—Sly creature!—Oh! my dear Catherine, you alone who know my heart can judge of my present happiness. Your brother is the most charming of men. I only wish I were more worthy of him.—But what will your excellent father and mother say?—Oh! heavens! when I think of them I am so agitated!"

Catherine's understanding began to awake: an idea of the truth suddenly darted into her mind; and, with the natural blush of so new an emotion, she cried out, "Good heaven!—my dear Isabella, what do you mean? Can you—can you really be in love with James?"

This bold surmise, however, she soon learnt comprehended but half the fact. The anxious affection, which she was accused of having continually watched in Isabella's every look and action, had, in the course of their yesterday's party, received the delightful confession of an equal love. Her heart and faith were alike engaged to James.—Never had Catherine listened to any thing so full of interest, wonder, and joy. Her brother and her friend engaged!—New to such circumstances, the importance of it appeared unspeakably great, and she contemplated it as one of those grand events, of which the ordinary course of life can hardly afford a return. The strength of her feelings she could not express; the nature of them, however, contented her friend. The happiness of having such a sister was their first effusion, and the fair ladies mingled in embraces and tears of joy

Delighting, however, as Catherine sincerely did in the prospect of the connection, it must be acknowledged that Isabella far surpassed her in tender anticipations.—"You will be so infinitely dearer to me, my Catherine, than either Anne or Maria: I feel that I shall be so much more attached to my dear Morland's family than to my own."

This was a pitch of friendship beyond Catherine.

"You are so like your dear brother," continued Isabella, "that I quite doted on you the first moment I saw you. But so it always is with me; the first moment settles every thing. The very first day that Morland came to us last Christmas—the very first moment I beheld him—my heart was irrecoverably gone. I remember I wore my yellow gown, with my hair done up in braids; and when I came into the drawing-room, and John introduced him, I thought I never saw any body so handsome before."

Here Catherine secretly acknowledged the power of love; for, though exceedingly fond of her brother, and partial to all his endowments, she had never in her life thought him handsome.

"I remember too, Miss Andrews drank tea with us that evening, and wore her puce-coloured sarsenet,[2] and she looked so heavenly, that I thought your brother must certainly fall in love with her; I could not sleep a wink all night for thinking of it. Oh! Catherine, the many sleepless nights I have had on your brother's account!—I would not have you suffer half what I have done! I am grown wretchedly thin I know; but I will not pain you by describing my anxiety; you have seen enough of it. I feel that I have betrayed myself perpetually;—so unguarded, in speaking of my

2. A fine pale yellow-beige silk, the color "puce" from the French meaning "flea."

partiality for the church!—But my secret I was always sure would be safe with *you*."

Catherine felt that nothing could have been safer; but ashamed of an ignorance little expected, she dared no longer contest the point, nor refuse to have been as full of arch penetration and affectionate sympathy as Isabella chose to consider her. Her brother she found was preparing to set off with all speed to Fullerton, to make known his situation and ask consent; and here was a source of some real agitation to the mind of Isabella. Catherine endeavoured to persuade her, as she was herself persuaded, that her father and mother would never oppose their son's wishes.—"It is impossible," said she, "for parents to be more kind, or more desirous of their children's happiness; I have no doubt of their consenting immediately."

"Morland says exactly the same," replied Isabella; "and yet I dare not expect it; my fortune will be so small; they never can consent to it. Your brother, who might marry any body!"

Here Catherine again discerned the force of love.

"Indeed, Isabella, you are too humble.—The difference of fortune can be nothing to signify."

"Oh! my sweet Catherine, in *your* generous heart I know it would signify nothing; but we must not expect such disinterestedness in many. As for myself, I am sure I only wish our situations were reversed. Had I the command of millions, were I mistress of the whole world, your brother would be my only choice."

This charming sentiment, recommended as much by sense as novelty, gave Catherine a most pleasing remembrance of all the heroines of her acquaintance; and she thought her friend never looked more lovely than in uttering the grand idea.—"I am sure they will consent," was her frequent declaration; "I am sure they will be delighted with you."

"For my own part," said Isabella, "my wishes are so moderate, that the smallest income in nature would be enough for me. Where people are really attached, poverty itself is wealth: grandeur I detest: I would not settle in London for the universe. A cottage in some retired village would be ecstasy. There are some charming little villas about Richmond."

"Richmond!" cried Catherine.—"You must settle near Fullerton. You must be near us."

"I am sure I shall be miserable if we do not. If I can but be near *you*, I shall be satisfied. But this is idle talking! I will not allow myself to think of such things, till we have your father's answer. Morland says that by sending it to-night to Salisbury, we may have it to-morrow.—To-morrow?—I know I shall never have courage to open the letter. I know it will be the death of me."

A reverie succeeded this conviction—and when Isabella spoke again, it was to resolve on the quality of her wedding-gown.

Their conference was put an end to by the anxious young lover himself, who came to breathe his parting sigh before he set off for Wiltshire. Catherine wished to congratulate him, but knew not what to say, and her eloquence was only in her eyes. From them however the eight parts of speech shone out most expressively, and James could combine them with ease. Impatient for the realization of all that he hoped at home, his adieus were not long; and they would have been yet shorter, had he not been frequently detained by the urgent entreaties of his fair one that he would go. Twice was he called almost from the door by her eagerness to have him gone. "Indeed, Morland, I must drive you away. Consider how far you have to ride. I cannot bear to see you linger so. For Heaven's sake, waste no more time. There, go, go—I insist on it."

The two friends, with hearts now more united than ever, were inseparable for the day; and in schemes of sisterly happiness the hours flew along. Mrs. Thorpe and her son, who were acquainted with every thing, and who seemed only to want Mr. Morland's consent to consider Isabella's engagement as the most fortunate circumstance imaginable for their family, were allowed to join their counsels, and add their quota of significant looks and mysterious expressions to fill up the measure of curiosity to be raised in the unprivileged younger sisters. To Catherine's simple feelings, this odd sort of reserve seemed neither kindly meant, nor consistently supported; and its unkindness she would hardly have forborn pointing out, had its inconsistency been less their friend;—but Anne and Maria soon set her heart at ease by the sagacity of their "I know what;" and the evening was spent in a sort of war of wit, a display of family ingenuity; on one side in the mystery of an affected secret, on the other of undefined discovery, all equally acute.

Catherine was with her friend again the next day, endeavouring to support her spirits, and while away the many tedious hours before the delivery of the letters; a needful exertion, for as the time of reasonable expectation drew near, Isabella became more and more desponding, and before the letter arrived, had worked herself into a state of real distress. But when it did come, where could distress be found? "I have had no difficulty in gaining the consent of my kind parents, and am promised that every thing in their power shall be done to forward my happiness," were the first three lines, and in one moment all was joyful security. The brightest glow was instantly spread over Isabella's features, all care and anxiety seemed removed, her spirits became almost too high for control, and she called herself without scruple the happiest of mortals.

Mrs. Thorpe, with tears of joy, embraced her daughter, her son, her visitor, and could have embraced half the inhibitants of Bath with satisfaction. Her heart was overflowing with tenderness. It was "dear John," and "dear Catherine" at every word;—"dear Anne and dear Maria" must immediately be made sharers in their felicity; and two "dears" at once before the name of Isabella were not more than that beloved child had now well earned. John himself was no skulker in joy. He not only bestowed on Mr. Morland the high commendation of being one of the finest fellows in the world, but swore off many sentences in his praise.

The letter, whence sprang all this felicity, was short, containing little more than this assurance of success; and every particular was deferred till James could write again. But for particulars Isabella could well afford to wait. The needful was comprised in Mr. Morland's promise; his honour was pledged to make every thing easy; and by what means their income was to be formed, whether landed property were to be resigned, or funded money made over, was a matter in which her disinterested spirit took no concern. She knew enough to feel secure of an honourable and speedy establishment, and her imagination took a rapid flight over its attendant felicities. She saw herself at the end of a few weeks, the gaze and admiration of every new acquaintance at Fullerton, the envy of every valued old friend in Putney, with a carriage at her command, a new name on her tickets,[3] and a brilliant exhibition of hoop rings on her finger.

3. Calling cards which people dropped off at houses to indicate they were interested in making social contact.

When the contents of the letter were ascertained, John Thorpe, who had only waited its arrival to begin his journey to London, prepared to set off. "Well, Miss Morland," said he, on finding her alone in the parlour, "I am come to bid you good bye." Catherine wished him a good journey. Without appearing to hear her, he walked to the window, fidgetted about, hummed a tune, and seemed wholly self-occupied.

"Shall not you be late at Devizes?"[4] said Catherine. He made no answer; but after a minute's silence burst out with, "A famous good thing this marrying scheme, upon my soul! A clever fancy of Morland's and Belle's. What do you think of it, Miss Morland? *I* say it is no bad notion."

"I am sure I think it a very good one."

"Do you?—that's honest, by heavens! I am glad you are no enemy to matrimony however. Did you ever hear the old song, 'Going to one wedding brings on another?' I say, you will come to Belle's wedding, I hope."[5]

"Yes; I have promised your sister to be with her, if possible."

"And then you know"—twisting himself about and forcing a foolish laugh—"I say, then you know, we may try the truth of this same old song."

"May we?—but I never sing. Well, I wish you a good journey. I dine with Miss Tilney to-day, and must now be going home."

"Nay, but there is no such confounded hurry.—Who knows when we may be together again?—Not but that I shall be down again by the end of a fortnight, and a devilish long fortnight it will appear to me."

"Then why do you stay away so long?" replied Catherine—finding that he waited for an answer.

"That is kind of you, however—kind and good-natured.—I shall not forget it in a hurry.—But you have more good-nature and all that, than any body living I believe. A monstrous deal of good-nature, and it is not only good-nature, but you have so much, so much of every thing; and then you have such—upon my soul I do not know any body like you."

---

4. A village, a rest stop, and an eating establishment between Bath and London.

5. Several alternative sources have been suggested such as John Gay's *The Wife of Bath* or Congreve, *Love for Love*. It is a common superstition.

"Oh! dear, there are a great many people like me, I dare say, only a great deal better. Good morning to you."

"But I say, Miss Morland, I shall come and pay my respects at Fullerton before it is long, if not disagreeable."

"Pray do.—My father and mother will be very glad to see you."

"And I hope—I hope, Miss Morland, *you* will not be sorry to see me."

"Oh! dear, not at all. There are very few people I am sorry to see. Company is always cheerful."

"That is just my way of thinking. Give me but a little cheerful company, let me only have the company of the people I love, let me only be where I like and with whom I like, and the devil take the rest, say I.—And I am heartily glad to hear you say the same. But I have a notion, Miss Morland, you and I think pretty much alike upon most matters."

"Perhaps we may; but it is more than I ever thought of. And as to *most matters*, to say the truth, there are not many that I know my own mind about."

"By Jove, no more do I. It is not my way to bother my brains with what does not concern me. My notion of things is simple enough. Let me only have the girl I like, say I, with a comfortable house over my head, and what care I for all the rest? Fortune is nothing. I am sure of a good income of my own; and if she had not a penny, why so much the better."

"Very true. I think like you there. If there is a good fortune on one side, there can be no occasion for any on the other. No matter which has it, so that there is enough. I hate the idea of one great fortune looking out for another. And to marry for money I think the wickedest thing in existence.—Good day.—We shall be very glad to see you at Fullerton, whenever it is convenient." And away she went. It was not in the power of all his gallantry to detain her longer. With such news to communicate, and such a visit to prepare for, her departure was not to be delayed by any thing in his nature to urge; and she hurried away, leaving him to the undivided consciousness of his own happy address, and her explicit encouragement.

The agitation which she had herself experienced on first learning her brother's engagement, made her expect to raise no inconsiderable emotion in Mr. and Mrs. Allen, by the communication of the wonderful event. How great was her disappointment! The important affair, which many words of preparation ushered in, had been foreseen by them both ever since her brother's arrival; and all that they felt on the occasion was comprehended in a wish for the young people's happiness, with a remark, on the gentleman's side, in favour of Isabella's beauty, and on the lady's, of her great good luck. It was to Catherine the most surprizing insensibility. The disclosure however of the great secret of James's going to Fullerton the day before, did raise some emotion in Mrs. Allen. She could not listen to that with perfect calmness; but repeatedly regretted the necessity of its concealment, wished she could have known his intention, wished she could have seen him before he went, as she should certainly have troubled him with her best regards to his father and mother, and her kind compliments to all the Skinners.

VOLUME II

CHAPTER I

Catherine's expectations of pleasure from her visit in Milsom-street were so very high, that disappointment was inevitable; and accordingly, though she was most politely received by General Tilney, and kindly welcomed by his daughter, though Henry was at home, and no one else of the party, she found, on her return, without spending many hours in the examination of her feelings, that she had gone to her appointment preparing for happiness which it had not afforded. Instead of finding herself improved in acquaintance with Miss Tilney, from the intercourse of the day, she seemed hardly so intimate with her as before; instead of seeing Henry Tilney to greater advantage than ever, in the ease of a family party, he had never said so little, nor been so little agreeable; and, in spite of their father's great civilities to her—in spite of his thanks, invitations, and compliments—it had been a release to get away from him. It puzzled her to account for all this. It could not be General Tilney's fault. That he was perfectly agreeable and good-natured, and altogether a very charming man, did not admit of a doubt, for he was tall and handsome, and Henry's father. *He* could not be accountable for his children's want of spirits, or for her want of enjoyment in his company. The former she hoped at last might have been accidental, and the latter she could only attribute to her own stupidity. Isabella, on hearing the particulars of the visit, gave a different explanation: "It was all pride, pride, insufferable haughtiness and pride!" She had long suspected the family to be very high, and this made it certain. Such insolence of behaviour as Miss Tilney's she had never heard of in her life! Not to do the honours of her house with common good-breeding!—To behave to her guest with such superciliousness!—Hardly even to speak to her!

"But it was not so bad as that, Isabella; there was no superciliousness; she was very civil."

"Oh! don't defend her! And then the brother, he, who had appeared so attached to you! Good heavens! well, some people's feelings are incomprehensible. And so he hardly looked once at you the whole day?"

"I do not say so; but he did not seem in good spirits."

"How contemptible! Of all things in the world inconstancy is my aversion. Let me entreat you never to think of him again, my dear Catherine; indeed he is unworthy of you."

"Unworthy! I do not suppose he ever thinks of me."

"That is exactly what I say; he never thinks of you.—Such fickleness! Oh! how different to your brother and to mine! I really believe John has the most constant heart."

"But as for General Tilney, I assure you it would be impossible for any body to behave to me with greater civility and attention; it seemed to be his only care to entertain and make me happy."

"Oh! I know no harm of him; I do not suspect him of pride. I believe he is a very gentleman-like man. John thinks very well of him, and John's judgment——"

"Well, I shall see how they behave to me this evening; we shall meet them at the Rooms."

"And must I go?"

"Do not you intend it? I thought it was all settled."

"Nay, since you make such a point of it, I can refuse you nothing. But do not insist upon my being very agreeable, for my heart, you know, will be some forty miles off. And as for dancing, do not mention it I beg; *that* is quite out of the question. Charles Hodges will plague me to death I dare say; but I shall cut him very short. Ten to one but he guesses the reason, and that is exactly what I want to avoid, so I shall insist on his keeping his conjecture to himself."

Isabella's opinion of the Tilneys did not influence her friend; she was sure there had been no insolence in the manners either of brother or sister; and she did not credit there being any pride in their hearts. The evening rewarded her confidence; she was met by one with the same kindness, and by the other with the same attention as heretofore: Miss Tilney took pains to be near her, and Henry asked her to dance.

Having heard the day before in Milsom-street, that their elder brother, Captain Tilney, was expected almost every hour, she was at no loss for the name of a very fashionable-looking, handsome young man, whom she had never seen before, and who now evidently belonged to their party. She looked at him with great admiration, and even supposed it possible, that some people might think him handsomer than his brother, though, in her eyes, his air was more assuming, and his countenance less prepossessing. His taste and manners were beyond a doubt decidedly inferior; for, within her hearing, he not only protested against every thought of dancing himself, but even laughed openly at Henry for finding it possible. From the latter circumstance it may be presumed, that, whatever might be our heroine's opinion of him, his admiration of her was not of a very dangerous kind; not likely to produce animosities between the brothers, nor persecutions to the lady. *He* cannot be the instigator of the three villians in horsemen's great coats, by whom she will hereafter be forced into a travelling chaise-and-four, which will drive off with incredible speed. Catherine, meanwhile, undisturbed by presentiments of such an evil, or of any evil at all, except that of having but a short set to dance down, enjoyed her usual happiness with Henry Tilney, listening with sparkling eyes to every thing he said; and, in finding him irresistible, becoming so herself.

At the end of the first dance, Captain Tilney came towards them again, and, much to Catherine's dissatisfaction, pulled his brother away. They retired whispering together; and, though her delicate sensibility did not take immediate alarm, and lay it down as fact, that Captain Tilney must have heard some malevolent misrepresentation of her, which he now hastened to communicate to his brother, in the hope of separating them for ever, she could not have her partner conveyed from her sight without very uneasy sensations. Her suspense was of full five minutes' duration; and she was beginning to think it a very long quarter of an hour, when they both returned, and an explanation was given, by Henry's requesting to know, if she thought her friend, Miss Thorpe, would have any objection to dancing, as his brother would be most happy to be introduced to her. Catherine, without hesitation, replied, that she was very sure Miss Thorpe did not mean to dance at all. The cruel reply was passed on to the other, and he immediately walked away.

"Your brother will not mind it I know," said she, "because I heard him say before, that he hated dancing; but it was very good-natured in him to think of it. I suppose he saw Isabella sitting down, and fancied she might wish for a partner; but he is quite mistaken, for she would not dance upon any account in the world."

Henry smiled, and said, "How very little trouble it can give you to understand the motive of other people's actions."

"Why?—What do you mean?"

"With you, it is not, How is such a one likely to be influenced? What is the inducement most likely to act upon such a person's feelings, age, situation, and probable habits of life considered?—but, how should *I* be influenced, what would be *my* inducement in acting so and so?"

"I do not understand you."

"Then we are on very unequal terms, for I understand you perfectly well."

"Me?—yes; I cannot speak well enough to be unintelligible."

"Bravo!—an excellent satire on modern language."

"But pray tell me what you mean."

"Shall I indeed?—Do you really desire it?—But you are not aware of the consequences; it will involve you in a very cruel embarrassment, and certainly bring on a disagreement between us."

"No, no; it shall not do either; I am not afraid."

"Well then, I only meant that your attributing my brother's wish of dancing with Miss Thorpe to good-nature alone, convinced me of your being superior in good-nature yourself to all the rest of the world."

Catherine blushed and disclaimed, and the gentleman's predictions were verified. There was a something, however, in his words which repaid her for the pain of confusion; and that something occupied her mind so much, that she drew back for some time, forgetting to speak or to listen, and almost forgetting where she was; till, roused by the voice of Isabella, she looked up and saw her with Captain Tilney preparing to give them hands across.

Isabella shrugged her shoulders and smiled, the only explanation of this extraordinary change which could at that time be given; but as it was not quite enough for Catherine's comprehension, she spoke her astonishment in very plain terms to her partner.

"I cannot think how it could happen! Isabella was so determined not to dance."

"And did Isabella never change her mind before?"

"Oh! but, because——and your brother!—After what you told him from me, how could he think of going to ask her?"

"I cannot take surprize to myself on that head. You bid me be surprized on your friend's account, and therefore I am; but as for my brother, his conduct in the business, I must own, has been no more than I believed him perfectly equal to. The fairness of your friend was an open attraction; her firmness, you know, could only be understood by yourself."

"You are laughing; but, I assure you, Isabella is very firm in general."

"It is as much as should be said of any one. To be always firm must be to be often obstinate. When properly to relax is the trial of judgment; and, without reference to my brother, I really think Miss Thorpe has by no means chosen ill in fixing on the present hour."

The friends were not able to get together for any confidential discourse till all the dancing was over; but then, as they walked about the room arm in arm, Isabella thus explained herself:—"I do not wonder at your surprize; and I am really fatigued to death. He is such a rattle!—Amusing enough, if my mind had been disengaged; but I would have given the world to sit still."

"Then why did not you?"

"Oh! my dear! it would have looked so particular; and you know how I abhor doing that. I refused him as long as I possibly could, but he would take no denial. You have no idea how he pressed me. I begged him to excuse me, and get some other partner—but no, not he; after aspiring to my hand, there was nobody else in the room he could bear to think of; and it was not that he wanted merely to dance, he wanted to be with *me*. Oh! such nonsense!—I told him he had taken a very unlikely way to prevail upon me; for, of all things in the world, I hated fine speeches and compliments;—and so——and so then I found there would be no peace if I did not stand up. Besides, I thought Mrs. Hughes, who introduced him, might take it ill if I did not: and your dear brother, I am sure he would have been miserable if I had sat down the whole evening. I am so glad it is over! My spirits are quite jaded with listening to his nonsense: and then,—being such a smart young fellow, I saw every eye was upon us."

"He is very handsome indeed."

"Handsome!—Yes, I suppose he may. I dare say people would admire him in general; but he is not at all in my style of beauty. I hate a florid complexion and dark eyes in a man. However, he is very well. Amazingly conceited, I am sure. I took him down several times you know in my way."

When the young ladies next met, they had a far more interesting subject to discuss. James Morland's second letter was then received, and the kind intentions of his father fully explained. A living, of which Mr. Morland was himself patron and incumbent, of about four hunded pounds yearly value, was to be resigned to his son as soon as he should be old enough to take it; no trifling deduction from the family income, no niggardly assignment to one of ten children. An estate of at least equal value, moreover, was assured as his future inheritance.

James expressed himself on the occasion with becoming gratitude; and the necessity of waiting between two and three years before they could marry, being, however unwelcome, no more than he had expected, was borne by him without discontent. Catherine, whose expectations had been as unfixed as her ideas of her father's income, and whose judgment was now entirely led by her brother, felt equally well satisfied, and heartily congratulated Isabella on having every thing so pleasantly settled.

"It is very charming indeed," said Isabella, with a grave face. "Mr. Morland has behaved vastly handsome indeed," said the gentle Mrs. Thorpe, looking anxiously at her daughter. "I only wish I could do as much. One could not expect more from him you know. If he finds he *can* do more by and bye, I dare say he will, for I am sure he must be an excellent good hearted man. Four hundred is but a small income to begin on indeed, but your wishes, my dear Isabella, are so moderate, you do not consider how little you ever want, my dear.'

"It is not on my own account I wish for more; but I cannot bear to be the means of injuring my dear Morland, making him sit down upon an income hardly enough to find one in the common necessaries of life. For myself, it is nothing; I never think of myself."

"I know you never do, my dear; and you will always find your reward in the affection it makes every body feel for you. There never was a young woman so beloved as you are by every body that knows you; and I dare say when Mr. Morland sees you, my dear child—but do not let us distress our dear Catherine by talking of such things. Mr. Morland has behaved so very handsome you know. I always heard he was a most excellent man; and you know, my dear, we are not to suppose but what, if you had had a suitable fortune, he would have come down with something more, for I am sure he must be a most liberal-minded man."

"Nobody can think better of Mr. Morland than I do, I am sure. But every body has their failing you know, and every body has a right to do what they like with their own money." Catherine was hurt by these insinuations. "I am very sure," said she, "that my father has promised to do as much as he can afford."

Isabella recollected herself. "As to that, my sweet Catherine, there cannot be a doubt, and you know me well enough to be sure that a much smaller income would satisfy me. It is not the want of more money that makes me just at present a little out of spirits; I hate money; and if our union could take place now upon only fifty pounds a year, I should not have a wish unsatisfied. Ah! my Catherine, you have found me out. There's the sting. The long, long, endless two years and half that are to pass before your brother can hold the living."

"Yes, yes, my darling Isabella," said Mrs. Thorpe, "we perfectly see into your heart. You have no disguise. We perfectly understand the present vexation; and every body must love you the better for such a noble honest affection."

Catherine's uncomfortable feelings began to lessen. She endeavoured to believe that the delay of the marriage was the only source of Isabella's regret; and when she saw her at their next interview as cheerful and amiable as ever, endeavoured to forget that she had for a minute thought otherwise. James soon followed his letter, and was received with the most gratifying kindness.

CHAPTER II

The Allens had now entered on the sixth week of their stay in Bath; and whether it should be the last, was for some time a question, to which Catherine listened with a beating heart. To have her acquaintance with the Tilneys end so soon, was an evil which nothing could counterbalance. Her whole happiness seemed at stake, while the affair was in suspense, and every thing secured when it was determined that the lodgings should be taken for another fortnight. What this additional fortnight was to produce to her beyond the pleasure of sometimes seeing Henry Tilney, made but a small part of Catherine's speculation. Once or twice indeed, since James's engagement had taught her what *could* be done, she had got so far as to indulge in a secret "perhaps," but in general the felicity of being with him for the present bounded her views: the present was now comprised in another three weeks, and her happiness being certain for that period, the rest of her life was at such a distance as to excite but little interest. In the course of the morning which saw this business arranged, she visited Miss Tilney, and poured forth her joyful feelings. It was doomed to be a day of trial. No sooner had she expressed her delight in Mr. Allen's lengthened stay, than Miss Tilney told her of her father's having just determined upon quitting Bath by the end of another week. Here was a blow! The past suspense of the morning had been ease and quiet to the present disappointment. Catherine's countenance fell, and in a voice of most sincere concern she echoed Miss Tilney's concluding words, "By the end of another week!"

"Yes, my father can seldom be prevailed on to give the waters what I think a fair trial. He has been disappointed of some friends' arrival whom he expected to meet here, and as he is now pretty well, is in a hurry to get home."

"I am very sorry for it," said Catherine dejectedly, "if I had known this before—"

"Perhaps," said Miss Tilney in an embarrassed manner, "you would be so good—it would make me very happy if—"

The entrance of her father put a stop to the civility, which Catherine was beginning to hope might introduce a desire of their corresponding. After addressing her with his usual politeness, he turned to his daughter and said, "Well, Eleanor, may I congratulate you on being successful in your application to your fair friend?"

"I was just beginning to make the request, sir, as you came in."

"Well, proceed by all means. I know how much your heart is in it. My daughter, Miss Morland," he continued, without leaving his daughter time to speak, "has been forming a very bold wish. We leave Bath, as she has perhaps told you, on Saturday se'nnight.[1] A letter from my steward tells me that my presence is wanted at home; and being disappointed in my hope of seeing the Marquis of Long-town and General Courteney here, some of my very old friends, there is nothing to detain me longer in Bath. And could we carry our selfish point with you, we should leave it without a single regret. Can you, in short, be prevailed on to quit this scene of public triumph and oblige your friend Eleanor with your company in Gloucestershire? I am almost ashamed to make the request, though its presumption would certainly appear greater to every creature in Bath than your-self. Modesty such as your's—but not for the world would I pain it by open praise. If you can be induced to honour us with a visit, you will make us happy beyond expression. 'Tis true, we can offer you nothing like the gaieties of this lively place; we can tempt you neither by amusement nor splendour, for our mode of living, as you see, is plain and unpretending; yet no endeavours shall be wanting on our side to make Northanger Abbey not wholly disagreeable."

Northanger Abbey!—These were thrilling words, and wound up Catherine's feelings to the highest point of ecstasy. Her grateful and gratified heart could hardly restrain its expressions within the language of tolerable calmness. To receive so flattering an invita-tion! To have her company so warmly solicited! Every thing hon-ourable and soothing, every present enjoyment, and every future hope was contained in it; and her acceptance, with only the saving clause of papa and mamma's approbation, was eagerly given.—"I will write home directly," said she, "and if they do not object, as I dare say they will not"—

General Tilney was not less sanguine, having already waited on her excellent friends in Pulteney-street, and obtained their sanction of his wishes. "Since they can consent to part with you," said he, "we may expect philisophy from all the world."

1. A week from Saturday.

Miss Tilney was earnest, though gentle, in her secondary civilities, and the affair became in a few minutes as nearly settled, as this necessary reference to Fullerton would allow.

The circumstances of the morning had led Catherine's feelings through the varieties of suspense, security, and disappointment; but they were now safely lodged in perfect bliss; and with spirits elated to rapture, with Henry at her heart, and Northanger Abbey on her lips, she hurried home to write her letter. Mr. and Mrs. Morland, relying on the discretion of the friends to whom they had already entrusted their daughter, felt no doubt of the propriety of an acquaintance which had been formed under their eye, and sent therefore by return of post their ready consent to her visit in Glouscestershire. This indulgence, though not more than Catherine had hoped for, completed her conviction of being favoured beyond every other human creature, in friends and fortune, circumstance and chance. Every thing seemed to co-operate for her advantage. By the kindness of her first friends, the Allens, she had been introduced into scenes, where pleasures of every kind had met her. Her feelings, her preferences had each known the happiness of a return. Wherever she felt attachment, she had been able to create it. The affection of Isabella was to be secured to her in a sister. The Tilneys, they, by whom above all, she desired to be favourably thought of, outstripped even her wishes in the flattering measures by which their intimacy was to be continued. She was to be their chosen visitor, she was to be for weeks under the same roof with the person whose society she mostly prized—and, in addition to all the rest, this roof was to be the roof of an abbey!—Her passion for ancient edifices was next in degee to her passion for Henry Tilney— and castles and abbeys made usually the charm of those reveries which his image did not fill. To see and explore either the ramparts and keep of the one, or the cloisters of the other, had been for many weeks a darling wish, though to be more than the visitor of an hour, had seemed too nearly impossible for desire. And yet, this was to happen. With all the chances against her of house, hall, place, park, court, and cottage, Northanger turned up an abbey, and she was to be its inhabitant. Its long, damp passages, its narrow cells and ruined chapel, were to be within her daily reach, and she could not entirely subdue the hope of some traditional legends, some awful memorials of an injured and ill-fated nun.

It was wonderful that her friends should seem so little elated by the possession of such a home; that the consciousness of it should be so meekly born. The power of early habit only could account for it. A distinction to which they had been born gave no pride. Their superiority of abode was no more to them than their superiority of person.

Many were the inquiries she was eager to make of Miss Tilney; but so active were her thoughts, that when these inquiries were answered, she was hardly more assured than before, of Northanger Abbey having been a richly-endowed convent at the time of the Reformation, of its having fallen into the hands of an ancestor of the Tilneys on its dissolution, of a large portion of the ancient building still making a part of the present dwelling although the rest was decayed, or of its standing low in a valley, sheltered from the north and east by rising woods of oak.

CHAPTER III

With a mind thus full of happiness, Catherine was hardly aware that two or three days had passed away, without her seeing Isabella for more than a few minutes together. She began first to be sensible of this, and to sigh for her conversation, as she walked along the Pump-room one morning, by Mrs. Allen's side, without any thing to say or to hear; and scarcely had she felt a five minutes' longing of friendship, before the object of it appeared, and inviting her to a secret conference, led the way to a seat. "This is my favourite place," said she, as they sat down on a bench between the doors, which commanded a tolerable view of every body entering at either, "it is so out of the way."

Catherine, observing that Isabella's eyes were continually bent towards one door or the other, as in eager expectation, and remembering how often she had been falsely accused of being arch, thought the present a fine opportunity for being really so; and therefore gaily said, "Do not be uneasy, Isabella. James will soon be here."

"Psha! my dear creature," she replied, "do not think me such a simpleton as to be always wanting to confine him to my elbow. It would be hideous to be always together; we should be the jest of the place. And so you are going to Northanger!—I am amazingly glad of it. It is one of the finest old places in England, I understand. I shall depend upon a most particular description of it."

"You shall certainly have the best in my power to give. But who are you looking for? Are your sisters coming?"

"I am not looking for any body. One's eyes must be somewhere, and you know what a foolish trick I have of fixing mine, when my thoughts are an hundred miles off. I am amazingly absent; I believe I am the most absent creature in the world. Tilney says it is always the case with minds of a certain stamp."

"But I thought, Isabella, you had something in particular to tell me?"

"Oh! yes, and so I have. But here is a proof of what I was saying. My poor head! I had quite forgot it. Well, the thing is this, I have just had a letter from John;—you can guess the contents."

"No, indeed, I cannot."

"My sweet love, do not be so abominably affected. What can he write about, but yourself? You know he is over head and ears in love with you."

"With *me*, dear Isabella!"

"Nay, my sweetest Catherine, this is being quite absurd! Modesty, and all that, is very well in its way, but really a little common honesty is sometimes quite as becoming. I have no idea of being so overstrained! It is fishing for compliments. His attentions were such as a child must have noticed. And it was but half an hour before he left Bath, that you gave him the most positive encouragement. He says so in this letter, says that he as good as made you an offer, and that you received his advances in the kindest way; and now he wants me to urge his suit, and say all manner of pretty things to you. So it is in vain to affect ignorance."

Catherine, with all the earnestness of truth, expressed her astonishment at such a charge, protesting her innocence of every thought of Mr. Thorpe's being in love with her, and the consequent impossibility of her having ever intended to encourage him. "As to any attentions on his side, I do declare, upon my honour, I never was sensible of them for a moment—except just his asking me to dance the first day of his coming. And as to making me an offer, or anything like it, there must be some unaccountable mistake. I could not have misunderstood a thing of that kind, you know!—and, as I ever wish to be believed, I solemnly protest that no syllable of such a nature ever passed between us. The last half hour before he went away!—It must be all and completely a mistake—for I did not see him once that whole morning."

"But *that* you certainly did, for you spent the whole morning in Edgar's Buildings—it was the day your father's consent came—and I am pretty sure that you and John were alone in the parlour, some time before you left the house."

"Are you?—Well, if you say it, it was so, I dare say—but for the life of me, I cannot recollect it.—I *do* remember now being with you, and seeing him as well as the rest—but that we were ever alone for five minutes—However, it is not worth arguing about, for whatever might pass on his side, you must be convinced, by my having no recollection of it, that I never thought, nor expected, nor wished for any thing of the kind from him. I am excessively concerned that he should have any regard for me—but indeed it has been quite unintentional on my side, I never had the smallest idea of it. Pray undeceive him as soon as you can, and tell him I beg his pardon—that is—I do not know what I ought to say—but make him understand what I mean, in the properest way. I would not speak disrespectfully of a brother of your's, Isabella, I am sure; but you know very well that if I could think of one man more than another—*he* is not the person." Isabella was silent. "My dear friend, you must not be angry with me. I cannot suppose your brother cares so very much about me. And, you know, we shall still be sisters."

"Yes, yes," (with a blush) "there are more ways than one of our being sisters.—But where am I wandering to?—Well, my dear Catherine, the case seems to be, that you are determined against poor John—is not it so?"

"I certainly cannot return his affection, and as certainly never meant to encourage it."

"Since that is the case, I am sure I shall not tease you any further. John desired me to speak to you on the subject, and therefore I have. But I confess, as soon as I read his letter, I thought it a very foolish, imprudent business, and not likely to promote the good of either; for what were you to live upon, supposing you came together? You have both of you something to be sure, but it is not a trifle that will support a family now-a-days; and after all that romancers may say, there is no doing without money. I only wonder John could think of it; he could not have received my last."

"You *do* acquit me then of any thing wrong?—You are convinced that I never meant to deceive your brother, never suspected him of liking me till this moment?"

"Oh! as to that," answered Isabella laughingly, "I do not pretend to determine what your thoughts and designs in time past may have been. All that is best known to yourself. A little harmless flirtation or so will occur, and one is often drawn on to give more encouragement than one wishes to stand by. But you may be assured that I am the last person in the world to judge you severely. All those things should be allowed for in youth and high spirits. What one means one day, you know, one may not mean the next. Circumstances change, opinions alter."

"But my opinion of your brother never did alter; it was always the same. You are describing what never happened."

"My dearest Catherine," continued the other without at all listening to her, "I would not for all the world be the means of hurrying you into an engagement before you knew what you were about. I do not think any thing would justify me in wishing you to sacrifice all your happiness merely to oblige my brother, because he is my brother, and who perhaps after all, you know, might be just as happy without you, for people seldom know what they would be at, young men especially, they are so amazingly changeable and inconstant. What I say is, why should a brother's happiness be dearer to me than a friend's? You know I carry my notions of friendship pretty high. But, above all things, my dear Catherine, do not be in a hurry. Take my word for it, that if you are in too great a hurry, you will certainly live to repent it. Tilney says, there is nothing people are so often deceived in, as the state of their own affections, and I believe he is very right. Ah! here he comes; never mind, he will not see us, I am sure."

Catherine, looking up, perceived Captain Tilney; and Isabella, earnestly fixing her eye on him as she spoke, soon caught his notice. He approached immediately, and took the seat to which her movements invited him. His first address made Catherine start. Though spoken low, she could distinguish, "What! always to be watched, in person or by proxy!"

"Psha, nonsense!" was Isabella's answer in the same half whisper. "Why do you put such things into my head? If I could believe it—my spirit, you know, is pretty independent."

•

"I wish your heart were independent. That would be enough for me."

"My heart, indeed! What can you have to do with hearts? You men have none of you any hearts."

"If we have not hearts, we have eyes; and they give us torment enough."

"Do they? I am sorry for it; I am sorry they find any thing so disagreeable in me. I will look another way. I hope this pleases you," (turning her back on him,) "I hope your eyes are not tormented now."

"Never more so; for the edge of a blooming cheek is still in view—at once too much and too little."

Catherine heard all this, and quite out of countenance could listen no longer. Amazed that Isabella could endure it, and jealous for her brother, she rose up, and saying she should join Mrs. Allen, proposed their walking. But for this Isabella showed no inclination. She was so amazingly tired, and it was so odious to parade about the Pump-room; and if she moved from her seat she should miss her sisters, she was expecting her sisters every moment; so that her dearest Catherine must excuse her, and must sit quietly down again. But Catherine could be stubborn too; and Mrs. Allen just then coming up to propose their returning home, she joined her and walked out of the Pump-room, leaving Isabella still sitting with Captain Tilney. With much uneasiness did she thus leave them. It seemed to her that Captain Tilney was falling in love with Isabella, and Isabella unconsciously encouraging him; unconsciously it must be, for Isabella's attachment to James was as certain and well acknowledged as her engagement. To doubt her truth or good intentions was impossible; and yet, during the whole of their conversation her manner had been odd. She wished Isabella had talked more like her usual self, and not so much about money; and had not looked so well pleased at the sight of Captain Tilney. How strange that she should not perceive his admiration! Catherine longed to give her a hint of it, to put her on her guard, and prevent all the pain which her too lively behaviour might otherwise create both for him and her brother.

The compliment of John Thorpe's affection did not make amends for this thoughtlessness in his sister. She was almost as far from believing as from wishing it to be sincere; for she had not forgotten that he could mistake, and his assertion of the offer and of her encouragement convinced her that his mistakes could sometimes be very egregious. In vanity therefore she gained but little, her chief profit was in wonder. That he should think it worth his while to fancy himself in love with her, was a matter of lively astonishment. Isabella talked of his attentions; *she* had never been sensible of any; but Isabella had said many things which she hoped had been spoken in haste, and would never be said again; and upon this she was glad to rest altogether for present ease and comfort.

CHAPTER IV

A few days passed away, and Catherine, though not allowing herself to suspect her friend, could not help watching her closely. The result of her observations was not agreeable. Isabella seemed an altered creature. When she saw her indeed surrounded only by their immediate friends in Edgar's Buildings or Pulteney-street, her change of manners was so trifling that, had it gone no farther, it might have passed unnoticed. A something of languid indifference, or of that boasted absence of mind which Catherine had never heard of before, would occasionally come across her; but had nothing worse appeared, *that* might only have spread a new grace and inspired a warmer interest. But when Catherine saw her in public, admitting Captain Tilney's attentions as readily as they were offered, and allowing him almost an equal share with James in her notice and smiles, the alteration became too positive to be passed over. What could be meant by such unsteady conduct? What her friend could be at was beyond her comprehension. Isabella could not be aware of the pain she was inflicting; but it was a degree of wilful thoughtlessness which Catherine could not but resent. James was the sufferer. She saw him grave and uneasy; and however careless of his present comfort the woman might be who had given him her heart, to *her* it was always an object. For poor Captain Tilney too she was greatly concerned. Though his looks did not please her, his name was a passport to her good will, and she thought with sincere compassion of his approaching disappointment; for, in spite of what she had believed herself to overhear in the Pump-room, his behaviour was so incompatible with a knowledge of Isabella's engagement, that she could not, upon reflection, imagine him aware of it. He might be jealous of her brother as a rival, but if more had seemed implied, the fault must have been in her misapprehension. She wished, by a gentle remonstrance, to remind Isabella of her situation, and make her aware of this double unkindness; but for remonstrance, either opportunity or comprehension was always against her. If able to suggest a hint, Isabella could never understand it. In this distress, the intended departure of the Tilney family became her chief consolation; their journey into Gloucestershire was to take place within a few days, and Captain Tilney's removal would at least restore peace to every heart but his own. But Captain Tilney had at present no intention of removing; he was not to be of the party to Northanger, he was to continue at Bath. When Catherine knew this, her resolution was directly made. She spoke to Henry Tilney on the subject, regretting his brother's evident partiality for Miss Thorpe, and entreating him to make known her prior engagement.

"My brother does know it," was Henry's answer.

"Does he?—then why does he stay here?"

He made no reply, and was beginning to talk of something else; but she eagerly continued, "Why do not you persuade him to go away? The longer he stays, the worse it will be for him at last. Pray advise him for his own sake, and for every body's sake, to leave Bath directly. Absence will in time make him comfortable again; but he can have no hope here, and it is only staying to be miserable." Henry smiled and said, "I am sure my brother would not wish to do that."

"Then you will persuade him to go away?"

"Persuasion is not at command; but pardon me, if I cannot even endeavour to persuade him. I have myself told him that Miss Thorpe is engaged. He knows what he is about, and must be his own master."

"No, he does not know what he is about," cried Catherine; "he does not know the pain he is giving my brother. Not that James has ever told me so, but I am sure he is very uncomfortable."

"And are you sure it is my brother's doing?"

"Yes, very sure."

"Is it my brother's attentions to Miss Thorpe, or Miss Thorpe's admission of them, that gives the pain?"

"Is not it the same thing?"

"I think Mr. Morland would acknowledge a difference. No man is offended by another man's admiration of the woman he loves; it is the woman only who can make it a torment."

Catherine blushed for her friend, and said, "Isabella is wrong. But I am sure she cannot mean to torment, for she is very much attached to my brother. She has been in love with him ever since they first met, and while my father's consent was uncertain, she fretted herself almost into a fever. You know she must be attached to him."

"I understand: she is in love with James, and flirts with Frederick."

"Oh! no, not flirts. A woman in love with one man cannot flirt with another."

"It is probable that she will neither love so well, nor flirt so well, as she might do either singly. The gentlemen must each give up a little."

After a short pause, Catherine resumed with "Then you do not believe Isabella so very much attached to my brother?"

"I can have no opinion on that subject."

"But what can your brother mean? If he knows her engagement, what can he mean by his behaviour?"

"You are a very close questioner."

"Am I?—I only ask what I want to be told."

"But do you only ask what I can be expected to tell?"

"Yes, I think so; for you must know your brother's heart."

"My brother's heart, as you term it, on the present occasion, I assure you I can only guess at."

"Well?"

"Well!—Nay, if it is to be guesswork, let us all guess for ourselves. To be guided by second-hand conjecture is pitiful. The premises are before you. My brother is a lively, and perhaps sometimes a thoughtless young man; he has had about a week's acquaintance with your friend, and he has known her engagement almost as long as he has known her."

"Well," said Catherine, after some moments' consideration, "*you* may be able to guess at your brother's intentions from all this; but I am sure I cannot. But is not your father uncomfortable about it?—Does not he want Captain Tilney to go away?—Sure, if your father were to speak to him, he would go."

"My dear Miss Morland," said Henry, "in this amiable solicitude for your brother's comfort, may you not be a little mistaken?

Are you not carried a little too far? Would he thank you, either on his own account or Miss Thorpe's, for supposing that her affection, or at least her good-behaviour, is only to be secured by her seeing nothing of Captain Tilney? Is he safe only in solitude?—or, is her heart constant to him only when unsolicited by any one else?—He cannot think this—and you may be sure that he would not have you think it. I will not say, 'Do not be uneasy,' because I know that you are so, at this moment; but be as little uneasy as you can. You have no doubt of the mutual attachment of your brother and your friend; depend upon it therefore, that real jealousy never can exist between them; depend upon it that no disagreement between them can be of any duration. Their hearts are open to each other, as neither heart can be to you; they know exactly what is required and what can be borne; and you may be certain, that one will never tease the other beyond what is known to be pleasant."

Perceiving her still to look doubtful and grave, he added, "Though Frederick does not leave Bath with us, he will probably remain but a very short time, perhaps only a few days behind us. His leave of absence will soon expire, and he must return to his regiment.—And what will then be their acquaintance?—The messroom will drink Isabella Thorpe for a fortnight, and she will laugh with your brother over poor Tilney's passion for a month."

Catherine would contend no longer against comfort. She had resisted its approaches during the whole length of a speech, but it now carried her captive. Henry Tilney must know best. She blamed herself for the extent of her fears, and resolved never to think so seriously on the subject again.

Her resolution was supported by Isabella's behaviour in their parting interview. The Thorpes spent the last evening of Catherine's stay in Pulteney-street, and nothing passed between the lovers to excite her uneasiness, or make her quit them in apprehension. James was in excellent spirits, and Isabella most engagingly placid. Her tenderness for her friend seemed rather the first feeling of her heart; but that at such a moment was allowable; and once she gave her lover a flat contradiction, and once she drew back her hand; but Catherine remembered Henry's instructions, and placed it all to judicious affection. The embraces, tears, and promises of the parting fair ones may be fancied.

CHAPTER V

Mr. and Mrs. Allen were sorry to lose their young friend, whose good humour and cheerfulness had made her a valuable companion, and in the promotion of whose enjoyment their own had been gently increased. Her happiness in going with Miss Tilney, however, prevented their wishing it otherwise; and, as they were to remain only one more week in Bath themselves, her quitting them now would not long be felt. Mr. Allen attended her to Milsom-street, where she was to breakfast, and saw her seated with the kindest welcome among her new friends; but so great was her agitation in finding herself as one of the family, and so fearful was she of not doing exactly what was right, and of not being able to preserve their good opinion, that, in the embarrassment of the first five minutes, she could almost have wished to return with him to Pulteney-street.

Miss Tilney's manners and Henry's smile soon did away some of her unpleasant feelings; but still she was far from being at ease; nor could the incessant attentions of the General himself entirely reassure her. Nay, perverse as it seemed, she doubted whether she might not have felt less, had she been less attended to. His anxiety for her comfort—his continual solicitations that she would eat, and his often-expressed fears of her seeing nothing to her taste—though never in her life before had she beheld half such variety on a breakfast-table—made it impossible for her to forget for a moment that she was a visitor. She felt utterly unworthy of such respect, and knew not how to reply to it. Her tranquillity was not improved by the General's impatience for the appearance of his eldest son, nor by the displeasure he expressed at his laziness when Captain Tilney at last came down. She was quite pained by the severity of his father's reproof, which seemed disproportionate to the offence; and much was her concern increased, when she found herself the principal cause of the lecture; and that his tardiness was chiefly resented from being disrespectful to her. This was placing her in a very uncomfortable situation, and she felt great compassion for Captain Tilney, without being able to hope for his good-will.

He listened to his father in silence, and attempted not any defence, which confirmed her in fearing, that the inquietude of his mind, on Isabella's account, might, by keeping him long sleepless, have been the real cause of his rising late.—It was the first time of her being decidedly in his company, and she had hoped to be now able to form her opinion of him; but she scarcely heard his voice while his father remained in the room; and even afterwards, so much were his spirits affected, she could distinguish nothing but these words, in a whisper to Eleanor, "How glad I shall be when you are all off."

The bustle of going was not pleasant.—The clock struck ten while the trunks were carrying down, and the General had fixed to be out of Milsom-street by that hour. His great coat, instead of being brought for him to put on directly, was spread out in the curricle in which he was to accompany his son. The middle seat of the chaise was not drawn out, though there were three people to go in it, and his daughter's maid had so crowded it with parcels, that Miss Morland would not have room to sit; and, so much was he influenced by this apprehension when he handed her in, that she had some difficulty in saving her own new writing-desk from being thrown out into the street.—At last, however, the door was closed upon the three females, and they set off at the sober pace in which the handsome, highly-fed four horses of a gentleman usually perform a journey of thirty miles: such was the distance of Northanger from Bath, to be now divided into two equal stages. Catherine's spirits revived as they drove from the door; for with Miss Tilney she felt no restraint; and, with the interest of a road entirely new to her, of an abbey before, and a curricle behind, she caught the last view of Bath without any regret, and met with every mile-stone before she expected it. The tediousness of a two hours' bait at Petty-France,[1] in which there was nothing to be done but to eat without being hungry, and loiter about without any thing to see, next followed—and her admiration of the style in which they travelled, of the fashionable chaise-and-four—postilions handsomely liveried, rising so regularly in their stirrups, and numerous out-riders properly mounted, sunk a little under this consequent inconvenience. Had their party been perfectly agreeable, the delay would have been nothing; but General Tilney, though so charming a man, seemed always a check upon his children's spirits, and scarcely any thing was said but by himself; the observation of which, with his

---

1. A small village where they stopped to feed and rest the horses.

discontent at whatever the inn afforded, and his angry impatience at the waiters, made Catherine grow every moment more in awe of him, and appeared to lengthen the two hours into four.—At last, however, the order of release was given; and much was Catherine then surprized by the General's proposal of her taking his place in his son's curricle for the rest of the journey:—the day was fine, and he was anxious for her seeing as much of the country as possible.

The remembrance of Mr. Allen's opinion, respecting young men's open carriages, made her blush at the mention of such a plan, and her first thought was to decline it; but her second was of greater deference for General Tilney's judgment; he could not propose any thing improper for her; and, in the course of a few minutes, she found herself with Henry in the curricle, as happy a being as ever existed. A very short trial convinced her that a curricle was the prettiest equipage in the world; the chaise-and-four wheeled off with some grandeur, to be sure, but it was a heavy and troublesome business, and she could not easily forget its having stopped two hours at Petty-France. Half the time would have been enough for the curricle, and so nimbly were the light horses disposed to move, that, had not the General chosen to have his own carriage lead the way, they could have passed it with ease in half a minute. But the merit of the curricle did not all belong to the horses;—Henry drove so well,—so quietly—without making any disturbance, without parading to her, or swearing at them; so different from the only gentleman-coachman whom it was in her power to compare him with!—And then his hat sat so well, and the innumerable capes of his great coat looked so becomingly important!—To be driven by him, next to being dancing with him, was certainly the greatest happiness in the world. In addition to every other delight, she had now that of listening to her own praise; of being thanked at least, on his sister's account, for her kindness in thus becoming her visitor; of hearing it ranked as real friendship, and described as creating real gratitude. His sister, he said, was uncomfortably circumstanced—she had no female companion—and, in the frequent absence of her father, was sometimes without any companion at all.

"But how can that be?" said Catherine, "are not you with her?"

"Northanger is not more than half my home; I have an establishment at my own house in Woodston, which is nearly twenty miles from my father's, and some of my time is necessarily spent there."

"How sorry you must be for that!"

"I am always sorry to leave Eleanor."

"Yes; but besides your affection for her, you must be so fond of the Abbey!—After being used to such a home as the abbey, an ordinary parsonage-house must be very disagreeable."

He smiled, and said, "You have formed a very favourable idea of the Abbey."

"To be sure I have. Is not it a fine old place, just like what one reads about?"

"And are you prepared to encounter all the horrors that a building such as 'what one reads about' may produce?—Have you a stout heart?—Nerves fit for sliding pannels and tapestry?"[2]

"Oh! yes—I do not think I should be easily frightened, because there would be so many people in the house—and besides, it has never been uninhabited and left deserted for years, and then the family come back to it unawares, without giving any notice, as generally happens."

"No, certainly.—We shall not have to explore our way into a hall dimly lighted by the expiring embers of a wood fire—nor be obliged to spread our beds on the floor of a room without windows, doors, or furniture. But you must be aware that when a young lady is (by whatever means) introduced into a dwelling of this kind, she is always lodged apart from the rest of the family. While they snugly repair to their own end of the house, she is formally conducted by Dorothy the ancient housekeeper up a different staircase, and along many gloomy passages, into an apartment never used since some cousin or kin died in it about twenty years before. Can you stand such a ceremony as this? Will not your mind misgive you, when you find yourself in this gloomy chamber—too lofty and extensive for you, with only the feeble rays of a single lamp to take in its size—its walls hung with tapestry exhibiting figures as large as life, and the bed, of dark green stuff or purple velvet, presenting even a funereal appearance. Will not your heart sink within you?"

---

2. The whole passage shows Henry's familiarity with popular gothic novels, drawing on familiar events and devices to feed Catherine's fantasy. Because the novelists often copied from one another, or repeated motifs in successive novels of their own, the details are familiar. Most, however, originate in Radcliffe's *Mysteries of Udolpho*, and the repetition is a parody of this imitative habit. Their smooth approach to the Abbey recalls the tortured and sublime ascent to Udolpho.

"Oh! but this will not happen to me, I am sure."

"How fearfully will you examine the furniture of your apartment!—And what will you discern?—Not tables, toilettes, wardrobes, or drawers, but on one side perhaps the remains of a broken lute, on the other a ponderous chest which no efforts can open, and over the fire-place the portrait of some handsome warrior, whose features will so incomprehensibly strike you, that you will not be able to withdraw your eyes from it. Dorothy meanwhile, no less struck by your appearance, gazes on you in great agitation, and drops a few unintelligible hints. To raise your spirits, moreover, she gives you reason to suppose that the part of the Abbey you inhabit is undoubtedly haunted, and informs you that you will not have a single domestic within call. With this parting cordial she curtseys off—you listen to the sound of her receding footsteps as long as the last echo can reach you—and when, with fainting spirits, you attempt to fasten your door, you discover, with increased alarm, that it has no lock."

"Oh! Mr. Tilney, how frightful!—This is just like a book!—But it cannot really happen to me. I am sure your housekeeper is not really Dorothy.—Well, what then?"

"Nothing further to alarm perhaps may occur the first night. After surmounting your *unconquerable* horror of the bed, you will retire to rest, and get a few hours' unquiet slumber. But on the second, or at farthest the *third* night after your arrival, you will probably have a violent storm. Peals of thunder so loud as to seem to shake the edifice to its foundation will roll round the neighbouring mountains—and during the frightful gusts of wind which accompany it, you will probably think you discern (for your lamp is not extinguished) one part of the hanging more violently agitated than the rest. Unable of course to repress your curiosity in so favourable a moment for indulging it, you will instantly arise, and throwing your dressing-gown around you, proceed to examine this mystery. After a very short search, you will discover a division in the tapestry so artfully constructed as to defy the minutest inspection, and on opening it, a door will immediately appear—which door being only secured by massy bars and a padlock, you will, after a few efforts, succeed in opening,—and, with your lamp in your hand, will pass through it into a small vaulted room."

"No, indeed; I should be too much frightened to do any such thing."

"What! not when Dorothy has given you to understand that there is a secret subterraneous communication between your apartment and the chapel of St. Anthony, scarcely two miles off—Could you shrink from so simple an adventure? No, no, you will proceed into this small vaulted room, and through this into several others, without perceiving any thing very remarkable in either. In one perhaps there may be a dagger, in another a few drops of blood, and in a third the remains of some instrument of torture; but there being nothing in all this out of the common way, and your lamp being nearly exhausted, you will return towards your own apartment. In repassing through the small vaulted room, however, your eyes will be attracted towards a large, old-fashioned cabinet of ebony and gold, which, though narrowly examining the furniture before, you had passed unnoticed. Impelled by an irresistible presentiment, you will eagerly advance to it, unlock its folding doors, and search into every drawer;—but for some time without discovering any thing of importance—perhaps nothing but a considerable hoard of diamonds. At last, however, by touching a secret spring, an inner compartment will open—a roll of paper appears:—you seize it—it contains many sheets of manuscript—you hasten with the precious treasure into your own chamber, but scarcely have you been able to decipher 'Oh! thou—whomsoever thou mayst be, into whose hands these memoirs of the wretched Matilda may fall'—when your lamp suddenly expires in the socket, and leaves you in total darkness."

"Oh! no, no—do not say so. Well, go on."

But Henry was too much amused by the interest he had raised, to be able to carry it farther; he could no longer command solemnity either of subject or voice, and was obliged to entreat her to use her own fancy in the perusal of Matilda's woes. Catherine, recollecting herself, grew ashamed of her eagerness, and began earnestly to assure him that her attention had been fixed without the smallest apprehension of really meeting with what he related. Miss Tilney, she was sure, would never put her into such a chamber as he had described!—She was not at all afraid.

As they drew near the end of their journey, her impatience for a sight of the Abbey—for some time suspended by his conversation on subjects very different—returned in full force, and every bend in the road was expected with solemn awe to afford a glimpse of its massy walls of grey stone, rising amidst a grove of ancient oaks, with the last beams of the sun playing in beautiful splendour on its high Gothic windows. But so low did the building stand, that she found herself passing through the great gates of the lodge into the very grounds of Northanger, without having discerned even an antique chimney.

She knew not that she had any right to be surprized, but there was a something in this mode of approach which she certainly had not expected. To pass between lodges of a modern appearance, to find herself with such ease in the very precincts of the Abbey, and driven so rapidly along a smooth, level road of fine gravel, without obstacle, alarm or solemnity of any kind, struck her as odd and inconsistent. She was not long at leisure however for such considerations. A sudden scud of rain driving full in her face, made it impossible for her to observe any thing further, and fixed all her thoughts on the welfare of her new straw bonnet:—and she was actually under the Abbey walls, was springing, with Henry's assistance, from the carriage, was beneath the shelter of the old porch, and had even passed on to the hall, where her friend and the General were waiting to welcome her, without feeling one awful foreboding of future misery to herself, or one moment's suspicion of any past scenes of horror being acted within the solemn edifice. The breeze had not seemed to waft the sighs of the murdered to her; it had wafted nothing worse than a thick mizzling rain; and having given a good shake to her habit, she was ready to be shown into the common drawing-room, and capable of considering where she was.

An abbey!—yes, it was delightful to be really in an abbey!—but she doubted, as she looked round the room, whether any thing within her observation, would have given her the consciousness. The furniture was in all the profusion and elegance of modern taste. The fire-place, where she had expected the ample width and ponderous carving of former times, was contracted to a Rumford,[3] with slabs of plain though handsome marble, and ornaments over it of the prettiest English china. The windows, to which she looked with peculiar dependence, from having heard the General talk of

3. A stove named after the American inventor, Count von Rumford, consisted of a metal barrier placed across the fireplace, heating rooms efficiently but detracting from the romance of an open fire.

his preserving them in their Gothic form with reverential care, were yet less what her fancy had portrayed. To be sure, the pointed arch was preserved—the form of them was Gothic—they might be even casements—but every pane was so large, so clear, so light.[4] To an imagination which had hoped for the smallest divisions, and the heaviest stone-work, for painted glass, dirt and cobwebs, the difference was very distressing.

The General, perceiving how her eye was employed, began to talk of the smallness of the room and simplicity of the furniture, where every thing being for daily use, pretended only to comfort, and flattering himself however that there were some apartments in the Abbey not unworthy her notice—and was proceeding to mention the costly gilding of one in particular, when taking out his watch, he stopped short to pronounce it with surprize within twenty minutes of five! This seemed the word of separation, and Catherine found herself hurried away by Miss Tilney in such a manner as convinced her that the strictest punctuality to the family hours would be expected at Northanger.

Returning through the large and lofty hall, they ascended a broad staircase of shining oak, which, after many flights and many landing-places, brought them upon a long wide gallery. On one side it had a range of doors, and it was lighted on the other by windows which Catherine had only time to discover looked into a quadrangle, before Miss Tilney led the way into a chamber, and scarcely staying to hope she would find it comfortable, left her with an anxious entreaty that she would make as little alteration as possible in her dress.

CHAPTER VI

A moment's glance was enough to satisfy Catherine that her apartment was very unlike the one which Henry had endeavoured to alarm her by the description of.—It was by no means unreasonably large, and contained neither tapestry nor velvet.—The walls were papered, the floor was carpeted; the windows were neither less perfect, nor more dim than those of the drawing-room below; the

---

4. Clear glass was another recent achievement in British manufacturing technology.

furniture, though not of the latest fashion, was handsome and comfortable, and the air of the room altogether far from uncheerful. Her heart instantaneously at ease on this point, she resolved to lose no time in particular examination of anything, as she greatly dreaded disobliging the General by any delay. Her habit therefore was thrown off with all possible haste, and she was preparing to unpin the linen package, which the chaise-seat had conveyed for her immediate accommodation, when her eye suddenly fell on a large high chest, standing back in a deep recess on one side of the fire-place. The sight of it made her start; and, forgetting every thing else, she stood gazing on it in motionless wonder, while these thoughts crossed her:—

"This is strange indeed! I did not expect such a sight as this!—An immense heavy chest!—What can it hold!—Why should it be placed here?—Pushed back too, as if meant to be out of sight!—I will look into it—cost me what it may, I will look into it—and directly too—by day-light.—If I stay till evening my candle may go out." She advanced and examined it closely: it was of cedar, curiously inlaid with some darker wood, and raised, about a foot from the ground, on a carved stand of the same. The lock was silver, though tarnished from age; at each end were the imperfect remains of handles also of silver, broken perhaps prematurely by some strange violence; and, on the centre of the lid, was a mysterious cypher, in the same metal. Catherine bent over it intently, but without being able to distinguish any thing with certainty. She could not, in whatever direction she took it, believe the last letter to be a *T;* and yet that it should be any thing else in that house was a circumstance to raise no common degree of astonishment. If not originally theirs, by what strange events could it have fallen into the Tilney family?

Her fearful curiosity was every moment growing greater; and seizing, with trembling hands, the hasp of the lock, she resolved at all hazards to satisfy herself at least as to its contents. With difficulty, for something seemed to resist her efforts, she raised the lid a few inches; but at that moment a sudden knocking at the door of the room made her, starting, quit her hold, and the lid closed with alarming violence. This ill-timed intruder was Miss Tilney's maid, sent by her mistress to be of use to Miss Morland; and though Catherine immediately dismissed her, it recalled her to the sense of what she ought to be doing, and forced her, in spite of her anxious desire to penetrate this mystery, to proceed in her dressing without further delay. Her progress was not quick, for her thoughts and her eyes were still bent on the object so well calculated to interest and alarm; and though she dared not waste a moment upon a second attempt, she could not remain many paces from the chest. At length, however, having slipped one arm into her gown, her toilette seemed so nearly finished, that the impatience of her curiosity might safely be indulged. One moment surely might be spared; and, so desperate should be the exertion of her strength, that, unless secured by supernatural means, the lid in one moment should be thrown back. With this spirit she sprang forward, and her confidence did not deceive her. Her resolute effort threw back the lid, and gave to her astonished eyes the view of a white cotton counterpane, properly folded, reposing at one end of the chest in undisputed possession!

She was gazing on it with the first blush of surprise, when Miss Tilney, anxious for her friend's being ready, entered the room, and to the rising shame of having harboured for some minutes an absurd expectation, was then added the shame of being caught in so idle a search. "That is a curious old chest, is not it?" said Miss Tilney, as Catherine hastily closed it and turned away to the glass. "It is impossible to say how many generations it has been here. How it came to be first put in this room I know not, but I have not had it moved, because I thought it might sometimes be of use in holding hats and bonnets. The worst of it is that its weight makes it difficult to open. In that corner, however, it is at least out of the way."

Catherine had no leisure for speech, being at once blushing, tying her gown, and forming wise resolutions with the most violent dispatch. Miss Tilney gently hinted her fear of being late; and in half a minute they ran down stairs together, in an alarm not wholly unfounded, for General Tilney was pacing the drawing-room, his watch in his hand, and having, on the very instant of their entering, pulled the bell with violence, ordered "Dinner to be on table *directly*!"

Catherine trembled at the emphasis with which he spoke, and sat pale and breathless, in a most humble mood, concerned for his children, and detesting old chests; and the General recovering his politeness as he looked at her, spent the rest of his time in scolding his daughter, for so foolishly hurrying her fair friend, who was absolutely out of breath from haste, when there was not the least occasion for hurry in the world: but Catherine could not at all get over the double distress of having involved her friend in a lecture and been a great simpleton herself, till they were happily seated at the dinner-table, when the General's complacent smiles, and a good appetite of her own, restored her to peace. The dining-parlour was a noble room, suitable in its dimensions to a much larger drawing-room than the one in common use, and fitted up in a style of luxury and expense which was almost lost on the unpractised eye of Catherine, who saw little more than its spaciousness and the number of their attendants. Of the former, she spoke aloud her admiration; and the General, with a very gracious countenance, acknowledged that it was by no means an ill-sized room; and further confessed, that, though as careless on such subjects as most people, he did look upon a tolerably large eating-room as one of the necessaries of life; he supposed, however, "that she must have been used to much better sized apartments at Mr. Allen's?"

"No indeed," was Catherine's honest assurance; "Mr. Allen's dining-parlour was not more than half as large:" and she had never seen so large a room as this in her life. The General's good-humour increased.—Why, as he *had* such rooms, he thought it would be simple not to make use of them; but, upon his honour, he believed there might be more comfort in rooms of only half their size. Mr. Allen's house, he was sure, must be exactly of the true size for rational happiness.

The evening passed without any further disturbance, and, in the occasional absence of General Tilney, with much positive cheerfulness. It was only in his presence that Catherine felt the smallest fatigue from her journey; and even then, even in moments of languor or restraint, a sense of general happiness preponderated, and she could think of her friends in Bath without one wish of being with them.

The night was stormy; the wind had been rising at intervals the whole afternoon; and by the time the party broke up, it blew and rained violently. Catherine, as she crossed the hall, listened to the tempest with sensations of awe; and when she heard it rage round a corner of the ancient building and close with sudden fury a distant door, felt for the first time that she was really in an Abbey.— Yes, these were characteristic sounds;—they brought to her recollection a countless variety of dreadful situations and horrid scenes, which such buildings had witnessed, and such storms ushered in; and most heartily did she rejoice in the happier circumstances attending her entrance within walls so solemn!—*She* had nothing to dread from midnight assassins or drunken gallants. Henry had certainly been only in jest in what he had told her that morning. In a house so furnished, and so guarded, she could have nothing to explore or to suffer; and might go to her bedroom as securely as if it had been her own chamber at Fullerton. Thus wisely fortifying her mind, as she proceeded up stairs, she was enabled, especially on perceiving that Miss Tilney slept only two doors from her, to enter her room with a tolerably stout heart; and her spirits were immediately assisted by the cheerful blaze of a wood fire. "How much better is this," said she, as she walked to the fender—"how much better to find a fire ready lit, than to have to wait shivering in the cold till all the family are in bed, as so many poor girls have been obliged to do, and then to have a faithful old servant frightening one by coming in with a faggot! How glad I am that Northanger is what it is! If it had been like some other places, I do not know that, in such a night as this, I could have answered for my courage:—but now, to be sure, there is nothing to alarm one."

She looked round the room. The window curtains seemed in motion. It could be nothing but the violence of the wind penetrating through the divisions of the shutters; and she stept boldly forward, carelessly humming a tune, to assure herself of its being so, peeped courageously behind each curtain, saw nothing on either low window seat to scare her, and on placing a hand against the shutter, felt the strongest conviction of the wind's force. A glance at the old chest, as she turned away from this examination, was not without its use; she scorned the causeless fears of an idle fancy, and began with a most happy indifference to prepare herself for bed. She should take her time; she should not hurry herself; she did not care if she were the last person up in the house. But she would not make up her fire; *that* would seem cowardly, as if she wished for the protection of light after she were in bed. The fire therefore died away, and Catherine, having spent the best part of an hour in her arrangements, was beginning to think of stepping into bed, when, on giving a parting glance round the room, she was struck by the appearance of a high, old-fashioned black cabinet, which, though in a situation conspicuous enough, had never caught her notice before. Henry's words, his description of the ebony cabinet which was to escape her observation at first, immediately rushed across her; and though there could be nothing really in it, there was something whimsical, it was certainly a very remarkable coincidence! She took her candle and looked closely at the cabinet. It was not absolutely ebony and gold; but it was Japan,[1] black and yellow Japan of the handsomest kind; and as she held her candle, the yellow had very much the effect of gold. The key was in the door, and she had a strange fancy to look into it; not however with the smallest expectation of finding any thing, but it was so very odd, after what Henry had said. In short, she could not sleep till she had examined it. So, placing the candle with great caution on a chair, she seized the key with a very tremulous hand and tried to turn it; but it resisted her utmost strength. Alarmed, but not discouraged, she tried it another way; a bolt flew, and she believed herself successful; but how strangely mysterious!—the door was still immoveable. She paused a moment in breathless wonder. The wind roared down the chimney, the rain beat in torrents against the windows, and every thing seemed to speak the awfulness of her situation. To retire to bed, however, unsatisfied on such a point, would be vain, since sleep must be impossible with the consciousness of a cabinet so mysteriously closed in her immediate vicinity. Again therefore she applied herself to the key, and after moving it in every possible way for some instants with the determined celerity of hope's last effort, the door suddenly yielded to her hand: her heart leaped with exultation at such a victory, and having thrown open each folding door, the second being secured only by bolts of less wonderful construction than the lock, though in that her eye could not discern any thing unusual, a double range of small drawers appeared in view, with some larger drawers above and below them; and in the centre, a small door, closed also with a lock and key, secured in all probability a cavity of importance.

Catherine's heart beat quick, but her courage did not fail her. With a cheek flushed by hope, and an eye straining with curiosity, her fingers grasped the handle of a drawer and drew it forth. It was entirely empty. With less alarm and greater eagerness she seized a second, a third, a fourth; each was equally empty. Not one was left

1. A hard, black, lacquered finish imported from Japan.

unsearched, and in not one was any thing found. Well read in the art of concealing a treasure, the possibility of false linings to the drawers did not escape her, and she felt round each with anxious acuteness in vain. The place in the middle alone remained now unexplored; and though she had never from the first had the smallest idea of finding any thing in any part of the cabinet, and was not in the least disappointed at her ill success thus far, it would be foolish not to examine it thoroughly while she was about it. It was some time however before she could unfasten the door, the same difficulty occurring in the management of this inner lock as of the outer; but at length it did open; and not vain, as hitherto, was her search; her quick eyes directly fell on a roll of paper pushed back into the further part of the cavity, apparently for concealment, and her feelings at that moment were indescribable. Her heart fluttered, her knees trembled, and her cheeks grew pale. She seized, with an unsteady hand, the precious manuscript, for half a glance sufficed to ascertain written characters; and while she acknowledged with awful sensations this striking exemplification of what Henry had foretold, resolved instantly to peruse every line before she attempted to rest.

The dimness of the light her candle emitted made her turn to it with alarm; but there was no danger of its sudden extinction, it had yet some hours to burn; and that she might not have any greater difficulty in distinguishing the writing than what its ancient date might occasion, she hastily snuffed it. Alas! it was snuffed and extinguished in one.[2] A lamp could not have expired with more awful effect. Catherine, for a few moments, was motionless with horror. It was done completely; not a remnant of light in the wick could give hope to the rekindling breath. Darkness impenetrable and immoveable filled the room. A violent gust of wind, rising with sudden fury, added fresh horror to the moment. Catherine trembled from head to foot. In the pause which succeeded, a sound like receding footsteps and the closing of a distant door struck on her affrighted ear. Human nature could support no more. A cold sweat stood on her forehead, the manuscript fell from her hand, and groping her way to the bed, she jumped hastily in, and sought some suspension of agony by creeping far underneath the clothes. To close her eyes in sleep that

2. Instead of pinching off the wick so it would burn longer, Catherine extinguished it.

night, she felt must be entirely out of the question. With a curiosity so justly awakened, and feelings in every way so agitated, repose must be absolutely impossible. The storm abroad so dreadful!—She had not been used to feel alarm from wind, but now every blast seemed fraught with awful intelligence. The manuscript so wonderfully found, so wonderfully accomplishing the morning's prediction, how was it to be accounted for?—What could it contain?—to whom could it relate?—by what means could it have been so long concealed?—and how singularly strange that it should fall to her lot to discover it! Till she had made herself mistress of its contents, however, she could have neither repose nor comfort; and with the sun's first rays she was determined to peruse it. But many were the tedious hours which must yet intervene. She shuddered, tossed about in her bed, and envied every quiet sleeper. The storm still raged, and various were the noises, more terrific even than the wind, which struck at intervals on her startled ear. The very curtains of her bed seemed at one moment in motion, and at another the lock of her door was agitated, as if by the attempt of somebody to enter. Hollow murmurs seemed to creep along the gallery, and more than once her blood was chilled by the sound of distant moans. Hour after hour passed away, and the wearied Catherine had heard three proclaimed by all the clocks in the house, before the tempest subsided, or she unknowingly fell fast asleep.

CHAPTER VII

The housemaid's folding back her window-shutters at eight o'clock the next day, was the sound which first roused Catherine; and she opened her eyes, wondering that they could ever have been closed, on objects of cheerfulness; her fire was already burning, and a bright morning had succeeded the tempest of the night. Instantaneously with the consciousness of existence, returned her recollection of the manuscript; and springing from the bed in the very moment of the maid's going away, she eagerly collected every scattered sheet which had burst from the roll on its falling to the ground, and flew back to enjoy the luxury of their perusal on her pillow. She now plainly saw that she must not expect a manuscript of equal length with the generality of what she had shuddered over in books, for the roll, seeming to consist entirely of small disjointed sheets, was altogether but of trifling size, and much less than she had supposed it to be at first.

Her greedy eye glanced rapidly over a page. She started at its import. Could it be possible, or did not her senses play her false?—An inventory of linen, in coarse and modern characters, seemed all that was before her! If the evidence of sight might be trusted, she held a washing-bill in her hand. She seized another sheet, and saw the same articles with little variation; a third, a fourth, and a fifth presented nothing new. Shirts, stockings, cravats and waistcoats faced her in each. Two others, penned by the same hand, marked an expenditure scarcely more interesting, in letters, hair-powder, shoe-string and breeches-ball.[1] And the larger sheet, which had inclosed the rest, seemed by its first cramp line, "To poultice chestnut mare,"—a farrier's bill![2] Such was the collection of papers, (left perhaps, as she could then suppose, by the negligence of a servant in the place whence she had taken them,) which had filled her with expectation and alarm, and robbed her of half her night's rest! She felt humbled to the dust. Could not the adventure of the chest have taught her wisdom? A corner of it catching her eye as she lay, seemed to rise up in judgment against her. Nothing could now be clearer than the absurdity of her recent fancies. To suppose that a manuscript of many generations back could have remained undiscovered in a room such as that, so modern, so habitable!—or that she should be the first to possess the skill of unlocking a cabinet, the key of which was open to all!

How could she have so imposed on herself?—Heaven forbid that Henry Tilney should ever know her folly! And it was in a great measure his own doing, for had not the cabinet appeared so exactly to agree with his description of her adventures, she should never have felt the smallest curiosity about it. This was the only comfort that occurred. Impatient to get rid of those hateful evidences of her folly, those detestable papers then scattered over the bed, she rose directly, and folding them up as nearly as possible in the same shape as before, returned them to the same spot within the cabinet, with a very hearty wish that no untoward accident might ever bring them forward again, to disgrace her even with herself.

1. Hair powder had been out of fashion for some time. Soap itself was a recent invention; the breeches-ball was a special blend for cleaning breeches, trousers.
2. Blacksmith.

Why the locks should have been so difficult to open however, was still something remarkable, for she could now manage them with perfect ease. In this there was surely something mysterious, and she indulged in the flattering suggestion for half a minute, till the possibility of the door's having been at first unlocked, and of being herself its fastener, darted into her head, and cost her another blush.

She got away as soon as she could from a room in which her conduct produced such unpleasant reflections, and found her way with all speed to the breakfast-parlour, as it had been pointed out to her by Miss Tilney the evening before. Henry was alone in it; and his immediate hope of her having been undisturbed by the tempest, with an arch reference to the character of the building they inhabited, was rather distressing. For the world would she not have her weakness suspected; and yet, unequal to an absolute falsehood, was constrained to acknowledge that the wind had kept her awake a little. "But we have a charming morning after it," she added, desiring to get rid of the subject; "and storms and sleeplessness are nothing when they are over. What beautiful hyacinths!³—I have just learnt to love a hyacinth."

"And how might you learn?—By accident or argument?"

"Your sister taught me; I cannot tell how. Mrs. Allen used to take pains, year after year, to make me like them; but I never could, till I saw them the other day in Milsom-street; I am naturally indifferent about flowers."

"But now you love a hyacinth. So much the better. You have gained a new source of enjoyment, and it is well to have as many holds upon happiness as possible. Besides, a taste for flowers is always desirable in your sex, as a means of getting you out of doors, and tempting you to more frequent exercise than you would otherwise take. And though the love of a hyacinth may be rather domestic, who can tell, the sentiment once raised, but you may in time come to love a rose?"

"But I do not want any such pursuit to get me out of doors. The pleasure of walking and breathing fresh air is enough for me, and in fine weather. I am out more than half my time.—Mamma says, I am never within."

3. Forcing bulbs for ornamental flowers indoors was a recent fashion in country homes, and, because bulbs were expensive, a great luxury.

"At any rate, however, I am pleased that you have learnt to love a hyacinth. The mere habit of learning to love is the thing; and a teachableness of disposition in a young lady is a great blessing.— Has my sister a pleasant mode of instruction?"

Catherine was saved the embarrassment of attempting an answer, by the entrance of the General, whose smiling compliments announced a happy state of mind, but whose gentle hint of sympathetic early rising did not advance her composure.

The elegance of the breakfast set forced itself on Catherine's notice when they were seated at table; and, luckily, it had been the General's choice. He was enchanted by her approbation of his taste, confessed it to be neat and simple, thought it right to encourage the manufacture of his country; and for his part, to his uncritical palate, the tea was as well flavoured from the clay of Staffordshire, as from that of Dresden or Sêve.[4] But this was quite an old set, purchased two years ago. The manufacture was much improved since that time; he had seen some beautiful specimens when last in town, and had he not been perfectly without vanity of that kind, might have been tempted to order a new set. He trusted, however, that an opportunity might ere long occur of selecting one— though not for himself. Catherine was probably the only one of the party who did not understand him.

Shortly after breakfast Henry left them for Woodston, where business required and would keep him two or three days. They all attended in the hall to see him mount his horse, and immediately on re-entering the breakfast-room, Catherine walked to a window in the hope of catching another glimpse of his figure. "This is a somewhat heavy call upon your brother's fortitude," observed the General to Eleanor. "Woodston will make but a sombre appearance to-day."

"Is it a pretty place?" asked Catherine.

"What say you, Eleanor?—speak your opinion, for ladies can best tell the taste of ladies in regard to places as well as men. I think it would be acknowledged by the most impartial eye to have many recommendations. The house stands among fine meadows facing

---

4. Staffordshire pottery, recently invented by Josiah Wedgwood and produced at his factory, Etruria, was made from the clays in the midlands. It was illustrated by artists such as Fuseli with Greek motifs for the domestic use of the middle classes, as opposed to the more elegant and traditional French or Austrian porcelain.

the south-east, with an excellent kitchen-garden in the same aspect; the walls surrounding which I built and stocked myself about ten years ago, for the benefit of my son. It is a family living, Miss Morland; and the property in the place being chiefly my own, you may believe I take care that it shall not be a bad one. Did Henry's income depend solely on this living, he would not be ill provided for. Perhaps it may seem odd, that with only two younger children, I should think any profession necessary for him; and certainly there are moments when we could all wish him disengaged from every tie of business. But though I may not exactly make converts of you young ladies, I am sure your father, Miss Morland, would agree with me in thinking it expedient to give every young man some employment. The money is nothing, it is not an object, but employment is the thing. Even Frederick, my eldest son, you see, who will perhaps inherit as considerable a landed property as any private man in the county, has his profession."

The imposing effect of this last argument was equal to his wishes. The silence of the lady proved it to be unanswerable.

Something had been said the evening before of her being shown over the house, and he now offered himself as her conductor; and though Catherine had hoped to explore it accompanied only by his daughter, it was a proposal of too much happiness itself, under any circumstances, not to be gladly accepted; for she had been already eighteen hours in the Abbey, and had seen only a few of its rooms. The netting-box, just leisurely drawn forth, was closed with joyful haste, and she was ready to attend him in a moment. And when they had gone over the house, he promised himself moreover the pleasure of accompanying her into the shrubberies and garden. She curtsied her acquiescence. But perhaps it might be more agreeable to her to make those her first object. The weather was at present favourable, and at this time of year the uncertainty was very great of its continuing so.—Which would she prefer? He was equally at her service.—Which did his daughter think would most accord with her fair friend's wishes?—But he thought he could discern.— Yes, he certainly read in Miss Morland's eyes a judicious desire of making use of the present smiling weather.—But when did she judge amiss?—The Abbey would be always safe and dry.—He yielded implicitly, and would fetch his hat and attend them in a moment. He left the room, and Catherine, with a disappointed, anxious face, began to speak of her unwillingness that he should be taking them out of doors against his own inclination, under a mistaken idea of pleasing her; but she was stopt by Miss Tilney's saying, with a little confusion, "I believe it will be wisest to take the morning while it is so fine; and do not be uneasy on my father's account, he always walks out at this time of day."

Catherine did not exactly know how this was to be understood. Why was Miss Tilney embarrassed? Could there be any unwillingness on the General's side to show her over the Abbey? The proposal was his own. And was not it odd that he should *always* take his walk so early? Neither her father nor Mr. Allen did so. It was certainly very provoking. She was all impatience to see the house, and had scarcely any curiosity about the grounds. If Henry had been with them indeed!—but now she should not know what was picturesque when she saw it. Such were her thoughts, but she kept them to herself, and put on her bonnet in patient discontent.

She was struck however, beyond her expectation, by the grandeur of the Abbey, as she saw it for the first time from the lawn. The whole building enclosed a large court; and two sides of the quadrangle, rich in Gothic ornaments, stood forward for admiration. The remainder was shut off by knolls of old trees, or luxuriant plantations,[5] and the steep woody hills rising behind to give it shelter, were beautiful even in the leafless month of March. Catherine had seen nothing to compare with it; and her feelings of delight were so strong, that without waiting for any better authority, she boldly burst forth in wonder and praise. The General listened with assenting gratitude; and it seemed as if his own estimation of Northanger had waited unfixed till that hour.

The kitchen-garden was to be next admired, and he led the way to it across a small portion of the park.

The number of acres contained in this garden was such as Catherine could not listen to without dismay, being more than

---

5. "Plantations" was a pretentious word for gardens, in this case an ornamental kitchen-garden. Such detail reveals General Tilney's self-indulgence and lack of social conscience, his growing tropical fruits when much of England, as Worral observes, was starving or subsisting on horse flesh, turnips, even nettles. Tilney's re-arranging functional land for the view, instead of crops, excluding other people, was recommended by Humphry Repton, whose *Fragments on the Theory and Practice of Landscape Gardening* appeared in 1816, when Austen was revising *Northanger Abbey*.

double the extent of all Mr. Allen's, as well her father's, including church-yard and orchard. The walls seemed countless in number, endless in length; a village of hot-houses seemed to arise among them, and a whole parish to be at work within the inclosure. The General was flattered by her looks of surprize, which told him almost as plainly, as he soon forced her to tell him in words, that she had never seen any gardens at all equal to them before;—and he then modestly owned that, without any ambition of that sort himself—without any solicitude about it,—he did believe them to be unrivalled in the kingdom. If he had a hobby-horse, it was *that*. He loved a garden. Though careless enough in most matters of eating, he loved good fruit—or if he did not, his friends and children did. There were great vexations however attending such a garden as his. The utmost care could not always secure the most valuable fruits. The pinery had yielded only one hundred in the last year. Mr. Allen, he supposed, must feel these inconveniences as well as himself.[6]

"No, not at all. Mr. Allen did not care about the garden, and never went into it."

With a triumphant smile of self-satisfaction, the General wished he could do the same, for he never entered his, without being vexed in some way or other, by its falling short of his plan.

"How were Mr. Allen's succession-houses worked?"[7] describing the nature of his own as they entered them.

"Mr. Allen had only one small hot-house, which Mrs. Allen had the use of for her plants in winter, and there was a fire in it now and then."

"He is a happy man!" said the General, with a look of very happy contempt.

Having taken her into every division, and led her under every wall, till she was heartily weary of seeing and wondering, he suffered the girls at last to seize the advantage of an outer door, and then expressing his wish to examine the effect of some recent alterations about the tea-house, proposed it as no unpleasant extension of their walk, if Miss Morland were not tired. "But

6. A pinery was a hothouse for growing pineapples. A hundred pineapples a year would be too much for any family to consume so he may have shared them with his servants or sold them.

7. A series of hot-houses with different temperatures for forcing plants out of season, another sign of luxury and excess.

where are you going, Eleanor?—Why do you chuse that cold, damp path to it? Miss Morland will get wet. Our best way is across the park."

"This is so favourite a walk of mine," said Miss Tilney, "that I always think it the best and nearest way. But perhaps it may be damp."

It was a narrow winding path through a thick grove of old Scotch firs; and Catherine, struck by its gloomy aspect, and eager to enter it, could not, even by the General's disapprobation, be kept from stepping forward. He perceived her inclination, and having again urged the plea of health in vain, was too polite to make further opposition. He excused himself however from attending them:—The rays of the sun were not too cheerful for him, and he would meet them by another course. He turned away; and Catherine was shocked to find how much her spirits were relieved by the separation. The shock however being less real than the relief, offered it no injury; and she began to talk with easy gaiety of the delightful melancholy which such a grove inspired.

"I am particularly fond of this spot," said her companion, with a sigh. "It was my mother's favourite walk."

Catherine had never heard Mrs. Tilney mentioned in the family before, and the interest excited by this tender remembrance, showed itself directly in her altered countenance, and in the attentive pause with which she waited for something more.

"I used to walk here so often with her!" added Eleanor; "though I never loved it then, as I have loved it since. At that time indeed I used to wonder at her choice. But her memory endears it now."

"And ought it not," reflected Catherine, "to endear it to her husband? Yet the General would not enter it." Miss Tilney continuing silent, she ventured to say, "Her death must have been a great affliction!"

"A great and increasing one," replied the other, in a low voice. "I was only thirteen when it happened; and though I felt my loss perhaps as strongly as one so young could feel it, I did not, I could not then know what a loss it was." She stopped for a moment, and then added, with great firmness, "I have no sister, you know—and though Henry—though my brothers are very affectionate, and Henry is a great deal here, which I am most thankful for, it is impossible for me not to be often solitary."

"To be sure you must miss him very much."

"A mother would have been always present. A mother would have been a constant friend; her influence would have been beyond all other."

"Was she a very charming woman? Was she handsome? Was there any picture of her in the Abbey? And why had she been so partial to that grove? Was it from dejection of spirits?"—were questions now eagerly poured forth;—the first three received a ready affirmative, the two others were passed by; and Catherine's interest in the deceased Mrs. Tilney augmented with every question, whether answered or not. Of her unhappiness in marriage, she felt persuaded. The General certainly had been an unkind husband. He did not love her walk:—could he therefore have loved her? And besides, handsome as he was, there was a something in the turn of his features which spoke his not having behaved well to her.

"Her picture, I suppose," blushing at the consummate art of her own question, "hangs in your father's room?"

"No;—it was intended for the drawing-room; but my father was dissatisfied with the painting, and for some time it had no place. Soon after her death I obtained it for my own, and hung it in my bed-chamber—where I shall be happy to show it you;—it is very like."—Here was another proof. A portrait—very like—of a departed wife, not valued by the husband!—He must have been dreadfully cruel to her!

Catherine attempted no longer to hide from herself the nature of the feelings which, in spite of all his attentions, he had previously excited; and what had been terror and dislike before, was now absolute aversion. Yes, aversion! His cruelty to such a charming woman made him odious to her. She had often read of such characters; characters, which Mr. Allen had been used to call unnatural and overdrawn; but here was proof positive of the contrary.

She had just settled this point, when the end of the path brought them directly upon the General; and in spite of all her virtuous indignation, she found herself again obliged to walk with him, listen to him, and even to smile when he smiled. Being no longer able however to receive pleasure from the surrounding objects, she soon began to walk with lassitude; the General perceived it, and with a concern for her health, which seemed to reproach her for her opinion of him, was most urgent for returning with his daughter to the house. He would follow them in a quarter of an hour. Again they parted—but Eleanor was called back in half a minute to receive a strict charge against taking her friend round the Abbey till his return. This second instance of his anxiety to delay what she so much wished for, struck Catherine as very remarkable.

CHAPTER VIII

An hour passed away before the General came in, spent, on the part of his young guest, in no very favourable consideration of his character.—This lengthened absence, these solitary rambles, did not speak a mind at ease, or a conscience void of reproach.—At length he appeared; and, whatever might have been the gloom of his meditations, he could still smile with *them*. Miss Tilney, understanding in part her friend's curiosity to see the house, soon revived the subject; and her father being, contrary to Catherine's expectations, unprovided with any pretence for further delay, beyond that of stopping five minutes to order refreshments to be in the room by their return, was at last ready to escort them.

They set forward; and, with a grandeur of air, a dignified step, which caught the eye, but could not shake the doubts of the well-read Catherine, he led the way across the hall, through the common drawing-room and one useless anti-chamber, into a room magnificent both in size and furniture—the real drawing-room, used only with company of consequence.—It was very noble—very grand—very charming!—was all that Catherine had to say, for her indiscriminating eye scarcely discerned the colour of the satin; and all minuteness of praise, all praise that had much meaning, was supplied by the General: the costliness or elegance of any room's fitting-up could be nothing to her; she cared for no furniture of a more modern date than the fifteenth century. When the General had satisfied his own curiosity, in a close examination of every well-known ornament, they proceeded into the library, an apartment, in its way, of equal magnificence, exhibiting a collection of books, on which an humble man might have looked with pride.—Catherine heard, admired, and wondered with more genuine feeling than before—gathered all that she could from this storehouse of knowledge, by running over the titles of half a shelf, and was ready to proceed. But suites of apartments did not spring up with her wishes.—Large as was the building, she had already visited the greatest part; though, on being told that, with the addition of the kitchen, the six or seven rooms she had now seen surrounded three sides of the court, she could scarcely believe it, or overcome the suspicion of their being many chambers secreted. It was some relief, however, that they were to return to the rooms in common use, by passing through a few of less importance, looking into the court, which, with occasional passages, not wholly unintricate, connected the different sides;—and she was further soothed in her progress, by being told, that she was treading what had once been a cloister, having traces of cells pointed out, and observing several doors, that were neither opened nor explained to her;—by finding herself successively in a billiard-room, and in the General's private apartment, without comprehending their connection, or being able to turn aright when she left them; and lastly, by passing through a dark little room, owning Henry's authority, and strewed with his litter of books, guns, and great coats.

From the dining-room of which, though already seen, and always to be seen at five o'clock, the General could not forego the pleasure of pacing out the length, for the more certain information of Miss Morland, as to what she neither doubted nor cared for, they proceeded by quick communication to the kitchen—the ancient kitchen of the convent, rich in the massy walls and smoke of former days, and in the stoves and hot closets of the present. The General's improving hand had not loitered here: every modern invention to facilitate the labour of the cooks, had been adopted within this, their spacious theatre; and, when the genius of others had failed, his own had often produced the perfection wanted. His endowments of this spot alone might at any time have placed him high among the benefactors of the convent.

With the walls of the kitchen ended all the antiquity of the Abbey; the fourth side of the quadrangle having, on account of its decaying state, been removed by the General's father, and the present erected in its place. All that was venerable ceased here. The new building was not only new, but declared itself to be so; intended only for offices, and enclosed behind by stable-yards, no uniformity of architecture had been thought necessary. Catherine could have raved at the hand which had swept away what must have been beyond the value of all the rest, for the purposes of mere domestic economy; and would willingly have been spared the mortification of a walk through scenes so fallen, had the General allowed it; but if he had a vanity, it was in the arrangement of his offices; and as he was convinced, that, to a mind like Miss Morland's, a view of the accommodations and comforts, by which the labours of her inferiors were softened, must always be gratifying, he should make no apology for leading her on. They took a slight survey of all; and Catherine was impressed, beyond her expectation, by their multiplicity and their convenience. The purposes for which a few shapeless pantries and a comfortless scullery were deemed sufficient at Fullerton, were here carried on in appropriate divisions, commodious and roomy. The number of servants continually appearing, did not strike her less than the number of their offices. Wherever they went, some pattened girl[1] stopped to curtsey, or some footman in *dishabille* sneaked off.[2] Yet this was an Abbey!— How inexpressibly different in these domestic arrangements from such as she had read about—from abbeys and castles, in which, though certainly larger than Northanger, all the dirty work of the house was to be done by two pair of female hands at the utmost. How they could get through it all, had often amazed Mrs. Allen; and, when Catherine saw what was necessary here, she began to be amazed herself.

They returned to the hall, that the chief staircase might be ascended, and the beauty of its wood, and ornaments of rich carving might be pointed out: having gained the top, they turned in an opposite direction from the gallery in which her room lay, and shortly entered one on the same plan, but superior in length and breadth. She was here shown successively into three large bed-chambers, with their dressing-rooms, most completely and handsomely fitted up; every thing that money and taste could do, to give comfort and elegance to apartments, had been bestowed on these; and, being furnished within the last five years, they were perfect in all that would be generally pleasing, and wanting in all that could give pleasure to Catherine. As they were surveying the last, the General, after slightly naming a few of the distinguished characters, by

---

1. The servant wore overshoes to protect her feet from the mud in the garden.

2. *Dishabille* was either a joke or a misprint for *déshabillé*, meaning undressed or out of uniform.

whom they had at times been honoured, turned with a smiling countenance to Catherine, and ventured to hope, that henceforward some of their earliest tenants might be "our friends from Fullerton." She felt the unexpected compliment, and deeply regretted the impossibility of thinking well of a man so kindly disposed towards herself, and so full of civility to all her family.

The gallery was terminated by folding doors, which Miss Tilney, advancing, had thrown open, and passed through, and seemed on the point of doing the same by the first door to the left, in another long reach of gallery, when the General, coming forwards, called her hastily, and, as Catherine thought, rather angrily back, demanding whither she were going?—And what was there more to be seen?—Had not Miss Morland already seen all that could be worth her notice?—And did she not suppose her friend might be glad of some refreshment after so much exercise? Miss Tilney drew back directly, and the heavy doors were closed upon the mortified Catherine, who, having seen, in a momentary glance beyond them, a narrower passage, more numerous openings, and symptoms of a winding staircase, believed herself at last within the reach of something worth her notice; and felt, as she unwillingly paced back the gallery, that she would rather be allowed to examine that end of the house, than see all the finery of all the rest.—The General's evident desire of preventing such an examination was an additional stimulant. Something was certainly to be concealed; her fancy, though it had trespassed lately once or twice, could not mislead her here; and what that something was, a short sentence of Miss Tilney's, as they followed the General at some distance down stairs, seemed to point out:—"I was going to take you into what was my mother's room—the room in which she died——" were all her words; but few as they were, they conveyed pages of intelligence to Catherine. It was no wonder that the General should shrink from the sight of such objects as that room must contain; a room in all probability never entered by him since the dreadful scene had passed, which released his suffering wife, and left him to the stings of conscience.

She ventured, when next alone with Eleanor, to express her wish of being permitted to see it, as well as all the rest of that side of the house; and Eleanor promised to attend her there, whenever they should have a convenient hour. Catherine understood her:—the

General must be watched from home, before that room could be entered. "It remains as it was, I suppose?" said she, in a tone of feeling.

"Yes, entirely."

"And how long ago may it be that your mother died?"

"She has been dead these nine years." And nine years, Catherine knew was a trifle of time, compared with what generally elapsed after the death of an injured wife, before her room was put to rights.

"You were with her, I suppose, to the last?"

"No," said Miss Tilney, sighing; "I was unfortunately from home.—Her illness was sudden and short; and, before I arrived it was all over."

Catherine's blood ran cold with the horrid suggestions which naturally sprang from these words. Could it be possible?—Could Henry's father?——And yet how many were the examples to justify even the blackest suspicions!—And, when she saw him in the evening, while she worked with her friend, slowly pacing the drawing-room for an hour together in silent thoughtfulness, with downcast eyes and contracted brow, she felt secure for all possibility of wronging him. It was the air and attitude of a Montoni![3]—What could more plainly speak the gloomy workings of a mind not wholly dead to every sense of humanity, in its fearful review of past scenes of guilt? Unhappy man!—And the anxiousness of her spirits directed her eyes towards his figure so repeatedly, as to catch Miss Tilney's notice. "My father," she whispered, "often walks about the room in this way; it is nothing unusual."

"So much the worse!" thought Catherine; such ill-timed exercise was of a piece with the strange unseasonableness of his morning walks, and boded nothing good.

After an evening, the little variety and seeming length of which made her peculiarly sensible of Henry's importance among them, she was heartily glad to be dismissed; though it was a look from the General not designed for her observation which sent his daughter to the bell. When the butler would have lit his master's candle, however, he was forbidden. The latter was not going to retire. "I have many pamphlets to finish," said he to Catherine, "before I can close my eyes; and perhaps may be poring over the affairs of the

3. Montoni, the villain in *The Mysteries of Udolpho*, intended to force Emily, the heroine, into a bad marriage in exchange for money.

nation for hours after you are asleep. Can either of us be more meetly employed? *My* eyes will be blinding for the good of others; and *yours* preparing by rest for future mischief."

But neither the business alleged, nor the magnificent compliment, could win Catherine from thinking, that some very different object must occasion so serious a delay of proper repose. To be kept up for hours, after the family were in bed, by stupid pamphlets, was not very likely. There must be some deeper cause: something was to be done which could be done only while the household slept; and the probability that Mrs. Tilney yet lived, shut up for causes unknown, and receiving from the pitiless hands of her husband a nightly supply of coarse food, was the conclusion which necessarily followed. Shocking as was the idea, it was at least better than a death unfairly hastened, as, in the natural course of things, she must ere long be released. The suddenness of her reputed illness; the absence of her daughter, and probably of her other children, at the time—all favoured the supposition of her imprisonment.—Its origin—jealousy perhaps, or wanton cruelty—was yet to be unravelled.

In revolving these matters, while she undressed, it suddenly struck her as not unlikely, that she might that morning have passed near the very spot of this unfortunate woman's confinement—might have been within a few paces of the cell in which she languished out her days; for what part of the Abbey could be more fitted for the purpose than that which yet bore the traces of monastic division? In the high-arched passage, paved with stone, which already she had trodden with peculiar awe, she well remembered the doors of which the General had given no account. To what might not those doors lead? In support of the plausibility of this conjecture, it further occurred to her, that the forbidden gallery, in which lay the apartments of the unfortunate Mrs. Tilney, must be, as certainly as her memory could guide her, exactly over this suspected range of cells, and the staircase by the side of those apartments of which she had caught a transient glimpse, communicating by some secret means with those cells, might well have favoured the barbarous proceedings of her husband. Down that staircase she had perhaps been conveyed in a state of well-prepared insensibility!

Catherine sometimes started at the boldness of her own surmises, and sometimes hoped or feared that she had gone too far;

but they were supported by such appearances as made their dismissal impossible.

The side of the quadrangle, in which she supposed the guilty scene to be acting, being, according to her belief, just opposite her own, it struck her that, if judiciously watched, some rays of light from the General's lamp might glimmer through the lower windows, as he passed to the prison of his wife; and, twice before she stepped into bed, she stole gently from her room to the corresponding window in the gallery, to see if it appeared; but all abroad was dark, and it must yet be too early. The various ascending noises convinced her that the servants must still be up. Till midnight, she supposed it would be in vain to watch; but then, when the clock had struck twelve, and all was quiet, she would, if not quite appalled by darkness, steal out and look once more. The clock struck twelve—and Catherine had been half an hour asleep.

CHAPTER IX

The next day afforded no opportunity for the proposed examination of the mysterious apartments. It was Sunday, and the whole time between morning and afternoon service was required by the General in exercise abroad or eating cold meat at home; and great as was Catherine's curiosity, her courage was not equal to a wish of exploring them after dinner, either by the fading light of the sky between six and seven o'clock, or by the yet more partial though stronger illumination of a treacherous lamp. The day was unmarked therefore by any thing to interest her imagination beyond the sight of a very elegant monument to the memory of Mrs. Tilney; which immediately fronted the family pew. By that her eye was instantly caught and long retained; and the perusal of the highly-strained epitaph, in which every virtue was ascribed to her by the inconsolable husband, who must have been in some way or other her destroyer, affected her even to tears.

That the General, having erected such a monument, should be able to face it, was not perhaps very strange, and yet that he could sit so boldly collected within its view, maintain so elevated an air, look so fearlessly around, nay, that he should even enter the church, seemed wonderful to Catherine. Not however that many instances of beings equally hardened in guilt might not be produced. She could remember dozens who had persevered in every possible vice, going on from crime to crime, murdering whomsoever they chose, without any feeling of humanity or remorse; till a violent death or a religious retirement closed their black career. The erection of the monument itself could not in the smallest degree affect her doubts of Mrs. Tilney's actual decease. Were she even to descend into the family vault where her ashes were supposed to slumber, were she to behold the coffin in which they were said to be enclosed—what could it avail in such a case? Catherine had read too much not to be perfectly aware of the ease with which a waxen figure[1] might be introduced, and a supposititious funeral carried on.

The succeeding morning promised something better. The General's early walk, ill-timed as it was in every other view, was favourable here; and when she knew him to be out of the house, she directly proposed to Miss Tilney the accomplishment of her promise. Eleanor was ready to oblige her; and Catherine reminding her as they went of another promise, their first visit in consequence was to the portrait in her bed-chamber. It represented a very lovely woman, with a mild and pensive countenance, justifying so far, the expectations of its new observer; but they were not in every respect answered, for Catherine had depended upon meeting with features, air, complexion that should be the very counterpart, the very image, if not of Henry's, of Eleanor's;—the only portraits of which she had been in the habit of thinking, bearing always an equal resemblance of mother and child. A face once taken was taken for generations. But here she was obliged to look and consider and study for a likeness. She contemplated it, however, in spite of this drawback, with much emotion; and, but for a yet stronger interest, would have left it unwillingly.

Her agitation as they entered the great gallery was too much for any endeavour at discourse; she could only look at her companion. Eleanor's countenance was dejected, yet sedate; and its composure spoke her inured to all the gloomy objects to which they were advancing. Again she passed through the folding doors, again her hand was upon the important lock, and Catherine, hardly able to

---

1. In *The Mysteries of Udolpho,* Emily, Catherine's counterpart, looks behind a black veil expecting to find a decomposing corpse and finds a wax figure instead.

breathe, was turning to close the former with fearful caution, when the figure, the dreaded figure of the General himself at the further end of the gallery, stood before her! The name of "Eleanor" at the same moment, in his loudest tone, resounded through the building, giving to his daughter the first intimation of his presence, and to Catherine terror upon terror. An attempt at concealment had been her first instinctive movement on perceiving him, yet she could scarcely hope to have escaped his eye; and when her friend, who with an apologizing look darted hastily by her, had joined and disappeared with him, she ran for safety to her own room, and, locking herself in, believed that she should never have courage to go down again. She remained there at least an hour, in the greatest agitation, deeply commiserating the state of her poor friend, and expecting a summons herself from the angry General to attend him in his own apartment. No summons however arrived; and at last, on seeing a carriage drive up to the Abbey, she was emboldened to descend and meet him under the protection of visitors. The breakfast-room was gay with company; and she was named to them by the General, as the friend of his daughter, in a complimentary style, which so well concealed his resentful ire, as to make her feel secure at least of life for the present. And Eleanor, with a command of countenance which did honour to her concern for his character, taking an early occasion of saying to her, "My father only wanted me to answer a note," she began to hope that she had either been unseen by the General, or that from some consideration of policy she should be allowed to suppose herself so. Upon this trust she dared still to remain in his presence, after the company left them, and nothing occurred to disturb it.

In the course of this morning's reflections, she came to a resolution of making her next attempt on the forbidden door alone. It would be much better in every respect that Eleanor should know nothing of the matter. To involve her in the danger of a second detection, to court her into an apartment which must wring her heart, could not be the office of a friend. The General's utmost anger could not be to herself what it might be to a daughter; and, besides, she thought the examination itself would be more satisfactory if made without any companion. It would be impossible to explain to Eleanor the suspicions, from which the other had, in all likelihood, been hitherto happily exempt; nor could she therefore, in *her* presence, search for those proofs of the General's cruelty, which however they might yet have escaped discovery, she felt confident of somewhere drawing forth, in the shape of some fragmented journal, continued to the last gasp. Of the way to the apartment she was now perfectly mistress; and as she wished to get it over before Henry's return, who was expected on the morrow, there was no time to be lost. The day was bright, her courage high; at four o'clock, the sun was now two hours above the horizon, and it would be only her retiring to dress half an hour earlier than usual.

It was done; and Catherine found herself alone in the gallery before the clocks had ceased to strike. It was no time for thought; she hurried on, slipped with the least possible noise through the folding doors, and without stopping to look or breathe, rushed forward to the one in question. The lock yielded to her hand, and, luckily, with no sullen sound that could alarm a human being. On tip-toe she entered; the room was before her; but it was some minutes before she could advance another step. She beheld what fixed her to the spot and agitated every feature.—She saw a large, well-proportioned apartment, an handsome dimity[2] bed, arranged as unoccupied with an housemaid's care, a bright Bath stove,[3] mahogany wardrobes and neatly-painted chairs, on which the warm beams of a western sun gaily poured through two sash windows! Catherine had expected to have her feelings worked, and worked they were. Astonishment and doubt first seized them; and a shortly succeeding ray of common sense added some bitter emotions of shame. She could not be mistaken as to the room; but how grossly mistaken in every thing else!—in Miss Tilney's meaning, in her own calculation! This apartment, to which she had given a date so ancient, a position so awful, proved to be one end of what the General's father had built. There were two other doors in the chamber, leading probably into dressing-closets; but she had no inclination to open either. Would the veil in which Mrs. Tilney had last walked, or the volume in which she had last read, remain to tell what nothing else was allowed to whisper? No: whatever might have been the General's crimes, he had certainly too much wit to let

2. An elegant heavy woven cotton fabric.

3. Like the Rumford, a modern stove built over a fireplace with a metal plate to direct the heat into the room.

them sue for detection. She was sick of exploring, and desired but to be safe in her own room, with her own heart only privy to its folly; and she was on the point of retreating as softly as she had entered, when the sound of footsteps, she could hardly tell where, made her pause and tremble. To be found there, even by a servant, would be unpleasant; but by the General, (and he seemed always at hand when least wanted,) much worse!—She listened—the sound had ceased; and resolving not to lose a moment, she passed through and closed the door. At that instant a door underneath was hastily opened; some one seemed with swift steps to ascend the stairs, by the head of which she had yet to pass before she could gain the gallery. She had no power to move. With a feeling of terror not very definable, she fixed her eyes on the staircase, and in a few moments it gave Henry to her view. "Mr. Tilney!" she exclaimed in a voice of more than common astonishment. He looked astonished too. "Good God!" she continued, not attending to his address, "how came you here?—how came you up that staircase?"

"How came I up that staircase!" he replied, greatly surprized. "Because it is my nearest way from the stable-yard to my own chamber; and why should I not come up it?"

Catherine recollected herself, blushed deeply, and could say no more. He seemed to be looking in her countenance for that explanation which her lips did not afford. She moved on towards the gallery. "And may I not, in my turn," said he, as he pushed back the folding doors, "ask how *you* came here?—This passage is at least as extraordinary a road from the breakfast-parlour to your apartment, as that staircase can be from the stables to mine."

"I have been," said Catherine, looking down, "to see your mother's room."

"My mother's room!—Is there any thing extraordinary to be seen there?"

"No, nothing at all.—I thought you did not mean to come back till to-morrow."

"I did not expect to be able to return sooner, when I went away; but three hours ago I had the pleasure of finding nothing to detain me.—You look pale.—I am afraid I alarmed you by running so fast up those stairs. Perhaps you did not know—you were not aware of their leading from the offices in common use?"

"No, I was not.—You have had a very fine day for your ride."

"Very;—and does Eleanor leave you to find your way into all the rooms in the house by yourself?"

"Oh! no; she showed me over the greatest part on Saturday— and we were coming here to these rooms—but only—" (dropping her voice)—"your father was with us."

"And that prevented you;" said Henry, earnestly regarding her.—"Have you looked into all the rooms in that passage?"

"No, I only wanted to see—-Is not it very late? I must go and dress."

"It is only a quarter past four," (showing his watch) "and you are not now in Bath. No theatre, no Rooms to prepare for. Half an hour at Northanger must be enough."

She could not contradict it, and therefore suffered herself to be detained, though her dread of further questions made her, for the first time in their acquaintance, wish to leave him. They walked slowly up the gallery. "Have you had any letter from Bath since I saw you?"

"No, and I am very much surprized. Isabella promised so faithfully to write directly."

"Promised so faithfully!—A faithful promise!—That puzzles me.—I have heard of a faithful performance. But a faithful promise— the fidelity of promising! It is a power little worth knowing however, since it can deceive and pain you. My mother's room is very commodious, is it not? Large and cheerful-looking, and the dressing-closets so well disposed! It always strikes me as the most comfortable apartment in the house, and I rather wonder that Eleanor should not take it for her own. She sent you to look at it, I suppose?"

"No."

"It has been your own doing entirely?"—Catherine said nothing—After a short silence, during which he had closely observed her, he added, "As there is nothing in the room in itself to raise curiosity, this must have proceeded from a sentiment of respect for my mother's character, as described by Eleanor, which does honour to her memory. The world, I believe, never saw a better woman. But it is not often that virtue can boast an interest such as this. The domestic, unpretending merits of a person never known, do not often create that kind of fervent, venerating tenderness which would prompt a visit like yours. Eleanor, I suppose, has talked of her a great deal?"

"Yes, a great deal. That is—no, not much, but what she did say, was very interesting. Her dying so suddenly," (slowly, and with hesitation it was spoken,) "and you—none of you being at home—and your father, I thought—perhaps had not been very fond of her."

"And from these circumstances," he replied, (his quick eye fixed on her's,) "you infer perhaps the probability of some negligence—some—" (involuntarily she shook her head) "—or it may be—of something still less pardonable." She raised her eyes towards him more fully than she had ever done before. "My mother's illness," he continued, "the seizure which ended in her death *was* sudden. The malady itself, one from which she had often suffered, a bilious fever—its cause therefore constitutional. On the third day, in short as soon as she could be prevailed on, a physician attended her, a very respectable man, and one in whom she had always placed great confidence. Upon his opinion of her danger, two others were called in the next day, and remained in almost constant attendance for four-and-twenty hours. On the fifth day she died. During the progress of her disorder, Frederick and I (*we* were both at home) saw her repeatedly; and from our own observation can bear witness to her having received every possible attention which could spring from the affection of those about her, or which her situation in life could command. Poor Eleanor *was* absent, and at such a distance as to return only to see her mother in her coffin."

"But your father," said Catherine, "was *he* afflicted?"

"For a time, greatly so. You have erred in supposing him not attached to her. He loved her, I am persuaded, as well as it was possible for him to—We have not all, you know, the same tenderness of disposition—and I will not pretend to say that while she lived, she might not often have had much to bear, but though his temper injured her, his judgment never did. His value of her was sincere; and, if not permanently, he was truly afflicted by her death."

"I am very glad of it," said Catherine, "it would have been very shocking!"——

"If I understand you rightly, you had formed a surmise of such horror as I have hardly words to—— Dear Miss Morland, consider the dreadful nature of the suspicions you have entertained. What have you been judging from? Remember the country and the age in which we live. Remember that we are English, that we are Christians. Consult your own understanding, your own sense of the

probable, you own observation of what is passing around you—
Does our education prepare us for such atrocities? Do our laws con-
nive at them? Could they be perpetrated without being known, in a
country like this, where social and literary intercourse is on such a
footing; where every man is surrounded by a neighbourhood of voluntary spies, and where roads and newspapers lay every thing open?
Dearest Miss Morland, what ideas have you been admitting?"

They had reached the end of the gallery; and with tears of
shame she ran off to her own room.

CHAPTER X

The visions of romance were over. Catherine was completely awakened. Henry's address, short as it had been, had more thoroughly
opened her eyes to the extravagance of her late fancies than all their
several disappointments had done. Most grievously was she humbled. Most bitterly did she cry. It was not only with herself that she
was sunk—but with Henry. Her folly, which now seemed even
criminal, was all exposed to him, and he must despise her for ever.
The liberty which her imagination had dared to take with the character of his father, could he ever forgive it? The absurdity of her curiosity and her fears, could they ever be forgotten? She hated herself more than she could express. He had—she thought he had,
once or twice before this fatal morning, shown something like affection for her.—But now—in short, she made herself as miserable
as possible for about half an hour, went down when the clock
struck five, with a broken heart, and could scarcely give an intelligible answer to Eleanor's inquiry, if she was well. The formidable
Henry soon followed her into the room, and the only difference in
his behaviour to her, was that he paid her rather more attention
than usual. Catherine had never wanted comfort more, and he
looked as if he was aware of it.

The evening wore away with no abatement of this soothing politeness; and her spirits were gradually raised to a modest tranquillity. She did not learn either to forget or defend the past; but she
learned to hope that it would never transpire farther, and that it
might not cost her Henry's entire regard. Her thoughts being still
chiefly fixed on what she had with such causeless terror felt and

done, nothing could shortly be clearer, than that it had been all a voluntary, self-created delusion, each trifling circumstance receiving importance from an imagination resolved on alarm, and every thing forced to bend to one purpose by a mind which, before she entered the Abbey, had been craving to be frightened. She remembered with what feelings she had prepared for a knowledge of Northanger. She saw that the infatuation had been created, the mischief settled long before her quitting Bath, and it seemed as if the whole might be traced to the influence of that sort of reading which she had there indulged.

Charming as were all Mrs. Radcliffe's works, and charming even as were the works of all her imitators, it was not in them perhaps that human nature, at least in the midland countries of England, was to be looked for. Of the Alps and Pyrenees, with their pine forests and their vices, they might give a faithful delineation; and Italy, Switzerland, and the South of France, might be as fruitful in horrors as they were there represented. Catherine dared not doubt beyond her own country, and even of that, if hard pressed, would have yielded the northern and western extremities. But in the central part of England there was surely some security for the existence even of a wife not beloved, in the laws of the land, and the manners of the age. Murder was not tolerated, servants were not slaves, and neither poison nor sleeping potions to be procured, like rhubarb, from every druggist. Among the Alps and Pyrenees, perhaps, there were no mixed characters. There, such as were not as spotless as an angel, might have the dispositions of a fiend. But in England it was not so; among the English, she believed, in their hearts and habits, there was a general though unequal mixture of good and bad. Upon this conviction, she would not be surprized if even in Henry and Eleanor Tilney, some slight imperfection might hereafter appear; and upon this conviction she need not fear to acknowledge some actual specks in the character of their father, who, though cleared from the grossly injurious suspicions which she must ever blush to have entertained, she did believe, upon serious consideration, to be not perfectly amiable.

Her mind made up on these several points, and her resolution formed, of always judging and acting in future with the greatest good sense, she had nothing to do but to forgive herself and be happier than ever; and the lenient hand of time did much for her by insensible gradations in the course of another day. Henry's astonishing generosity and nobleness of conduct, in never alluding in the slightest way to what had passed, was of the greatest assistance to her; and sooner than she could have supposed it possible in the beginning of her distress, her spirits became absolutely comfortable, and capable, as heretofore, of continual improvement by any thing he said. There were still some subjects indeed, under which she believed they must always tremble;—the mention of a chest or a cabinet, for instance—and she did not love the sight of Japan in any shape: but even *she* could allow, that an occasional memento of past folly, however painful, might not be without use.

The anxieties of common life began soon to succeed to the alarms of romance. Her desire of hearing from Isabella grew every day greater. She was quite impatient to know how the Bath world went on, and how the Rooms were attended; and especially was she anxious to be assured of Isabella's having matched some fine netting-cotton, on which she had left her intent; and of her continuing on the best terms with James. Her only dependence for information of any kind was on Isabella. James had protested against writing to her till his return to Oxford; and Mrs. Allen had given her no hopes of a letter till she had got back to Fullerton.—But Isabella had promised and promised again; and when she promised a thing, she was so scrupulous in performing it! this made it so particularly strange!

For nine successive mornings, Catherine wondered over the repetition of a disappointment, which each morning became more severe: but, on the tenth, when she entered the breakfast-room, her first object was a letter, held out by Henry's willing hand. She thanked him as heartily as if he had written it himself. " 'Tis only from James, however," as she looked at the direction. She opened it; it was from Oxford; and to this purpose:—

Dear Catherine,

Though, God knows, with little inclination for writing, I think it my duty to tell you, that every thing is at an end between Miss Thorpe and me.—I left her and Bath yesterday, never to see either again. I shall not enter into particulars, they would only pain you more. You will soon hear enough from another quarter to know where lies the blame; and I hope will acquit your brother of every thing but the folly of too easily thinking his affection returned. Thank God! I am undeceived in time! But it is a heavy blow!—After my father's consent had been so kindly given—but no more of this. She has made me miserable for ever! Let me soon hear from you, dear Catherine; you are my only friend; *your* love I do build upon. I wish your visit at Northanger may be over before Captain Tilney makes his engagement known, or you will be uncomfortably circumstanced.—Poor Thorpe is in town: I dread the sight of him; his honest heart would feel so much. I have written to him and my father. Her duplicity hurts me more than all; till the very last, if I reasoned with her, she declared herself as much attached to me as ever, and laughed at my fears. I am ashamed to think how long I bore with it; but if ever man had reason to believe himself loved, I was that man. I cannot understand even now what she would be at, for there could be no need of my being played off to make her secure of Tilney. We parted at last by mutual consent—happy for me had we never met! I can never expect to know such another woman! Dearest Catherine, beware how you give your heart.

Believe me, &c.

Catherine had not read three lines before her sudden change of countenance, and short exclamations of sorrowing wonder, declared her to be receiving unpleasant news; and Henry, earnestly watching her through the whole letter, saw plainly that it ended no better than it began. He was prevented, however, from even looking his surprize by his father's entrance. They went to breakfast directly; but Catherine could hardly eat any thing. Tears filled her eyes, and even ran down her cheeks as she sat. The letter was one moment in her hand, then in her lap, and then in her pocket: and she looked as if she knew not what she did. The General, between his cocoa and his newspaper, had luckily no leisure for noticing her; but to the other two her distress was equally visible. As soon as she dared leave the table she hurried away to her own room; but the house-maids were busy in it, and she was obliged to come down again. She turned into the drawing-room for privacy, but Henry and Eleanor had likewise retreated thither, and were at that moment deep in consultation about her. She drew back, trying to beg their pardon, but was, with gentle violence, forced to return; and the others withdrew, after Eleanor had affectionately expressed a wish of being of use or comfort to her.

After half an hour's free indulgence of grief and reflection, Catherine felt equal to encountering her friends; but whether she should make her distress known to them was another consideration. Perhaps, if particularly questioned, she might just give an idea—just distantly hint at it—but not more. To expose a friend, such a friend as Isabella had been to her—and then their own brother so closely concerned in it!—She believed she must wave the subject altogether. Henry and Eleanor were by themselves in the breakfast-room; and each, as she entered it, looked at her anxiously. Catherine took her place at the table, and, after a short silence, Eleanor said, "No bad news from Fullerton, I hope? Mr. and Mrs. Morland—your brothers and sisters—I hope they are none of them ill?"

"No, I thank you," (sighing as she spoke,) "they are all very well. My letter was from my brother at Oxford."

Nothing further was said for a few minutes; and then speaking through her tears, she added, "I do not think I shall ever wish for a letter again!"

"I am sorry," said Henry, closing the book he had just opened; "if I had suspected the letter of containing any thing unwelcome, I should have given it with very different feelings."

"It contained something worse than any body could suppose!— Poor James is so unhappy!—You will soon know why."

"To have so kind-hearted, so affectionate a sister," replied Henry, warmly, "must be a comfort to him under any distress."

"I have one favour to beg," said Catherine, shortly afterwards, in an agitated manner, "that, if your brother should be coming here, you will give me notice of it, that I may go away."

"Our brother!—Frederick!"

"Yes; I am sure I should be very sorry to leave you so soon, but something has happened that would make it very dreadful for me to be in the same house with Captain Tilney."

Eleanor's work was suspended while she gazed with increasing astonishment; but Henry began to suspect the truth, and something, in which Miss Thorpe's name was included, passed his lips.

"How quick you are!" cried Catherine: "you have guessed it, I declare!—And yet, when we talked about it in Bath, you little thought of its ending so. Isabella—no wonder *now* I have not heard from her—Isabella has deserted my brother, and is to marry your's! Could you have believed there had been such inconstancy and fickleness, and every thing that is bad in the world?"

"I hope, so far as concerns my brother, you are misinformed. I hope he has not had any material share in bringing on Mr. Morland's disappointment. His marrying Miss Thorpe is not probable. I think you must be deceived so far. I am very sorry for Mr. Morland—sorry that any one you love should be unhappy; but my surprize would be greater at Frederick's marrying her, than at any other part of the story."

"It is very true, however; you shall read James's letter yourself.—Stay——there is one part——" recollecting with a blush the last line.

"Will you take the trouble of reading to us the passages which concern my brother?"

"No, read it yourself," cried Catherine, whose second thoughts were clearer. "I do not know what I was thinking of," (blushing again that she had blushed before,)—"James only means to give me good advice."

He gladly received the letter; and, having read it through, with close attention, returned it saying, "Well, if it is to be so, I can only say that I am sorry for it. Frederick will not be the first man who has chosen a wife with less sense than his family expected. I do not envy his situation, either as a lover or a son."

Miss Tilney, at Catherine's invitation, now read the letter likewise; and, having expressed also her concern and surprize, began to inquire into Miss Thorpe's connections and fortune.

"Her mother is a very good sort of woman," was Catherine's answer.

"What was her father?"

"A lawyer, I believe.—They live at Putney."

"Are they a wealthy family?"

"No, not very. I do not believe Isabella has any fortune at all: but that will not signify in your family.—Your father is so very liberal! He told me the other day, that he only valued money as it allowed him to promote the happiness of his children." The brother and sister loked at each other. "But," said Eleanor, after a short pause, "would it be to promote his happiness, to enable him to marry such a girl?—She must be an unprincipled one, or she could not have used your brother so.—And how strange an infatuation on Frederick's side! A girl who, before his eyes, is violating an engagement voluntarily entered into with another man! Is not it inconceivable, Henry? Frederick too, who always wore his heart so proudly! who found no woman good enough to be loved!"

"That is the most unpromising circumstance, the strongest presumption against him. When I think of his past declarations, I give him up.—Moreover, I have too good an opinion of Miss Thorpe's prudence, to suppose that she would part with one gentleman before the other was secured. It is all over with Frederick indeed! He is a deceased man—defunct in understanding. Prepare for your sister-in-law, Eleanor, and such a sister-in-law as you must delight in!—Open, candid, artless, guileless, with affections strong but simple, forming no pretensions, and knowing no disguise."

"Such a sister-in-law, Henry, I should delight in," said Eleanor, with a smile.

"But perhaps," observed Catherine, "though she has behaved so ill by our family, she may behave better by your's. Now she has really got the man she likes, she may be constant."

"Indeed I am afraid she will," replied Henry; "I am afraid she will be very constant, unless a baronet should come in her way; that is Frederick's only chance.—I will get the Bath paper, and look over the arrivals."

"You think it is all for ambition then?—And, upon my word, there are some things that seem very like it. I cannot forget, that, when she first knew what my father would do for them, she seemed quite disappointed that it was not more. I never was so deceived in any one's character in my life before."

"Among all the great variety that you have known and studied."

"My own disappointment and loss in her is very great; but, as for poor James, I suppose he will hardly ever recover it."

"Your brother is certainly very much to be pitied at present; but we must not, in our concern for his sufferings, undervalue your's. You feel, I suppose, that, in losing Isabella, you lose half yourself: you feel a void in your heart which nothing else can occupy. Society is becoming irksome; and as for the amusements in which you were wont to share at Bath, the very idea of them without her is abhorrent. You would not, for instance, now go to a ball for the world. You feel that you have no longer any friend to whom you can speak with unreserve; on whose regard you can place dependence; or whose counsel, in any difficulty, you could rely on. You feel all this?"

"No," said Catherine, after a few moments' reflection, "I do not—ought I? To say the truth, though I am hurt and grieved, that I cannot still love her, that I am never to hear from her, perhaps never to see her again, I do not feel so very, very much afflicted as one would have thought."

"You feel, as you always do, what is most to the credit of human nature.—Such feelings ought to be investigated, that they may know themselves."

Catherine, by some chance or other, found her spirits so very much relieved by this conversation, that she could not regret her being led on, though so unaccountably, to mention the circumstance which had produced it.

CHAPTER XI

From this time, the subject was frequently canvassed by the three young people; and Catherine found, with some surprize, that her two young friends were perfectly agreed in considering Isabella's want of consequence and fortune as likely to throw great difficulties in the way of her marrying their brother. Their persuasion that the General would, upon this ground alone, independent of the objection that might be raised against her character, oppose the connection, turned her feelings moreover with some alarm towards herself. She was as insignificant, and perhaps as portionless as Isabella; and if the heir of the Tilney property had not grandeur and wealth enough in himself, at what point of interest were the demands of his younger brother to rest? The very painful reflections to which this thought led, could only be dispersed by a dependence on the effect of that particular partiality, which, as she was given to understand by his words as well as his actions, she had from the first been so fortunate as to excite in the General; and by a recollection of some most generous and disinterested sentiments on the subject of money, which she had more than once heard him utter, and which tempted her to think his disposition in such matters misunderstood by his children.

They were so fully convinced, however, that their brother would not have the courage to apply in person for his father's consent, and so repeatedly assured her that he had never in his life been less likely to come to Northanger than at the present time, that she suffered her mind to be at ease as to the necessity of any sudden removal of her own. But as it was not to be supposed that Captain Tilney, whenever he made his application, would give his father any just idea of Isabella's conduct, it occurred to her as highly expedient that Henry should lay the whole business before him as it really was, enabling the General by that means to form a cool and impartial opinion, and prepare his objections on a fairer ground than inequality of situations. She proposed it to him accordingly; but he did not catch at the measure so eagerly as she had expected. "No," said he, "my father's hands need not be strengthened, and Frederick's confession of folly need not be forestalled. He must tell his own story."

"But he will tell only half of it."

"A quarter would be enough."

A day or two passed away and brought no tidings of Captain Tilney. His brother and sister knew not what to think. Sometimes it appeared to them as if his silence would be the natural result of the suspected engagement, and at others that it was wholly incompatible with it. The General, meanwhile, though offended every morning by Frederick's remissness in writing, was free from any real anxiety about him; and had no more pressing solicitude than that of making Miss Morland's time at Northanger pass pleasantly. He often expressed his uneasiness on this head, feared the sameness of every day's society and employments would disgust her with the place, wished the Lady Frasers had been in the country, talked every now and then of having a large party to dinner, and once or twice began even to calculate the number of young dancing people in the neighbourhood. But then it was such a dead time of year, no wild-fowl, no game, and the Lady Frasers were not in the country. And it all ended, at last, in his telling Henry one morning, that when he next went to Woodston, they would take him by surprize there some day or other, and eat their mutton with him. Henry was greatly honoured and very happy, and Catherine was quite delighted with the scheme. "And when do you think, sir, I may look forward to this pleasure?—I must be at Woodston on Monday to attend the parish meeting, and shall probably be obliged to stay two or three days."

"Well, well, we will take our chance some one of those days. There is no need to fix. You are not to put yourself at all out of your way. Whatever you may happen to have in the house will be enough. I think I can answer for the young ladies making allowance for a bachelor's table. Let me see; Monday will be a busy day with you, we will not come on Monday; and Tuesday will be a busy one with me. I expect my surveyor from Brockham with his report in the morning; and afterwards I cannot in decency fail attending the club. I really could not face my acquaintance if I staid away now; for, as I am known to be in the country, it would be taken exceedingly amiss; and it is a rule with me, Miss Morland, never to give offence to any of my neighbours, if a small sacrifice of time and attention can prevent it. They are a set of very worthy men. They have half a buck from Northanger twice a year; and I dine with them whenever I can. Tuesday, therefore, we may say is out of the question. But on Wednesday, I think, Henry, you may expect us; and we shall be with you early, that we may have time to look about us. Two hours and three quarters will carry us to Woodston, I suppose; we shall be in the carriage by ten; so, about a quarter before one on Wednesday, you may look for us."

A ball itself could not have been more welcome to Catherine than this little excursion, so strong was her desire to be acquainted with Woodston; and her heart was still bounding with joy, when Henry, about an hour afterwards, came booted and great coated into the room where she and Eleanor were sitting, and said, "I am come, young ladies, in a very moralizing strain, to observe that our pleasures in this world are always to be paid for, and that we often purchase them at a great disadvantage, giving ready-monied actual happiness for a draft on the future, that may not be honoured. Witness myself, at this present hour. Because I am to hope for the satisfaction of seeing you at Woodston on Wednesday, which bad weather, or twenty other causes may prevent, I must go away directly, two days before I intended it."

"Go away!" said Catherine, with a very long face; "and why?"

"Why!—How can you ask the question?—Because no time is to be lost in frightening my old housekeeper out of her wits,—because I must go and prepare a dinner for you to be sure."

"Oh! not seriously!"

"Aye, and sadly too—for I had much rather stay."

"But how can you think of such a thing, after what the General said? when he so particularly desired you not to give yourself any trouble, because *any thing* would do."

Henry only smiled. "I am sure it is quite unnecessary upon your sister's account and mine. You must know it to be so; and the General made such a point of your providing nothing extraordinary:—besides, if he had not said half so much as he did, he has always such an excellent dinner at home, that sitting down to a middling one for one day could not signify."

"I wish I could reason like you, for his sake and my own. Good bye. As to-morrow is Sunday, Eleanor, I shall not return."

He went; and, it being at any time a much simpler operation to Catherine to doubt her own judgment than Henry's, she was very soon obliged to give him credit for being right, however disagreeable to her his going. But the inexplicability of the General's conduct dwelt much on her thoughts. That he was very particular in his eating, she had, by her own unassisted observation, already discovered; but why he should say one thing so positively, and mean another all the while, was most unaccountable! How were people, at that rate, to be understood? Who but Henry could have been aware of what his father was at?

From Saturday to Wednesday, however, they were now to be without Henry. This was the sad finale of every reflection:—and Captain Tilney's letter would certainly come in his absence; and Wednesday she was very sure would be wet. The past, present, and future, were all equally in gloom. Her brother so unhappy, and her loss in Isabella so great; and Eleanor's spirits always affected by Henry's absence! What was there to interest or amuse her? She was tired of the woods and the shrubberies—always so smooth and so dry; and the Abbey in itself was no more to her now than any other house. The painful remembrance of the folly it had helped to nourish and perfect, was the only emotion which could spring from a consideration of the building. What a revolution in her ideas! she, who had so longed to be in an abbey! Now, there was nothing so charming to her imagination as the unpretending comfort of a well-connected[1] Parsonage, something like Fullerton, but better: Fullerton had its faults, but Woodston probably had none.—If Wednesday should ever come!

1. Conveniently designed.

It did come, and exactly when it might be reasonably looked for. It came—it was fine—and Catherine trod on air. By ten o'clock, the chaise-and-four conveyed the trio from the Abbey; and, after an agreeable drive of almost twenty miles, they entered Woodston, a large and populous village, in a situation not unpleasant. Catherine was ashamed to say how pretty she thought it, as the General seemed to think an apology necessary for the flatness of the country, and the size of the village; but in her heart she preferred it to any place she had ever been at, and looked with great admiration at every neat house above the rank of a cottage, and at all the little chandler's shops[2] which they passed. At the further end of the village, and tolerably disengaged from the rest of it, stood the Parsonage, a new-built substantial stone house, with its semi-circular sweep and green gates; and, as they drove up to the door, Henry, with the friends of his solitude, a large Newfoundland puppy and two or three terriers, was ready to receive and make much of them.

Catherine's mind was too full, as she entered the house, for her either to observe or to say a great deal; and, till called on by the General for her opinion of it, she had very little idea of the room in which she was sitting. Upon looking round it then, she perceived in a moment that it was the most comfortable room in the world; but she was too guarded to say so, and the coldness of her praise disappointed him.

"We are not calling it a good house," said he.—"We are not comparing it with Fullerton and Northanger—We are considering it as a mere Parsonage, small and confined, we allow, but decent perhaps, and habitable; and altogether not inferior to the generality;—or, in other words, I believe there are few country parsonages in England half so good. It may admit of improvement, however. Far be it from me to say otherwise; and any thing in reason—a bow thrown out, perhaps—though, between ourselves, if there is one thing more than another my aversion, it is a patched-on bow."[3]

Catherine did not hear enough of this speech to understand or be pained by it; and other subjects being studiously brought forward and supported by Henry, at the same time that a tray full of refreshments was introduced by his servant, the General was shortly restored to his complacency, and Catherine to all her usual ease of spirits.

The room in question was of a commodious, well-proportioned size, and handsomely fitted up as a dining-parlour; and on their quitting it to walk round the grounds, she was shown, first into a smaller apartment, belonging peculiarly to the master of the house, and made unusually tidy on the occasion; and afterwards into what was to be the drawing-room, with the appearance of which, though unfurnished, Catherine was delighted enough even to satisfy the General. It was a prettily-shaped room, the windows reaching to the ground, and the view from them pleasant, though only over green meadows; and she expressed her admiration at the moment with all the honest simplicity with which she felt it. "Oh! why do not you fit up this room, Mr. Tilney? What a pity not to have it fitted up! It is the prettiest room I ever saw;—it is the prettiest room in the world!"

"I trust," said the General, with a most satisfied smile, "that it will very speedily be furnished: it waits only for a lady's taste!"

"Well, if it was my house, I should never sit any where else. Oh! what a sweet little cottage there is among the trees—apple trees too! It is the prettiest cottage!"—

"You like it—you approve it as an object—it is enough. Henry, remember that Robinson is spoken to about it. The cottage remains."[4]

Such a compliment recalled all Catherine's consciousness, and silenced her directly; and, though pointedly applied to by the General for her choice of the prevailing colour of the paper and hangings, nothing like an opinion on the subject could be drawn from her. The influence of fresh objects and fresh air, however, was of great use in dissipating these embarrassing associations; and, having reached the ornamental part of the premises, consisting of a walk round two sides of a meadow, on which Henry's genius had begun to act about half a year ago, she was sufficiently recovered to think it prettier than any pleasure-ground she had ever been in before, though there was not a shrub in it higher than the green bench in the corner.

---

4. Country gentry "improved" their grounds by moving the laborers' cottages further away from the main house where they had been placed for mutual defense during feudal times.

A saunter into other meadows, and through part of the village, with a visit to the stables to examine some improvements, and a charming game of play with a litter of puppies just able to roll about, brought them to four o'clock, when Catherine scarcely thought it could be three. At four they were to dine, and at six to set off on their return. Never had any day passed so quickly!

She could not but observe that the abundance of the dinner did not seem to create the smallest astonishment in the General; nay, that he was even looking at the side-table for cold meat which was not there. His son and daughter's observations were of a different kind. They had seldom seen him eat so heartily at any table but his own; and never before known him so little disconcerted by the melted butter's being oiled.

At six o'clock, the General having taken his coffee, the carriage again received them; and so gratifying had been the tenor of his conduct throughout the whole visit, so well assured was her mind on the subject of his expectations, that, could she have felt equally confident of the wishes of his son, Catherine would have quitted Woodston with little anxiety as to the How or the When she might return to it.

CHAPTER XII

The next morning brought the following very unexpected letter from Isabella:—

Bath, April——

My dearest Catherine,

I received your two kind letters with the greatest delight, and have a thousand apologies to make for not answering them sooner. I really am quite ashamed of my idleness; but in this horrid place one can find time for nothing. I have had my pen in my hand to begin a letter to you almost every day since you left Bath, but have always been prevented by some silly trifler or other. Pray write to me soon, and direct to my own home. Thank God! we leave this vile place to-morrow. Since you went away, I have had no pleasure in it—the dust is beyond any thing; and every body one cares for is gone. I believe if I could see you

I should not mind the rest, for you are dearer to me than any body can conceive. I am quite uneasy about your dear brother, not having heard from him since he went to Oxford; and am fearful of some misunderstanding. Your kind offices will set all right:—he is the only man I ever did or could love, and I trust you will convince him of it. The spring fashions are partly down; and the hats the most frightful you can imagine. I hope you spend your time pleasantly, but am afraid you never think of me. I will not say all that I could of the family you are with, because I would not be ungenerous, or set you against those you esteem; but it is very difficult to know whom to trust, and young men never know their minds two days together. I rejoice to say, that the young man whom, of all others, I particulary abhor, has left Bath. You will know, from this description, I must mean Captain Tilney, who, as you may remember, was amazingly disposed to follow and tease me, before you went away. Afterwards he got worse, and became quite my shadow. Many girls might have been taken in, for never were such attentions; but I knew the fickle sex too well. He went away to his regiment two days ago, and I trust I shall never be plagued with him again. He is the greatest coxcomb I ever saw, and amazingly disagreeable. The last two days he was always by the side of Charlotte Davis: I pitied his taste, but took no notice of him. The last time we met was in Bath-street, and I turned directly into a shop that he might not speak to me;—I would not even look at him. He went into the Pump-room afterwards; but I would not have followed him for all the world. Such a contrast between him and your brother!—pray send me some news of the latter—I am quite unhappy about him, he seemed so uncomfortable when he went away, with a cold, or something that affected his spirits. I would write to him myself, but have mislaid his direction; and, as I hinted above, am afraid he took something in my conduct amiss. Pray explain every thing to his satisfaction; or, if he still harbours any doubt, a line from himself to me, or a call at Putney when next in town, might set all to rights. I have not been to the Rooms this age, nor to the Play, except going in last night with the Hodges's, for a frolic, at half-price: they teased me into it; and I was determined they should not say I shut myself up because Tilney was gone. We happened to sit by the Mitchells, and they pretended to be quite surprized to see me out. I knew their spite:—at one time they could not be civil to me, but now they are all friendship; but I am not such a fool as to be taken in by them. You know I have a pretty good spirit of my own. Anne Mitchell had tried to put on a turban like mine, as I wore it the week before at the Concert, but made wretched work of it—it happened to become my odd face I believe, at least Tilney told me so at the time, and said every eye was upon me; but he is the last man whose word I would take. I wear nothing but purple now: I know I look hideous in it, but no matter—it is your dear brother's favourite colour. Lose no time, my dearest, sweetest Catherine, in writing to him and to me,

Who ever am, &c.

Such a strain of shallow artifice could not impose even upon Catherine. Its inconsistencies, contradictions, and falsehood, struck her from the very first. She was ashamed of Isabella, and ashamed of having ever loved her. Her professions of attachment were now as disgusting as her excuses were empty, and her demands impudent. Write to James on her behalf!—No, James should never hear Isabella's name mentioned by her again.

On Henry's arrival from Woodston, she made known to him and Eleanor their brother's safety, congratulating them with sincerity on it, and reading aloud the most material passages of her letter with strong indignation. When she had finished it,—"So much for Isabella," she cried, "and for all our intimacy! She must think me an idiot, or she could not have written so; but perhaps this has served to make her character better known to me than mine is to her. I see what she has been about. She is a vain coquette, and her tricks have not answered. I do not believe she had ever any regard either for James or for me, and I wish I had never known her."

"It will soon be as if you never had," said Henry.

"There is but one thing that I cannot understand. I see that she has had designs on Captain Tilney, which have not succeeded; but I do not understand what Captain Tilney has been about all this time. Why should he pay her such attentions as to make her quarrel with my brother, and then fly off himself?"

"I have very little to say for Frederick's motives, such as I believe them to have been. He has his vanities as well as Miss Thorpe, and the chief difference is, that, having a stronger head, they have not yet injured himself. If the *effect* of his behaviour does not justify him with you, we had better not seek after the cause."

"Then you do not suppose he ever really cared about her?"

"I am persuaded that he never did."

"And only made believe to do so for mischief's sake?"

Henry bowed his assent.

"Well, then, I must say that I do not like him at all. Though it has turned out so well for us, I do not like him at all. As it happens, there is no great harm done, because I do not think Isabella has any heart to lose. But, suppose he had made her very much in love with him?"

"But we must first suppose Isabella to have had a heart to lose,—consequently to have been a very different creature; and, in that case, she would have met with very different treatment."

"It is very right that you should stand by your brother."

"And if you would stand by *your's*, you would not be much distressed by the disappointment of Miss Thorpe. But your mind is warped by an innate principle of general integrity, and therefore not accessible to the cool reasonings of family partiality, or a desire of revenge."

Catherine was complimented out of further bitterness. Frederick could not be unpardonably guilty, while Henry made himself so agreeable. She resolved on not answering Isabella's letter; and tried to think no more of it.

CHAPTER XIII

Soon after this, the General found himself obliged to go to London for a week; and he left Northanger earnestly regretting that any necessity should rob him even for an hour of Miss Morland's company, and anxiously recommending the study of her comfort and amusement to his children as their chief object in his absence. His departure gave Catherine the first experimental conviction that a loss may be sometimes a gain. The happiness with which their time now passed, every employment voluntary, every laugh indulged, every meal a scene of ease and good-humour, walking where they liked and when they liked, their hours, pleasures and fatigues at their own command, made her thoroughly sensible of the restraint which the General's presence had imposed, and most thankfully feel their present release from it. Such ease and such delights made her love the place and the people more and more every day; and had it not been for a dread of its soon becoming expedient to leave the one, and an apprehension of not being equally beloved by the other, she would at each moment of each day have been perfectly happy; but she was now in the fourth week of her visit; before the General came home, the fourth week would be turned, and perhaps it might seem an intrusion if she stayed much longer. This was a painful consideration whenever it occurred; and eager to get rid of such a weight on her mind, she very soon resolved to speak to Eleanor about it at once, propose going away, and be guided in her conduct by the manner in which her proposal might be taken.

Aware that if she gave herself much time, she might feel it difficult to bring forward so unpleasant a subject, she took the first opportunity of being suddenly alone with Eleanor, and of Eleanor's being in the middle of a speech about something very different, to start forth her obligation of going away very soon. Eleanor looked and declared herself much concerned. She had hoped for the pleasure of her company for a much longer time—had been misled (perhaps by her wishes) to suppose that a much longer visit had been promised—and could not but think that if Mr. and Mrs. Morland were aware of the pleasure it was to her to have her there, they would be too generous to hasten her return.—Catherine explained.—Oh! as to *that*, papa and mamma were in no hurry at all. As long as she was happy, they would always be satisfied.

Then why, might she ask, in such a hurry herself to leave them? Oh! because she had been there so long.

"Nay, if you can use such a word, I can urge you no farther. If you think it long—"

"Oh! no, I do not indeed. For my own pleasure, I could stay with you as long again."—And it was directly settled that, till she had, her leaving them was not even to be thought of. In having this cause of uneasiness so pleasantly removed, the force of the other was likewise weakened. The kindness, the earnestness of Eleanor's manner in pressing her to stay, and Henry's gratified look on being told that her stay was determined, were such sweet proofs of her importance with them, as left her only just so much solicitude as the human mind can never do comfortably without. She did—almost always—believe that Henry loved her, and quite always that his father and sister loved and even wished her to belong to them; and believing so far, her doubts and anxieties were merely sportive irritations.

Henry was not able to obey his father's injunction of remaining wholly at Northanger in attendance on the ladies, during his absence in London; the engagements of his curate at Woodston obliging him to leave them on Saturday for a couple of nights. His loss was not now what it had been while the General was at home; it lessened their gaiety, but did not ruin their comfort; and the two girls agreeing in occupation, and improving in intimacy, found themselves so well-sufficient for the time to themselves, that it was eleven o'clock, rather a late hour at the Abbey, before they quitted the supper-room on the day of Henry's departure. They had just reached the head of the stairs, when it seemed, as far as the thickness of the walls would allow them to judge, that a carriage was driving up to the door, and the next moment confirmed the idea by the loud noise of the house-bell. After the first perturbation of surprize had passed away, in a "Good Heaven! what can be the matter?" it was quickly decided by Eleanor to be her eldest brother, whose arrival was often as sudden, if not quite so unseasonable, and accordingly she hurried down to welcome him.

Catherine walked on to her chamber, making up her mind as well as she could, to a further acquaintance with Captain Tilney, and comforting herself under the unpleasant impression his conduct had given her, and the persuasion of his being by far too fine a gentleman to approve of her, that at least they should not meet under such circumstances as would make their meeting materially painful. She trusted he would never speak of Miss Thorpe; and indeed, as he must by this time be ashamed of the part he had acted, there could be no danger of it; and as long as all mention of Bath scenes were avoided, she thought she could behave to him very civilly. In such considerations time passed away, and it was certainly in his favour that Eleanor should be so glad to see him, and have so much to say, for half an hour was almost gone since his arrival, and Eleanor did not come up.

At that moment Catherine thought she heard her step in the gallery, and listened for its continuance; but all was silent. Scarcely, however, had she convicted her fancy of error, when the noise of something moving close to her door made her start; it seemed as if some one was touching the very doorway—and in another moment a slight motion of the lock proved that some hand must be on it. She trembled a little at the idea of any one's approaching so cautiously; but resolving not to be again overcome by trivial appearances of alarm, or misled by a raised imagination, she stepped quietly forward, and opened the door. Eleanor, and only Eleanor, stood there. Catherine's spirits however were tranquillized but for an instant, for Eleanor's cheeks were pale, and her manner greatly agitated. Though evidently intending to come in, it seemed an effort to enter the room, and a still greater to speak when there. Catherine, supposing some uneasiness on Captain Tilney's account, could only express her concern by silent attention; obliged her to be seated, rubbed her temples with lavender-water, and hung over her with affectionate solicitude. "My dear Catherine, you must not— you must not indeed—" were Eleanor's first connected words. "I am quite well. This kindness distracts me—I cannot bear it—I come to you on such an errand!"

"Errand!—to me!"

"How shall I tell you!—Oh! how shall I tell you!"

A new idea now darted into Catherine's mind, and turning as pale as her friend, she exclaimed, "'Tis a messenger from Woodston!"

"You are mistaken, indeed," returned Eleanor, looking at her most compassionately—"it is no one from Woodston. It is my father himself." Her voice faltered, and her eyes were turned to the ground as she mentioned his name. His unlooked-for return was enough in itself to make Catherine's heart sink, and for a few moments she hardly supposed there were any thing worse to be told. She said nothing; and Eleanor endeavouring to collect herself and speak with firmness, but with eyes still cast down, soon went on. "You are too good, I am sure, to think the worse of me for the part I am obliged to perform. I am indeed a most unwilling messenger. After what has so lately passed, so lately been settled between us— how joyfully, how thankfully on my side!—as to your continuing here as I hoped for many, many weeks longer, how can I tell you that your kindness is not to be accepted—and that the happiness your company has hitherto given us is to be repaid by——but I must not trust myself with words. My dear Catherine, we are to part. My father has recollected an engagement that takes our whole family away on Monday. We are going to Lord Longtown's, near

Hereford, for a fortnight. Explanation and apology are equally impossible. I cannot attempt either."

"My dear Eleanor," cried Catherine, suppressing her feelings as well as she could, "do not be so distressed. A second engagement must give way to a first. I am very, very sorry we are to part—so soon, and so suddenly too; but I am not offended, indeed I am not. I can finish my visit here you know at any time; or I hope you will come to me. Can you, when you return from this lord's, come to Fullerton?"

"It will not be in my power, Catherine."

"Come when you can, then."—

Eleanor made no answer; and Catherine's thoughts recurring to something more directly interesting, she added, thinking aloud, "Monday—so soon as Monday;—and you *all* go. Well, I am certain of——I shall be able to take leave however. I need not go till just before you do, you know. Do not be distressed, Eleanor, I can go on Monday very well. My father and mother's having no notice of it is of very little consequence. The General will send a servant with me, I dare say, half the way—and then I shall soon be at Salisbury, and then I am only nine miles from home."

"Ah, Catherine! were it settled so, it would be somewhat less intolerable, though in such common attentions you would have received but half what you ought. But—how can I tell you?— To-morrow morning is fixed for your leaving us, and not even the hour is left to your choice; the very carriage is ordered, and will be here at seven o'clock, and no servant will be offered you."

Catherine sat down, breathless and speechless. "I could hardly believe my senses, when I heard it;—and no displeasure, no resentment that you can feel at this moment, however justly great, can be more than I myself——but I must not talk of what I felt. Oh! that I could suggest any thing in extenuation! Good God! what will your father and mother say! After courting you from the protection of real friends to this—almost double distance from your home, to have you driven out of the house, without the considerations even of decent civility! Dear, dear Catherine, in being the bearer of such a message, I seem guilty myself of all its insult; yet, I trust you will acquit me, for you must have been long enough in this house to see that I am but a nominal mistress of it, that my real power is nothing."

"Have I offended the General?" said Catherine in a faltering voice. "Alas! for my feelings as a daughter, all that I know, all that

I answer for is, that you can have given him no just cause of offence. He certainly is greatly, very greatly discomposed; I have seldom seen him more so. His temper is not happy, and something has now occurred to ruffle it in an uncommon degree; some disappointment, some vexation, which just at this moment seems important; but which I can hardly suppose you to have any concern in, for how is it possible?"

It was with pain that Catherine could speak at all; and it was only for Eleanor's sake that she attempted it. "I am sure," said she, "I am very sorry if I have offended him. It was the last thing I would willingly have done. But do not be unhappy, Eleanor. An engagement you know must be kept. I am only sorry it was not recollected sooner, that I might have written home. But it is of very little consequence."

"I hope, I earnestly hope that to your real safety it will be of none; but to every thing else it is of the greatest consequence; to comfort, appearance, propriety, to your family, to the world. Were your friends, the Allens, still in Bath, you might go to them with comparative ease; a few hours would take you there; but a journey of seventy miles, to be taken post by you, at your age, alone, unattended!"

"Oh, the journey is nothing. Do not think about that. And if we are to part, a few hours sooner or later, you know, makes no difference. I can be ready by seven. Let me be called in time." Eleanor saw that she wished to be alone; and believing it better for each that they should avoid any further conversation, now left her with "I shall see you in the morning."

Catherine's swelling heart needed relief. In Eleanor's presence friendship and pride had equally restrained her tears, but no sooner was she gone than they burst forth in torrents. Turned from the house, and in such a way!—Without any reason that could justify, any apology that could atone for the abruptness, the rudeness, nay, the insolence of it. Henry at a distance—not able even to bid him farewell. Every hope, every expectation from him suspended, at least, and who could say how long?—Who could say when they might meet again?—And all this by such a man as General Tilney, so polite, so well-bred, and heretofore so particularly fond of her! It was as incomprehensible as it was mortifying and grievous. From what it could arise, and where it would end, were considerations of equal perplexity and alarm. The manner in which it was done so grossly uncivil; hurrying her away without any reference to her own convenience, or allowing her even the appearance of choice as to the time or mode of her travelling; of two days, the earliest fixed on, and of that almost the earliest hour, as if resolved to have her gone before he was stirring in the morning, that he might not be obliged even to see her. What could all this mean but an intentional affront? By some means or other she must have had the misfortune to offend him. Eleanor had wished to spare her from so painful a notion, but Catherine could not believe it possible that any injury or any misfortune could provoke such ill-will against a person not connected, or, at least, not supposed to be connected with it.

Heavily passed the night. Sleep, or repose that deserved the name of sleep, was out of the question. That room, in which her disturbed imagination had tormented her on her first arrival, was again the scene of agitated spirits and unquiet slumbers. Yet how different now the source of her inquietude from what it had been then—how mournfully superior in reality and substance! Her anxiety had foundation in fact, her fears in probability; and with a mind so occupied in the contemplation of actual and natural evil, the solitude of her situation, the darkness of her chamber, the antiquity of the building were felt and considered with the smallest emotion; and though the wind was high, and often produced strange and sudden noises throughout the house, she heard it all as she lay awake, hour after hour, without curiosity or terror.

Soon after six Eleanor entered her room, eager to show attention or give assistance where it was possible; but very little remained to be done. Catherine had not loitered; she was almost dressed, and her packing almost finished. The possibility of some conciliatory message from the General occurred to her as his daughter appeared. What so natural, as that anger should pass away and repentance succeed it? and she only wanted to know how far, after what had passed, an apology might properly be received by her. But the knowledge would have been useless here, it was not called for; neither clemency nor dignity was put to the trial—Eleanor brought no message. Very little passed between them on meeting; each found her greatest safety in silence, and few and trivial were the sentences exchanged while they remained up stairs, Catherine in busy agitation completing her dress, and Eleanor with more good-will than experience intent upon filling the trunk. When every thing was done they left the room, Catherine lingering only half a minute behind her friend to throw a parting glance on every well-known cherished object, and went down to the breakfast-parlour, where breakfast was prepared. She tried to eat, as well to save herself from the pain of being urged, as to make her friend comfortable; but she had no appetite, and could not swallow many mouthfuls. The contrast between this and her last breakfast in that room, gave her fresh misery, and strengthened her distaste for every thing before her. It was not four-and-twenty hours ago since they had met there to the same repast, but in circumstances how different! With what cheerful ease, what happy, though false security, had she then looked around her, enjoying every thing present, and fearing little in future, beyond Henry's going to Woodston for a day! Happy, happy breakfast! for Henry had been there, Henry had sat by her and helped her. These reflections were long indulged undisturbed by any address from her companion, who sat as deep in thought as herself; and the appearance of the carriage was the first thing to startle and recall them to the present moment. Catherine's colour rose at the sight of it; and the indignity with which she was treated striking at that instant on her mind with peculiar force, made her for a short time sensible only of resentment. Eleanor seemed now impelled into resolution and speech.

"You *must* write to me, Catherine," she cried, "you *must* let me hear from you as soon as possible. Till I know you to be safe at home, I shall not have an hour's comfort. For *one* letter, at all risks, all hazards, I must entreat. Let me have the satisfaction of knowing that you are safe at Fullerton, and have found your family well, and then, till I can ask for your correspondence as I ought to do, I will not expect more. Direct to me at Lord Longtown's, and, I must ask it, under cover to Alice."

"No, Eleanor, if you are not allowed to receive a letter from me, I am sure I had better not write. There can be no doubt of my getting home safe."

Eleanor only replied, "I cannot wonder at your feelings. I will not importune you. I will trust to your own kindness of heart when I am at a distance from you." But this, with the look of sorrow accompanying it, was enough to melt Catherine's pride in a moment, and she instantly said, "Oh, Eleanor, I *will* write to you indeed."

There was yet another point which Miss Tilney was anxious to settle, though somewhat embarrassed in speaking of. It had occurred to her, that after so long an absence from home, Catherine might not be provided with money enough for the expenses of her journey, and, upon suggesting it to her with most affectionate offers of accommodation, it proved to be exactly the case. Catherine had never thought on the subject till that moment; but, upon examining her purse, was convinced that but for this kindness of her friend, she might have been turned from the house without even the means of getting home; and the distress in which she must have been thereby involved filling the minds of both, scarcely another word was said by either during the time of their remaining together. Short, however, was that time. The carriage was soon announced to be ready; and Catherine, instantly rising, a long and affectionate embrace supplied the place of language in bidding each other adieu; and, as they entered the hall, unable to leave the house without some mention of one whose name had not yet been spoken by either, she paused a moment, and with quivering lips just made it intelligible that she left "her kind remembrance for her absent friend." But with this approach to his name ended all possibility of restraining her feelings; and, hiding her face as well as she could with her handkerchief, she darted across the hall, jumped into the chaise, and in a moment was driven from the door.

CHAPTER XIV

Catherine was too wretched to be fearful. The journey in itself had no terrors for her; and she began it without either dreading its length, or feeling its solitariness.[1] Leaning back in one corner of the carriage, in a violent burst of tears, she was conveyed some miles beyond the walls of the Abbey before she raised her head; and the highest point of ground within the park was almost closed from her view before she was capable of turning her eyes towards it. Unfortunately, the road she now travelled was the same which

1. The trip lasted about eleven hours, during which time Catherine was alone in a dangerous and uncomfortable public conveyance used to transport mail. In both 1798 and in 1817, discharged soldiers, homeless beggars, vagrants, robbers, criminals of all sorts were common on the roads, and people who traveled in public coaches were in great danger, especially a defenseless young girl traveling alone. Alert to imaginary dangers, she fails to recognize the real ones.

only ten days ago she had so happily passed along in going to and from Woodston; and, for fourteen miles, every bitter feeling was rendered more severe by the review of objects on which she had first looked under impressions so different. Every mile, as it brought her nearer Woodston, added to her sufferings, and when within the distance of five, she passed the turning which led to it, and thought of Henry, so near, yet so unconscious, her grief and agitation were excessive.

The day which she had spent at that place had been one of the happiest of her life. It was there, it was on that day that the General had made use of such expressions with regard to Henry and herself, had so spoken and so looked as to give her the most positive conviction of his actually wishing their marriage. Yes, only ten days ago had he elated her by his pointed regard—had he even confused her by his too significant reference! And now—what had she done, or what had she omitted to do, to merit such a change?

The only offence against him of which she could accuse herself, had been such as was scarcely possible to reach his knowledge. Henry and her own heart only were privy to the shocking suspicions which she had so idly entertained; and equally safe did she believe her secret with each. Designedly, at least, Henry could not have betrayed her. If, indeed, by any strange mischance his father should have gained intelligence of what she had dared to think and look for, of her causeless fancies and injurious examinations, she could not wonder at any degree of his indignation. If aware of her having viewed him as a murderer, she could not wonder at his even turning her from his house. But a justification so full of torture to herself, she trusted would not be in his power.

Anxious as were all her conjectures on this point, it was not, however, the one on which she dwelt most. There was a thought yet nearer, a more prevailing, more impetuous concern. How Henry would think, and feel, and look, when he returned on the morrow to Northanger and heard of her being gone, was a question of force and interest to rise over every other, to be never ceasing, alternately irritating and soothing; it sometimes suggested the dread of his calm acquiescence, and at others was answered by the sweetest confidence in his regret and resentment. To the General, of course, he would not dare to speak; but to Eleanor—what might he not say to Eleanor about her?

In this unceasing recurrence of doubts and inquiries, on any one article of which her mind was incapable of more than momentary repose, the hours passed away, and her journey advanced much faster than she looked for. The pressing anxieties of thought, which prevented her from noticing any thing before her, when once beyond the neighbourhood of Woodston, saved her at the same time from watching her progress; and though no object on the road could engage a moment's attention, she found no stage of it tedious. From this, she was preserved too by another cause, by feeling no eagerness for her journey's conclusion; for to return in such a manner to Fullerton was almost to destroy the pleasure of a meeting with those she loved best, even after an absence such as her's—an eleven weeks absence. What had she to say that would not humble herself and pain her family; that would not increase her own grief by the confession of it, extend an useless resentment, and perhaps involve the innocent with the guilty in undistinguishing ill-will? She could never do justice to Henry and Eleanor's merit; she felt it too strongly for expression; and should a dislike be taken against them, should they be thought of unfavourably, on their father's account, it would cut her to the heart.

With these feelings, she rather dreaded than sought for the first view of that well-known spire which would announce her within twenty miles of home. Salisbury she had known to be her point on leaving Northanger; but after the first stage she had been indebted to the post-masters for the names of the places which were then to conduct her to it; so great had been her ignorance of her route. She met with nothing, however, to distress or frighten her. Her youth, civil manners and liberal pay, procured her all the attention that a traveller like herself could require; and stopping only to change horses, she travelled on for about eleven hours without accident or alarm, and between six and seven o'clock in the evening found herself entering Fullerton.

A heroine returning, at the close of her career, to her native village, in all the triumph of recovered reputation, and all the dignity of a countess, with a long train of noble relations in their several phaetons, and three waiting-maids in a travelling chaise-and-four, behind her, is an event on which the pen of the contriver may well delight to dwell; it gives credit to every conclusion, and the author must share in the glory she so liberally bestows.—But my affair is widely different; I bring back my heroine to her home in solitude and disgrace; and no sweet elation of spirits can lead me into minuteness. A heroine in a hack post-chaise, is such a blow upon sentiment, as no attempt at grandeur or pathos can withstand. Swiftly therefore shall her post-boy drive through the village, amid the gaze of Sunday groups, and speedy shall be her descent from it.

But, whatever might be the distress of Catherine's mind, as she thus advanced towards the Parsonage, and whatever the humiliation of her biographer in relating it, she was preparing enjoyment of no everyday nature for those to whom she went; first, in the appearance of her carriage—and secondly, in herself. The chaise of a traveller being a rare sight in Fullerton, the whole family were immediately at the window; and to have it stop at the sweep-gate was a pleasure to brighten every eye and occupy every fancy—a pleasure quite unlooked for by all but the two youngest children, a boy and girl of six and four years old, who expected a brother or sister in every carriage. Happy the glance that first distinguished Catherine!—Happy the voice that proclaimed the discovery!—But whether such happiness were the lawful property of George or Harriet could never be exactly understood.

Her father, mother, Sarah, George, and Harriet, all assembled at the door, to welcome her with affectionate eagerness, was a sight to awaken the best feelings of Catherine's heart; and in the embrace of each, as she stepped from the carriage, she found herself soothed beyond any thing that she had believed possible. So surrounded, so caressed, she was even happy! In the joyfulness of family love every thing for a short time was subdued, and the pleasure of seeing her, leaving them at first little leisure for calm curiosity, they were all seated round the tea-table, which Mrs. Morland had hurried for the comfort of the poor traveller, whose pale and jaded looks soon caught her notice, before any inquiry so direct as to demand a positive answer was addressed to her.

Reluctantly, and with much hesitation, did she then begin what might perhaps, at the end of half an hour, be termed by the courtesy of her hearers, an explanation; but scarcely, within that time, could they at all discover the cause, or collect the particulars of her sudden return. They were far from being an irritable race; far from any quickness in catching, or bitterness in resenting affronts:—but here, when the whole was unfolded, was an insult not to be overlooked, nor, for the first half hour, to be easily pardoned. Without suffering any romantic alarm, in the consideration of their daughter's long and lonely journey, Mr. and Mrs. Morland could not but feel that it might have been productive of much unpleasantness to her; that it was what they could never have voluntarily suffered; and that, in forcing her on such a measure, General Tilney had acted neither honourably nor feelingly—neither as a gentleman nor as a parent. Why he had done it, what could have provoked him to such a breach of hospitality, and so suddenly turned all his partial regard for their daughter into actual ill-will, was a matter which they were at least as far from divining as Catherine herself; but it did not oppress them by any means so long; and, after a due course of useless conjecture, that, "it was a strange business, and that he must be a very strange man," grew enough for all their indignation and wonder; though Sarah indeed still indulged in the sweets of incomprehensibility, exclaiming and conjecturing with youthful ardour.—"My dear, you give yourself a great deal of needless trouble," said her mother at last; "depend upon it, it is something not at all worth understanding."

"I can allow for his wishing Catherine away, when he recollected this engagement," said Sarah, "but why not do it civilly?"

"I am sorry for the young people," returned Mrs. Morland; "they must have a sad time of it; but as for any thing else, it is no matter now; Catherine is safe at home, and our comfort does not depend upon General Tilney." Catherine sighed. "Well," continued her philosophic mother, "I am glad I did not know of your journey at the time; but now it is all over perhaps there is no great harm done. It is always good for young people to be put upon exerting themselves; and you know, my dear Catherine, you always were a sad little shatter-brained creature; but now you must have been forced to have your wits about you, with so much changing of chaises and so forth; and I hope it will appear that you have not left any thing behind you in any of the pockets."

Catherine hoped so too, and tried to feel an interest in her own amendment, but her spirits were quite worn down; and, to be silent and alone becoming soon her only wish, she readily agreed to her mother's next counsel of going early to bed. Her parents seeing nothing in her ill-looks and agitation but the natural consequence of mortified feelings, and of the unusual exertion and fatigue of such a journey, parted from her without any doubt of their being soon slept away; and though, when they all met the next morning, her recovery was not equal to their hopes, they were still perfectly unsuspicious of their being any deeper evil. They never once thought of her heart, which, for the parents of a young lady of seventeen, just returned from her first excursion from home, was odd enough!

As soon as breakfast was over, she sat down to fulfil her promise to Miss Tilney, whose trust in the effect of time and distance on her friend's disposition was already justified, for already did Catherine reproach herself with having parted from Eleanor coldly; with having never enough valued her merits or kindness; and never enough commiserated her for what she had been yesterday left to endure. The strength of these feelings, however, was far from assisting her pen; and never had it been harder for her to write than in addressing Eleanor Tilney. To compose a letter which might at once do justice to her sentiments and her situation, convey gratitude without servile regret, be guarded without coldness, and honest without resentment—a letter which Eleanor might not be pained by the perusal of—and, above all, which she might not blush herself, if Henry should chance to see, was an undertaking to frighten away all her powers of performance; and, after long thought and much perplexity, to be very brief was all that she could determine on with any confidence of safety. The money therefore which Eleanor had advanced was inclosed with little more than grateful thanks, and the thousand good wishes of a most affectionate heart.

"This has been a strange acquaintance," observed Mrs. Morland, as the letter was finished; "soon made and soon ended.—I am sorry it happens so, for Mrs. Allen thought them very pretty kind of young people; and you were sadly out of luck too in your Isabella. Ah! poor James! Well, we must live and learn; and the next new friends you make I hope will be better worth keeping."

Catherine coloured as she warmly answered, "No friend can be better worth keeping than Eleanor."

"If so, my dear, I dare say you will meet again some time or other; do not be uneasy. It is ten to one but you are thrown together again in the course of a few years; and then what a pleasure it will be!"

Mrs. Morland was not happy in her attempt at consolation. The hope of meeting again in the course of a few years could only put into Catherine's head what might happen within that time to make a meeting dreadful to her. She could never forget Henry Tilney, or think of him with less tenderness than she did at that

moment; but he might forget her; and in that case to meet!——Her
eyes filled with tears as she pictured her acquaintance so renewed;
and her mother, perceiving her comfortable suggestions to have had
no good effect, proposed, as another expedient for restoring her
spirits, that they should call on Mrs. Allen.

The two houses were only a quarter of a mile apart; and, as
they walked, Mrs. Morland quickly dispatched all that she felt on
the score of James's disappointment. "We are sorry for him," said
she; "but otherwise there is no harm done in the match going off;
for it could not be a desirable thing to have him engaged to a girl
whom we had not the smallest acquaintance with, and who was so
entirely without fortune; and now, after such behaviour, we cannot
think at all well of her. Just at present it comes hard to poor James;
but that will not last for ever; and I dare say he will be a discreeter
man all his life, for the foolishness of his first choice."

This was just such a summary view of the affair as Catherine
could listen to; another sentence might have endangered her complaisance, and made her reply less rational; for soon were all her
thinking powers swallowed in the reflection of her own change of
feelings and spirits since last she had trodden that well-known
road. It was not three months ago since, wild with joyful expectation, she had there run backwards and forwards some ten times a-
day, with an heart light, gay, and independent; looking forward to
pleasures untasted and unalloyed, and free from the apprehension
of evil as from the knowledge of it. Three months ago had seen her
all this; and now, how altered a being did she return!

She was received by the Allens with all the kindness which her
unlooked-for appearance, acting on a steady affection, would naturally call forth; and great was their surprize, and warm their displeasure, on hearing how she had been treated,—though Mrs. Morland's account of it was no inflated representation, no studied
appeal to their passions. "Catherine took us quite by surprize yesterday evening," said she. "She travelled all the way post by herself,
and knew nothing of coming till Saturday night; for General Tilney,
from some odd fancy or other, all of a sudden grew tired of having
her there, and almost turned her out of the house. Very unfriendly,
certainly; and he must be a very odd man;—but we are so glad to
have her amongst us again! And it is a great comfort to find that she
is not a poor helpless creature, but can shift very well for herself."

Mr. Allen expressed himself on the occasion with the reasonable resentment of a sensible friend; and Mrs. Allen thought his expressions quite good enough to be immediately made use of again by herself. His wonder, his conjectures, and his explanations, became in succession her's, with the addition of this single remark—"I really have not patience with the General"—to fill up every accidental pause. And, "I really have not patience with the General," was uttered twice after Mr. Allen left the room, without any relaxation of anger, or any material digression of thought. A more considerable degree of wandering attended the third repetition; and, after completing the fourth, she immediately added, "Only think, my dear, of my having got that frightful great rent in my best Mechlin[2] so charmingly mended, before I left Bath, that one can hardly see where it was. I must show it you some day or other. Bath is a nice place, Catherine, after all. I assure you I did not above half like coming away. Mrs. Thorpe's being there was such a comfort to us, was not it? You know you and I were quite forlorn at first."

"Yes, but *that* did not last long," said Catherine, her eyes brightening at the recollection of what had first given spirit to her existence there.

"Very true: we soon met with Mrs. Thorpe, and then we wanted for nothing. My dear, do not you think these silk gloves wear very well? I put them on new the first time of our going to the Lower Rooms, you know, and I have worn them a great deal since. Do you remember that evening?"

"Do I! Oh! perfectly."

"It was very agreeable, was not it? Mr. Tilney drank tea with us, and I always thought him a great addition, he is so very agreeable. I have a notion you danced with him, but am not quite sure. I remember I had my favourite gown on."

Catherine could not answer; and, after a short trial of other subjects, Mrs. Allen again returned to—"I really have not patience with the General! Such an agreeable, worthy man as he seemed to be! I do not suppose, Mrs. Morland, you ever saw a better-bred man in your life. His lodgings were taken the very day after he left them, Catherine. But no wonder; Milsom-street you know."—

2. A fine lace from Flanders.

As they walked home again, Mrs. Morland endeavoured to impress on her daughter's mind the happiness of having such steady well-wishers as Mr. and Mrs. Allen, and the very little consideration which the neglect or unkindness of slight acquaintance like the Tilneys ought to have with her, while she could preserve the good opinion and affection of her earliest friends. There was a great deal of good sense in all this; but there are some situations of the human mind in which good sense has very little power; and Catherine's feelings contradicted almost every position her mother advanced. It was upon the behaviour of these very slight acquaintance that all her present happiness depended; and while Mrs. Morland was successfully confirming her own opinions by the justness of her own representations, Catherine was silently reflecting that *now* Henry must have arrived at Northanger; *now* he must have heard of her departure; and *now*, perhaps, they were all setting off for Hereford.

CHAPTER XV

Catherine's disposition was not naturally sedentary, nor had her habits been ever very industrious; but whatever might hitherto have been her defects of that sort, her mother could not but perceive them now to be greatly increased. She could neither sit still, nor employ herself for ten minutes together, walking round the garden and orchard again and again, as if nothing but motion was voluntary; and it seemed as if she could even walk about the house rather than remain fixed for any time in the parlour. Her loss of spirits was a yet greater alteration. In her rambling and her idleness she might only be a caricature of herself; but in her silence and sadness she was the very reverse of all that she had been before.

For two days Mrs. Morland allowed it to pass even without a hint; but when a third night's rest had neither restored her cheerfulness, improved her in useful activity, nor given her a greater inclination for needle-work, she could no longer refrain from the gentle reproof of, "My dear Catherine, I am afraid you are growing quite a fine lady. I do not know when poor Richard's cravats would be done, if he had no friend but you. Your head runs too much upon Bath; but there is a time for every thing—a time for balls and plays, and a time for work. You have had a long run of amusement, and now you must try to be useful."

Catherine took up her work directly, saying, in a dejected voice, that her head did not run upon Bath——much."

"Then you are fretting about General Tilney, and that is very simple of you; for ten to one whether you ever see him again. You should never fret about trifles." After a short silence—"I hope, my Catherine, you are not getting out of humour with home because it is not so grand as Northanger. That would be turning your visit into an evil indeed. Wherever you are you should always be contented, but especially at home, because there you must spend the most of your time. I did not quite like, at breakfast, to hear you talk so much about the French-bread at Northanger."

"I am sure I do not care about the bread. It is all the same to me what I eat."

"There is a very clever Essay in one of the books up stairs upon much such a subject, about young girls that have been spoilt for home by great acquaintance—*The Mirror*,[1] I think. I will look it out for you some day or other, because I am sure it will do you good."

Catherine said no more, and, with an endeavour to do right, applied to her work; but, after a few minutes, sunk again; without knowing it herself, into languor and listlessness, moving herself in her chair, from the irritation of weariness, much oftener than she moved her needle.—Mrs. Morland watched the progress of this relapse; and seeing, in her daughter's absent and dissatisfied look, the full proof of that repining spirit to which she had now begun to attribute her want of cheerfulness, hastily left the room to fetch the book in question, anxious to lose no time in attacking so dreadful a malady. It was some time before she could find what she looked for; and other family matters occurring to detain her, a quarter of an hour had elapsed ere she returned down stairs with the volume from which so much was hoped. Her avocations above having shut out all noise but what she created herself, she knew not that a visitor had

---

1. *The Mirror*, a periodical edited by Henry McKenzie (1745–1831). Mrs. Morland is alluding to Essay 12, "Consequences to Little Folks of Intimacy with Great Ones in a Letter from John Homespun" (March 6, 1779), in which John Homespun claims his daughters have been spoiled by their recent visit to a great lady, staying up late, copying her fashion, using French phrases, playing cards, and questioning the immortality of the soul.

arrived within the last few minutes, till, on entering the room, the first object she beheld was a young man whom she had never seen before. With a look of much respect, he immediately rose, and being introduced to her by her conscious daughter as "Mr. Henry Tilney," with the embarrassment of real sensibility began to apologise for his appearance there, acknowledging that after what had passed he had little right to expect a welcome at Fullerton, and stating his impatience to be assured of Miss Morland's having reached her home in safety, as the cause of his intrusion. He did not address himself to an uncandid judge or a resentful heart. Far from comprehending him or his sister in their father's misconduct, Mrs. Morland had been always kindly disposed towards each, and instantly, pleased by his appearance, received him with the simple professions of unaffected benevolence; thanking him for such an attention to her daughter, assuring him that the friends of her childen were always welcome there, and entreating him to say not another word of the past.

He was not ill inclined to obey this request, for, though his heart was greatly relieved by such unlooked-for mildness, it was not just at that moment in his power to say any thing to the purpose. Returning in silence to his seat, therefore, he remained for some minutes most civilly answering all Mrs. Morland's common remarks about the weather and roads. Catherine meanwhile,—the anxious, agitated, happy, feverish Catherine,—said not a word; but her glowing cheek and brightened eye made her mother trust that this good-natured visit would at least set her heart at ease for a time, and gladly therefore did she lay aside the first volume of *The Mirror* for a future hour.

Desirous of Mr. Morland's assistance, as well in giving encouragement, as in finding conversation for her guest, whose embarrassment on his father's account she earnestly pitied, Mrs. Morland had very early dispatched one of the children to summon him; but Mr. Morland was from home—and being thus without any support, at the end of a quarter of an hour she had nothing to say. After a couple of minutes unbroken silence, Henry, turning to Catherine for the first time since her mother's entrance, asked her, with sudden alacrity, if Mr. and Mrs. Allen were now at Fullerton? and on developing, from amidst all her perplexity of words in reply, the meaning, which one short syllable would have given, immediately expressed his intention of paying his respects to them, and, with a rising colour, asked her if she would have the goodness to show him the way. "You may see the house from this window, sir," was information on Sarah's side, which produced only a bow of acknowledgment from the gentleman, and a silencing nod from her mother; for Mrs. Morland, thinking it probable, as a secondary consideration in his wish of waiting on their worthy neighbours, that he might have some explanation to give of his father's behaviour, which it must be more pleasant for him to communicate only to Catherine, would not on any account prevent her accompanying him. They began their walk, and Mrs. Morland was not entirely mistaken in his object in wishing it. Some explanation on his father's account he had to give; but his first purpose was to explain himself, and before they reached Mr. Allen's grounds he had done it so well, that Catherine did not think it could ever be repeated too often. She was assured of his affection; and that heart in return was solicited, which, perhaps, they pretty equally knew was already entirely his own; for, though Henry was now sincerely attached to her, though he felt and delighted in all the excellencies of her character and truly loved her society, I must confess that his affection originated in nothing better than gratitude, or, in other words, that a persuasion of her partiality for him had been the only cause of giving her a serious thought. It is a new circumstance in romance, I acknowledge, and dreadfully derogatory of an heroine's dignity; but if it be as new in common life, the credit of a wild imagination will at least be all my own.

A very short visit to Mrs. Allen, in which Henry talked at random, without sense or connection, and Catherine, wrapt in the contemplation of her own unutterable happiness, scarcely opened her lips, dismissed them to the ecstasies of another *tête-à-tête*; and before it was suffered to close, she was enabled to judge how far he was sanctioned by parental authority in his present application. On his return from Woodston, two days before, he had been met near the Abbey by his impatient father, hastily informed in angry terms of Miss Morland's departure, and ordered to think of her no more.

Such was the permission upon which he had now offered her his hand. The affrighted Catherine, amidst all the terrors of expectation, as she listened to this account, could not but rejoice in the kind caution with which Henry had saved her from the necessity of a conscientious rejection, by engaging her faith before he mentioned the subject; and as he proceeded to give the particulars, and explain the motives of his father's conduct, her feelings soon hardened into even a triumphant delight. The General had had nothing to accuse her of, nothing to lay to her charge, but her being the involuntary, unconscious object of a deception which his pride could not pardon, and which a better pride would have been ashamed to own. She was guilty only of being less rich than he had supposed her to be. Under a mistaken persuasion of her possessions and claims, he had courted her acquaintance in Bath, solicited her company at Northanger, and designed her for his daughter-in-law. On discovering his error, to turn her from the house seemed the best, though to his feelings an inadequate proof of his resentment towards herself, and his contempt of her family.

John Thorpe had first misled him. The General, perceiving his son one night at the theatre to be paying considerable attention to Miss Morland, had accidentally inquired of Thorpe, if he knew more of her than her name. Thorpe, most happy to be on speaking terms with a man of General Tilney's importance, had been joyfully and proudly communicative;—and being at that time not only in daily expectation of Morland's engaging Isabella, but likewise pretty well resolved upon marrying Catherine himself, his vanity induced him to represent the family as yet more wealthy than his vanity and avarice had made him believe them. With whomsoever he was, or was likely to be connected, his own consequence always required that theirs should be great, and as his intimacy with any acquaintance grew, so regularly grew their fortune. The expectations of his friend Morland, therefore, from the first over-rated, had ever since his introduction to Isabella, been gradually increasing; and by merely adding twice as much for the grandeur of the moment, by doubling what he chose to think the amount of Mr. Morland's preferment, trebling his private fortune, bestowing a rich aunt, and sinking half the children, he was able to represent the whole family to the General in a most respectable light. For Catherine, however, the peculiar object of the General's curiosity, and his own speculations, he had yet something more in reserve, and the ten or fifteen thousand pounds which her father could give her, would be a pretty addition to Mr. Allen's estate. Her intimacy there had made him seriously determine on her being handsomely legacied hereafter; and to speak of her therefore as the almost acknowledged future heiress of Fullerton naturally followed. Upon such intelligence the General had proceeded; for never had it occurred to him to doubt its authority. Thorpe's interest in the family by his sister's approaching connection with one of its members, and his own views on another, (circumstances of which he boasted with almost equal openness,) seemed sufficient vouchers for his truth; and to these were added the absolute facts of the Allens being wealthy and childless, of Miss Morland's being under their care, and—as soon as his acquaintance allowed him to judge—of their treating her with parental kindness. His resolution was soon formed. Already had he discerned a liking towards Miss Morland in the countenance of his son; and thankful for Mr. Thorpe's communication, he almost instantly determined to spare no pain in weakening his boasted interest and ruining his dearest hopes. Catherine herself could not be more ignorant at the time of all this, than his own children. Henry and Eleanor, perceiving nothing in her situation likely to engage their father's particular respect, had seen with astonishment the suddenness, continuance and extent of his attention; and though latterly, from some hints which had accompanied an almost positive command to his son of doing every thing in his power to attach her, Henry was convinced of his father's believing it to be an advantageous connection, it was not till the late explanation at Northanger that they had the smallest idea of the false calculations which had hurried him on. That they were false, the General had learnt from the very person who had suggested them, from Thorpe himself, whom he had chanced to meet again in town, and who, under the influence of exactly opposite feelings, irritated by Catherine's refusal, and yet more by the failure of a very recent endeavour to accomplish a reconciliation between Morland and Isabella, convinced that they were separated for ever, and spurning a friendship which could no longer be serviceable, hastened to contradict all that he had said before to the advantage of the Morlands;— confessed himself to have been totally mistaken in his opinion of their circumstances and character, misled by the rhodomontade of his friend to believe his father a man of substance and credit, whereas the transactions of the two or three last weeks proved him to be neither; for after coming eagerly forward on the first overture of a marriage between the families, with the most liberal proposals, he had, on being brought to the point by the shrewdness of the relator, been constrained to acknowledge himself incapable of giving the young people even a decent support. They were, in fact, a necessitous family; numerous too almost beyond example; by no means respected in their own neighbourhood, as he had lately had particular opportunities of discovering; aiming at a style of life which their fortune could not warrant; seeking to better themselves by wealthy connections; a forward, bragging, scheming race.

The terrified General pronounced the name of Allen with an inquiring look; and here too Thorpe had learnt his error. The Allens, he believed, had lived near them too long, and he knew the young man on whom the Fullerton estate must devolve. The General needed no more. Enraged with almost every body in the world but himself, he set out the next day for the Abbey, where his performances have been seen.

I leave it to my readers' sagacity to determine how much of all this it was possible for Henry to communicate at this time to Catherine, how much of it he could have learnt from his father, in what points his own conjectures might assist him, and what portion must yet remain to be told in a letter from James. I have united for their ease what they must divide for mine. Catherine, at any rate, heard enough to feel, that in suspecting General Tilney of either murdering or shutting up his wife, she had scarcely sinned against his character, or magnified his cruelty.

Henry, in having such things to relate of his father, was almost as pitiable as in their first avowal to himself. He blushed for the narrow-minded counsel which he was obliged to expose. The conversation between them at Northanger had been of the most unfriendly kind. Henry's indignation on hearing how Catherine had been treated, on comprehending his father's views, and being ordered to acquiesce in them, had been open and bold. The General, accustomed on every ordinary occasion to give the law in his family, prepared for no reluctance but of feeling, no opposing desire that should dare to clothe itself in words, could ill brook the opposition of his son, steady as the sanction of reason and the dictate of conscience could make it. But, in such a cause, his anger, though it must shock, could not intimidate Henry, who was sustained in his purpose by a conviction of its justice. He felt himself bound as much in honour as in affection to Miss Morland, and believing that heart to be his own which he had been directed to gain, no unworthy retraction of a tacit consent, no reversing decree of unjustifiable anger, could shake his fidelity, or influence the resolutions it prompted.

He steadily refused to accompany his father into Herefordshire, an engagement formed almost at the moment, to promote the dismissal of Catherine, and as steadily declared his intention of offering her his hand. The General was furious in his anger, and they parted in dreadful disagreement. Henry, in an agitation of mind which many solitary hours were required to compose, had returned almost instantly to Woodston; and, on the afternoon of the following day, had begun his journey to Fullerton.

CHAPTER XVI

Mr. and Mrs. Morland's surprize on being applied to by Mr. Tilney, for their consent to his marrying their daughter, was, for a few minutes, considerable; it having never entered their heads to suspect an attachment on either side; but as nothing, after all, could be more natural than Catherine's being beloved, they soon learnt to consider it with only the happy agitation of gratified pride, and, as far as they alone were concerned, had not a single objection to start. His pleasing manners and good sense were self-evident recommendations; and having never heard evil of him, it was not their way to suppose any evil could be told. Good-will supplying the place of experience, his character needed no attestation. "Catherine would make a sad heedless young housekeeper to be sure," was her mother's foreboding remark; but quick was the consolation of there being nothing like practice.

There was but one obstacle, in short, to be mentioned; but till that one was removed, it must be impossible for them to sanction the engagement. Their tempers were mild, but their principles were steady, and while his parent so expressly forbad the connection, they could not allow themselves to encourage it. That the General should come forward to solicit the alliance, or that he should even very heartily approve it, they were not refined enough to make any parading stipulation; but the decent appearance of consent must be yielded, and that once obtained—and their own hearts made them trust that it could not be very long denied—their willing approbation was instantly to follow. His *consent* was all that they wished for. They were no more inclined than entitled to demand his *money*. Of a very considerable fortune, his son was, by marriage settlements, eventually secure; his present income was an income of independence and comfort, and under every pecuniary view, it was a match beyond the claims of their daughter.

The young people could not be surprized at a decision like this. They felt and they deplored—but they could not resent it; and they parted, endeavouring to hope that such a change in the General, as each believed almost impossible, might speedily take place, to unite them again in the fulness of privileged affection. Henry returned to what was now his only home, to watch over his young plantations, and extend his improvements for her sake, to whose share in them he looked anxiously forward; and Catherine remained at Fullerton to cry. Whether the torments of absence were softened by a clandestine correspondence, let us not inquire. Mr. and Mrs. Morland never did—they had been too kind to exact any promise; and whenever Catherine received a letter, as, at that time, happened pretty often, they always looked another way.

The anxiety, which in this state of their attachment must be the portion of Henry and Catherine, and of all who loved either, as to its final event, can hardly extend, I fear, to the bosom of my readers, who will see in the tell-tale compression of the pages before them, that we are all hastening together to perfect felicity. The means by which their early marriage was effected can be the only doubt: what probable circumstance could work upon a temper like the General's? The circumstance which chiefly availed, was the marriage of his daughter with a man of fortune and consequence, which took place in the course of the summer—an accession of dignity that threw him into a fit of good-humour, from which he did not recover till after Eleanor had obtained his forgiveness of Henry, and his permission for him "to be a fool if he liked it!"

The marriage of Eleanor Tilney, her removal from all the evils of such a home as Northanger had been made by Henry's banishment, to the home of her choice and the man of her choice, is an event which I expect to give general satisfaction among all her acquaintance. My own joy on the occasion is very sincere. I know no one more entitled, by unpretending merit, or better prepared by habitual suffering, to receive and enjoy felicity. Her partiality for this gentleman was not of recent origin; and he had been long withheld only by inferiority of situation from addressing her. His unexpected accession to title and fortune had removed all his difficulties; and never had the General loved his daughter so well in all her hours of companionship, utility, and patient endurance, as when he first hailed her, "Your Ladyship!" Her husband was really deserving of her;

independent of his peerage, his wealth, and his attachment, being to a precision the most charming young man in the world. Any further definition of his merits must be unnecessary; the most charming young man in the world is instantly before the imagination of us all. Concerning the one in question therefore I have only to add—(aware that the rules of composition forbid the introduction of a character not connected with my fable)—that this was the very gentleman whose negligent servant left behind him that collection of washing-bills, resulting from a long visit at Northanger, by which my heroine was involved in one of her most alarming adventures.

The influence of the Viscount and Viscountess in their brother's behalf was assisted by that right understanding of Mr. Morland's circumstances which, as soon as the General would allow himself to be informed, they were qualified to give. It taught him that he had been scarcely more misled by Thorpe's first boast of the family wealth, than by his subsequent malicious overthrow of it; that in no sense of the word were they necessitous or poor, and that Catherine would have three thousand pounds. This was so material an amendment of his late expectations, that it greatly contributed to smooth the descent of his pride; and by no means without its effect was the private intelligence, which he was at some pains to procure, that the Fullerton estate, being entirely at the disposal of its present proprietor, was consequently open to every greedy speculation.

On the strength of this, the General, soon after Eleanor's marriage, permitted his son to return to Northanger, and thence made him the bearer of his consent, very courteously worded in a page full of empty professions to Mr. Morland. The event which it authorized soon followed. Henry and Catherine were married, the bells rang and every body smiled; and, as this took place within a twelvemonth from the first day of their meeting, it will not appear, after all the dreadful delays occasioned by the General's cruelty, that they were essentially hurt by it. To begin perfect happiness at the respective ages of twenty-six and eighteen, is to do pretty well; and professing myself moreover convinced, that the General's unjust interference, so far from being really injurious to their felicity, was perhaps rather conducive to it, by improving their knowledge of each other, and adding strength to their attachment, I leave it to be settled by whomsoever it may concern, whether the tendency of this work be altogether to recommend parental tyranny, or reward filial disobedience.

CONTEXTS

The Romance Plot

Like the gothic romances Austen parodies, *Northanger Abbey* embodies a tale derived from ancient courtship rituals describing the adventures of a favorite daughter abandoned or sent off by her father to confront danger, find a mate, and rescue the family. She trespasses, enters a forbidden room, eats a forbidden fruit, opens a forbidden chest, and must, therefore, be redeemed by some kind of task or ordeal that often includes a visit to the underworld. This motif or plot appears in the tales of Orpheus and Eurydice, Demeter and Persephone, Genesis, Pandora, "Beauty and the Beast," "Cinderella," and "Blue Beard," to name a few, tales familiar either in the oral tradition or through the collections by Charles Perrault and the anonymous *Arabian Nights*. The same plot or motif appears in Austen's novels as well as Ann Radcliffe's, Mary Shelley's, and poems by Coleridge, Wordsworth, and Keats. In January, 1798, while Austen was writing *Northanger Abbey*, George Colman the Younger's powerful dramatization "Blue-Beard; or Female Curiosity" was presented in London, where it was successful, profitable, and controversial, and again in 1799, at the Orchard Street Theater in Bath, with the haunting scene of a huge skeleton under the inscription "The Punishment of Curiosity."

"Cupid and Psyche" was the most familiar and elaborate version of this tale. Derived from myth and oral narratives, it appeared in *The Golden Ass or Metamorphosis* by Lucius Apuleius (123–170 A.D.) a Roman philosopher and rhetorician. He framed the account as an "old wive's tale" told by an old woman to a young one who had been abducted and held for ransom by a band of robbers, explaining its appeal to both readers and authors of gothic romance. Like *The Arabian Nights*, which originated in Baghdad in the ninth century A.D., the narrator of Apuleius's version is a woman who uses the tale to comfort or distract, in a scene of great danger. Apuleius's timing is interesting: once a compelling myth, a religious tale with ritual associations, this version, written about two centuries after the birth of Christ and the introduction of Christianity, is secularized, socialized, turned to entertainment, like many folk tales and fairy tales originating in religious teachings and practice. In the Romantic period the tale inspired many poems, including Mary Tighe's *Psyche or the Legend of Love* (1805) and Keats's "Ode to Psyche" (1820). Anne Williams's *Art of Darkness: A Poetics of Gothic* (1995) traces the analogies between this tale and *The Mysteries of Udolpho*. Although one among many, I offer the version from Thomas Bulfinch, *The Age of Fable; or, Stories of Gods and Heroes* (1855).

Cupid and Psyche

A certain king and queen had three daughters. The charms of the two elder were more than common, but the beauty of the youngest was so wonderful that the poverty of language is unable to express its due praise. The fame of her beauty was so great that strangers from neighboring countries came in crowds to enjoy the sight, and looked on her with amazement, paying her that homage which is due only to Venus herself. In fact Venus found her altars deserted, while men turned their devotion to this young virgin. As she passed along, the people sang her praises, and strewed her way with chaplets and flowers.

This homage to the exaltation of a mortal gave great offense to the real Venus. Shaking her ambrosial locks with indignation, she exclaimed, "Am I then to be eclipsed in my honors by a mortal girl? In vain then did that royal shepherd, whose judgment was approved by Jove himself, give me the palm of beauty over my illustrious rivals, Pallas and Juno. But she shall not so quietly usurp my honors. I will give her cause to repent of so unlawful a beauty."

Thereupon she calls her winged son Cupid, mischievous enough in his own nature, and rouses and provokes him yet more by her complaints. She points out Psyche to him and says, "My dear son, punish that contumacious beauty; give your mother a revenge as sweet as her injuries are great; infuse into the bosom of that haughty girl a passion for some low, mean, unworthy being, so that she may reap a mortification as great as her present exultation and triumph."

Cupid prepared to obey the commands of his mother. There are two fountains in Venus's garden, one of sweet waters, the other of bitter. Cupid filled two amber vases, one from each fountain, and suspending them from the top of his quiver, hastened to the chamber of Psyche, whom he found asleep. He shed a few drops from the bitter fountain over her lips, though the sight of her almost moved him to pity; then touched her side with the point of his arrow. At the touch she awoke, and opened her eyes upon Cupid (himself invisible), which so startled him that in his confusion he wounded himself with his own arrow. Heedless of his wound, his whole thought now was to repair the mischief he had done, and he poured the balmy drops of joy over all her silken ringlets.

Psyche, henceforth frowned upon by Venus, derived no benefit from all her charms. True, all eyes were cast eagerly upon her, and every mouth spoke her praises; but neither king, royal youth, nor plebeian presented himself to demand her in marriage. Her two elder sisters of moderate charms had now long been married to two royal princes; but Psyche, in her lonely apartment, deplored her solitude, sick of that beauty which, while it procured abundance of flattery, had failed to awaken love.

Her parents, afraid that they had unwittingly incurred the anger of the gods, consulted the oracle of Apollo, and received this answer, "The virgin is destined for the bride of no mortal lover. Her future husband awaits her on the top of the mountain. He is a monster whom neither gods nor men can resist."

This dreadful decree of the oracle filled all the people with dismay, and her parents abandoned themselves to grief. But Psyche said, "Why, my dear parents, do you now lament me? You should rather have grieved when the people showered upon me undeserved honors, and with one voice called me a Venus. I now perceive that I am a victim to that name. I submit. Lead me to that rock to which my unhappy fate has destined me."

Accordingly, all things being prepared, the royal maid took her place in the procession, which more resembled a funeral than a nuptial pomp, and with her parents, amid the lamentations of the people, ascended the mountain, on the summit of which they left her alone, and with sorrowful hearts returned home.

While Psyche stood on the ridge of the mountain, panting with fear and with eyes full of tears, the gentle Zephyr raised her from the earth and bore her with an easy motion into a flowery dale. By degrees her mind became composed, and she laid herself down on the grassy bank to sleep.

When she awoke refreshed with sleep, she looked round and beheld near a pleasant grove of tall and stately trees. She entered it, and in the midst discovered a fountain, sending forth clear and crystal waters, and fast by, a magnificent palace whose august front impressed the spectator that it was not the work of mortal hands, but the happy retreat of some god. Drawn by admiration and wonder, she approached the building and ventured to enter.

Every object she met filled her with pleasure and amazement. Golden pillars supported the vaulted roof, and the walls were enriched with carvings and paintings representing beasts of the chase and rural scenes, adapted to delight the eye of the beholder. Proceeding onward, she perceived that besides the apartments of state there were others filled with all manner of treasures, and beautiful and precious productions of nature and art.

While her eyes were thus occupied, a voice addressed her, though she saw no one, uttering these words, "Sovereign lady, all that you see is yours. We whose voices you hear are your servants and shall obey all your commands with our utmost care and diligence. Retire, therefore, to your chamber and repose on your bed of down, and when you see fit, repair to the bath. Supper awaits you in the adjoining alcove when it pleases you to take your seat there."

Psyche gave ear to the admonitions of her vocal attendants, and after repose and the refreshment of the bath, seated herself in the alcove, where a table immediately presented itself, without any visible aid from waiters or servants, and covered with the greatest delicacies of food and the most nectareous wines. Her ears too were feasted with music from invisible performers; of whom one sang, another played on the lute, and all closed in the wonderful harmony of a full chorus.

She had not yet seen her destined husband. He came only in the hours of darkness and fled before the dawn of morning, but his accents were full of love, and inspired a like passion in her. She often begged him to stay and let her behold him, but he would not consent. On the contrary he charged her to make no attempt to see him, for it was his pleasure, for the best of reasons, to keep concealed.

"Why should you wish to behold me?" he said. "Have you any doubt of my love? Have you any wish ungratified? If you saw me, perhaps you would fear me, perhaps adore me, but all I ask of you is to love me. I would rather you would love me as an equal than adore me as a god."

This reasoning somewhat quieted Psyche for a time, and while the novelty lasted she felt quite happy. But at length the thought of her parents, left in ignorance of her fate, and of her sisters, precluded from sharing with her the delights of her situation, preyed on her mind and made her begin to feel her palace as but a splendid prison. When her husband came one night, she told him her distress, and at last drew from him an unwilling consent that her sisters should be brought to see her.

So, calling Zephyr, she acquainted him with her husband's commands, and he, promptly obedient, soon brought them across the mountain down to their sister's valley. They embraced her and she returned their caresses.

"Come," said Psyche, "enter with me my house and refresh yourselves with whatever your sister has to offer."

Then taking their hands she led them into her golden palace, and committed them to the care of her numerous train of attendant voices, to refresh them in her baths and at her table, and to show them all her treasures. The view of these celestial delights caused envy to enter their bosoms, at seeing their young sister possessed of such state and splendor, so much exceeding their own.

They asked her numberless questions, among others what sort of a person her husband was. Psyche replied that he was a beautiful youth, who generally spent the daytime in hunting upon the mountains.

The sisters, not satisfied with this reply, soon made her confess that she had never seen him. Then they proceeded to fill her bosom with dark suspicions. "Call to mind," they said, "the Pythian oracle that declared you destined to marry a direful and tremendous monster. The inhabitants of this valley say that your husband is a terrible and monstrous serpent, who nourishes you for a while with dainties that he may by and by devour you. Take our advice. Provide yourself with a lamp and a sharp knife; put them in concealment that your husband may not discover them, and when he is sound asleep, slip out of bed, bring forth your lamp, and see for yourself whether what they say is true or not. If it is, hesitate not to cut off the monster's head, and thereby recover your liberty."

Psyche resisted these persuasions as well as she could, but they did not fail to have their effect on her mind, and when her sisters were gone, their words and her own curiosity were too strong for her to resist. So she prepared her lamp and a sharp knife, and hid them out of sight of her husband. When he had fallen into his first sleep, she silently rose and uncovering her lamp beheld not a hideous monster, but the most beautiful and charming of the gods, with his golden ringlets wandering over his snowy neck and crimson cheek, with two dewy wings on his shoulders, whiter than snow, and with shining feathers like the tender blossoms of spring.

As she leaned the lamp over to have a better view of his face, a drop of burning oil fell on the shoulder of the god. Startled, he opened his eyes and fixed them upon her. Then, without saying a word, he spread his white wings and flew out of the window. Psyche, in vain endeavoring to follow him, fell from the window to the ground.

Cupid, beholding her as she lay in the dust, stopped his flight for an instant and said, "Oh foolish Psyche, is it thus you repay my love? After I disobeyed my mother's commands and made you my wife, will you think me a monster and cut off my head? But go; return to your sisters, whose advice you seem to think preferable to mine. I inflict no other punishment on you than to leave you for ever. Love cannot dwell with suspicion." So saying, he fled away, leaving poor Psyche prostrate on the ground, filling the place with mournful lamentations.

When she had recovered some degree of composure she looked around her, but the palace and gardens had vanished, and she found herself in the open field not far from the city where her sisters dwelt. She repaired thither and told them the whole story of her misfortunes, at which, pretending to grieve, those spiteful creatures inwardly rejoiced.

"For now," said they, "he will perhaps choose one of us." With this idea, without saying a word of her intentions, each of them rose early the next morning and ascended the mountain, and having reached the top, called upon Zephyr to receive her and bear her to his lord; then leaping up, and not being sustained by Zephyr, fell down the precipice and was dashed to pieces.

Psyche meanwhile wandered day and night, without food or repose, in search of her husband. Casting her eyes on a lofty mountain having on its brow a magnificent temple, she sighed and said to herself, "Perhaps my love, my lord, inhabits there," and directed her steps thither.

She had no sooner entered than she saw heaps of corn, some in loose ears and some in sheaves, with mingled ears of barley. Scattered about, lay sickles and rakes, and all the instruments of harvest, without order, as if thrown carelessly out of the weary reapers' hands in the sultry hours of the day.

This unseemly confusion the pious Psyche put an end to, by separating and sorting everything to its proper place and kind, believing that she ought to neglect none of the gods, but endeavor by her piety to engage them all in her behalf. The holy Ceres, whose temple it was, finding her so religiously employed, thus spoke to her, "Oh Psyche, truly worthy of our pity, though I cannot shield you from the frowns of Venus, yet I can teach you how best to allay her displeasure. Go, then, and voluntarily surrender yourself to your lady and sovereign, and try by modesty and submission to win her forgiveness, and perhaps her favor will restore you the husband you have lost."

Psyche obeyed the commands of Ceres and took her way to the temple of Venus, endeavoring to fortify her mind and ruminating on what she should say and how best propitiate the angry goddess, feeling that the issue was doubtful and perhaps fatal.

Venus received her with angry countenance. "Most undutiful and faithless of servants," said she, "do you at last remember that you really have a mistress? Or have you rather come to see your sick husband, yet laid up of the wound given him by his loving wife? You are so ill favored and disagreeable that the only way you can merit your lover must be by dint of industry and diligence. I will make trial of your housewifery." Then she ordered Psyche to be led to the storehouse of her temple, where was laid up a great quantity of wheat, barley, millet, vetches, beans, and lentils prepared for food for her pigeons, and said, "Take and separate all these grains, putting all of the same kind in a parcel by themselves, and see that you get it done before evening." Then Venus departed and left her to her task.

But Psyche, in a perfect consternation at the enormous work, sat stupid and silent, without moving a finger to the inextricable heap.

While she sat despairing, Cupid stirred up the little ant, a native of the fields, to take compassion on her. The leader of the anthill, followed by whole hosts of his six-legged subjects, approached the heap, and with the utmost diligence taking grain by grain, they separated the pile, sorting each kind to its parcel; and when it was all done, they vanished out of sight in a moment.

Venus at the approach of twilight returned from the banquet of the gods, breathing odors and crowned with roses. Seeing the task done, she exclaimed, "This is no work of yours, wicked one, but his, whom to your own and his misfortune you have enticed." So saying, she threw her a piece of black bread for her supper and went away.

Next morning Venus ordered Psyche to be called and said to her, "Behold yonder grove which stretches along the margin of the water. There you will find sheep feeding without a shepherd, with golden-shining fleeces on their backs. Go, fetch me a sample of that precious wool gathered from every one of their fleeces."

Psyche obediently went to the riverside, prepared to do her best to execute the command. But the river god inspired the reeds with harmonious murmurs, which seemed to say, "Oh maiden, severely tried, tempt not the dangerous flood, nor venture among the formidable rams on the other side, for as long as they are under the influence of the rising sun, they burn with a cruel rage to destroy mortals with their sharp horns or rude teeth. But when the noontide sun has driven the cattle to the shade, and the serene spirit of the flood has lulled them to rest, you may then cross in safety, and you will find the woolly gold sticking to the bushes and the trunks of the trees."

Thus the compassionate river god gave Psyche instructions how to accomplish her task, and by observing his directions she soon returned to Venus with her arms full of the golden fleece; but she received not the approbation of her implacable mistress, who said, "I know very well it is by none of your own doings that you have succeeded in this task, and I am not satisfied yet that you have any capacity to make yourself useful. But I have another task for you. Here, take this box and go your way to the infernal shades, and give this box to Proserpine and say, 'My mistress Venus desires you to send her a little of your beauty, for in tending her sick son she has lost some of her own.' Be not too long on your errand, for I must paint myself with it to appear at the circle of the gods and goddesses this evening."

Psyche was now satisfied that her destruction was at hand, being obliged to go with her own feet directly down to Erebus. Wherefore, to make no delay of what was not to be avoided, she goes to the top of a high tower to precipitate herself headlong, thus to descend the shortest way to the shades below. But a voice from the tower said to her, "Why, poor unlucky girl, do you design to put an end to your days in so dreadful a manner? And what cowardice makes you sink under this last danger who have been so miraculously supported in all your former?" Then the voice told her how by a certain cave she might reach the realms of Pluto, and how to avoid all the dangers of the road, to pass by Cerberus, the three-headed dog, and prevail on Charon, the ferryman, to take her across the black river and bring her back again. But the voice added, "When Proserpine has given you the box filled with her beauty, of all things this is chiefly to be observed by you, that you never once open or look into the box nor allow your curiosity to pry into the treasure of the beauty of the goddesses."

Psyche, encouraged by this advice, obeyed it in all things, and taking heed to her ways traveled safely to the kingdom of Pluto. She was admitted to the palace of Proserpine, and without accepting the delicate seat or delicious banquet that was offered her, but contented with coarse bread for her food, she delivered her message from Venus. Presently the box was returned to her, shut and filled with the precious commodity. Then she returned the way she came, and glad was she to come out once more into the light of day.

But having got so far successfully through her dangerous task a longing desire seized her to examine the contents of the box. "What," said she, "shall I, the carrier of this divine beauty, not take the least bit to put on my cheeks to appear to more advantage in the eyes of my beloved husband!" So she carefully opened the box, but found nothing there of any beauty at all, but an infernal and truly Stygian sleep, which being thus set free from its prison, took possession of her, and she fell down in the midst of the road, a sleepy corpse without sense or motion.

But Cupid, being now recovered from his wound, and not able longer to bear the absence of his beloved Psyche, slipping through the smallest crack of the window of his chamber which happened to be left open, flew to the spot where Psyche lay, and gathering up the sleep from her body closed it again in the box, and waked Psyche with a light touch of one of his arrows. "Again," said he, "have you almost perished by the same curiosity. But now perform exactly the task imposed on you by my mother, and I will take care of the rest."

Then Cupid, as swift as lightning penetrating the heights of heaven, presented himself before Jupiter with his supplication. Jupiter lent a favoring ear, and pleaded the cause of the lovers so earnestly with Venus that he won her consent. On this he sent Mercury to bring Psyche up to the heavenly assembly, and when she arrived, handing her a cup of ambrosia, he said, "Drink this, Psyche, and be immortal; nor shall Cupid ever break away from the knot in which he is tied, but these nuptials shall be perpetual."

Thus Psyche became at last united to Cupid, and in due time they had a daughter born to them whose name was Pleasure.

Gothic Romance, Sensibility and the Sublime

Horace Walpole (1717–1797)

In the seventeenth century, "gothic" meant crude, rough, and barbaric, a derisive term usually applied to architecture. In 1749, Horace Walpole, the son of the powerful Prime Minister and a Member of Parliament (1741–67), initiated gothic as a fashion when he remodeled a cottage at Strawberry Hill on the Thames near Windsor into a "gothic" castle with artificial battlements, towers, stained glass windows, pointed arches, and furnished it with armor, weapons, a decorative baptismal font, and a plaster mantle painted to look like stone. More a stage-set than a home, it grew and collapsed over the years, initiating a trend in building ruins, "follies" such as Blaize Castle in Northanger Abbey, *representing both worldly status and its futility, the invention of personal and public histories that didn't exist, the weight of a past in which the owners did not share. Walpole studied the antique, the real and the imaginary, and published books on early English life, letters, painting and architecture in his own Strawberry Hill Press. One evening, the story goes, in 1765, while dozing in his castle, Walpole dreamt of a giant hand encased in armor on the staircase, and that evening, he began writing* The Castle of Otranto. *Finished and published anonymously two months later, it became a formula for gothic romance which is still used in novels and films.*

Claiming to have found the manuscript in "the library of an ancient Catholic family in the north of England," printed in Italian in 1529, Walpole offers a fast-paced tale, events taking priority over character, atmosphere and special effects over plot. The story takes place during the Crusades, between 1095 and 1243, when Prince Manfred of Otranto arranges for his fifteen-year-old son, Conrad, to marry in order to avoid the mysterious prophecy that he will lose his castle "whenever the real owner should be grown too large to inhabit it." After his son is crushed on the eve of his marriage by a giant plumed helmet, Manfred unjustly accuses a peasant, Theodore, imprisons him under the helmet from which he must either magically escape or starve. The scene initiates a series of events in which otherwise inanimate objects express the wishes of an implacable spiritual world: the nose on a statue bleeds; an armor-clad foot appears in a gallery; a skeleton dressed as a monk offers advice; an ancestral portrait sighs, descends from its frame, and walks out of the novel. The supernatural events are intensified by the familiar Greek tragic themes of false inheritance, retribution, mistaken identity, and incest, a mighty summing up of everything that has been known to terrorize civilized people in the Western world.

To protect his castle and produce an heir, Manfred tries to divorce his good wife, Hippolita, and marry Isabella, his dead son's bride. Theodore, the imprisoned young man, turns out to be the rightful heir to the castle, with whom Matilda, Manfred's daughter, falls in love. Seeing them together and believing the woman is Isabella, he stabs her, unwittingly killing his own daughter. Manfred and Hippolita withdraw to separate convents. Isabella's father offers her to Theodore, who, still overcome by grief at the loss of Matilda, agrees to marry her so "he could for ever indulge the melancholy that had taken possession of his soul."

Displaced by Enlightenment rationality, gothic brought the spiritual world back through things; possessions which, in this first age of consumerism, took over people's lives, shaped and expressed them, and became instruments of revenge. The gothic pattern also reflects an odd sexual fantasy, appealing to women and to men, in which an insensitive male villain overpowers a helpless, vulnerable, and terrified virgin to be saved in the end by a mild-mannered, effeminate "hero." Stylistically, gothic romances are so exaggerated that even the most gruesome incidents seem to be burlesques of the very characters and actions that are supposed to cause terror. The following excerpt is from the opening chapter.

from *The Castle of Otranto*

MANFRED, Prince of Otranto, had one son and one daughter: the latter, a most beautiful virgin, aged eighteen, was called Matilda. Conrad, the son, was three years younger, a homely youth, sickly, and of no promising disposition; yet he was the darling of his father, who never showed any symptoms of affection to Matilda. Manfred had contracted a marriage for his son with the Marquis of Vicenza's daughter, Isabella; and she had already been delivered by her guardians into the hands of Manfred, that he might celebrate the wedding as soon as Conrad's infirm state of health would permit.

Manfred's impatience for this ceremonial was remarked by his family and neighbours. The former, indeed, apprehending the severity of their Prince's disposition, did not dare to utter their surmises on this precipitation. Hippolita, his wife, an amiable lady, did sometimes venture to represent the danger of marrying their only son so early, considering his great youth, and greater infirmities; but she never received any other answer than reflections on her own sterility, who had given him but one heir. His tenants and subjects were less cautious in their discourses. They attributed this hasty wedding to the Prince's dread of seeing accomplished an ancient prophecy, which was said to have pronounced that the castle and lordship of Otranto "should pass from the present family, whenever the real owner should be grown too large to inhabit it." It was difficult to make any sense of this prophecy; and still less easy to conceive what it had to do with the marriage in question. Yet these mysteries, or contradictions, did not make the populace adhere the less to their opinion.

Young Conrad's birthday was fixed for his espousals. The company was assembled in the chapel of the Castle, and everything ready for beginning the divine office, when Conrad himself was missing. Manfred, impatient of the least delay, and who had not observed his son retire, dispatched one of his attendants to summon the young Prince. The servant, who had not stayed long enough to have crossed the court to Conrad's apartment, came running back breathless, in a frantic manner, his eyes staring, and foaming at the month. He said nothing, but pointed to the court.

The company were struck with terror and amazement. The Princess Hippolita, without knowing what was the matter, but anxious for her son, swooned away. Manfred, less apprehensive than enraged at the procrastination of the nuptials, and at the folly of his domestic, asked imperiously what was the matter? The fellow made no answer, but continued pointing towards the courtyard; and at last, after repeated questions put to him, cried out, "Oh! the helmet! the helmet!"

In the meantime, some of the company had run into the court, from whence was heard a confused noise of shrieks, horror, and surprise. Manfred, who began to be alarmed at not seeing his son, went himself to get information of what occasioned this strange confusion. Matilda remained endeavouring to assist her mother, and Isabella stayed for the same purpose, and to avoid showing any impatience for the bridegroom, for whom, in truth, she had conceived little affection.

The first thing that struck Manfred's eyes was a group of his servants endeavouring to raise something that appeared to him a mountain of sable plumes. He gazed without believing his sight.

"What are ye doing?" cried Manfred, wrathfully; "where is my son?"

A volley of voices replied, "Oh! my Lord! the Prince! the Prince! the helmet! the helmet!"

Shocked with these lamentable sounds, and dreading he knew not what, he advanced hastily,—but what a sight for a father's eyes!— he beheld his child dashed to pieces, and almost buried under an enormous helmet, an hundred times more large than any casque ever made for human being, and shaded with a proportionable quantity of black feathers.

The horror of the spectacle, the ignorance of all around how this misfortune had happened, and above all, the tremendous phenomenon before him, took away the Prince's speech. Yet his silence lasted longer than even grief could occasion. He fixed his eyes on what he wished in vain to believe a vision; and seemed less attentive to his loss, than buried in meditation on the stupendous object that had occasioned it. He touched, he examined the fatal casque; nor could even the bleeding mangled remains of the young Prince divert the eyes of Manfred from the portent before him.

William Beckford (1760–1844)

Like Walpole, William Beckford was the son of a powerful politician, Member of Parliament, the author of a gothic novel and a castle-builder. Born in 1760, the son of the Lord Mayor of London, at age ten Beckford inherited a vast fortune that included Jamaican sugar plantations and at least a thousand slaves. Talented, learned, well-traveled, Beckford was also ill-natured, hedonistic, extravagant, and perverse, the model of a gothic villain. He celebrated his coming of age with a three-day festival at Fonthill, his family estate, transformed by a famous stage designer into an oriental palace reminiscent of The Arabian Nights—*a collection of tales which had fascinated Beckford as it did Jane Austen and nearly every other writer in the eighteenth century. After scandalous affairs with a young viscount and with his cousin's wife, and repeatedly exiled to the Continent, Beckford married Lady Margaret Gordon, who died giving birth to his second daughter. Shortly after, he wrote* The History of Caliph Vathek *(1786), in French, in three days, he says, though it is actually the work of a year, a book so full of mayhem and butchery that, he confesses in the Preface, he trembled while writing it. Again, architecture expresses character: the book is set in a compound of palaces with a tower at the center, where Vathek, his many wives, his mother Carathis, a necromancer (a parody of Beckford's own strict Methodist mother), and their one-eyed mute slaves and eunuchs conduct elaborate sacrifices, the most spectacular a bonfire of venomous oils, skeletons, mummies, and 140 dedicated subjects who, believing that Vathek is in danger, climb the tower and are pushed into the pyre.*

In 1796, driven back to England by the wars in Europe, Beckford published Modern Novel Writing or the Elegant Enthusiast *(1796) and* Azemia *(1797), novels which satirize the gothic romance, the government, and the war. To establish his presence, he hired James Wyatt, the foremost British architect, who renovated Fonthill into a gothic abbey of monumental proportions, with a huge tower, the largest in England, that collapsed almost immediately. An arrogant and tasteless appropriation of space, labor, and materials, Beckford filled it with dwarf-servants dressed in costumes, odd things and inventions, elaborate gardens, artificial ponds, and wild animals roaming freely—more of a theme park, a Neverland, than the palatial ancestral estate modeled after Salisbury Cathedral that he imagined. Although privacy was one of his obsessions, he nonetheless sold tickets, granted tours, and had Fonthill painted by the popular artists of his day, including Turner.*

In 1810, one of Beckford's daughters married Lord Douglas, and the other daughter, Margaret, whom Jane Austen called "cousin," eloped with Colonel James Orde on May 15, 1811, suggesting, according to some critics, the elopements in Pride and Prejudice *and* Mansfield Park *(Halperin 198) and eliciting Austen's cryptic comment, "The Papers say that her Father disinherits her, but I think too well of an Orde, to suppose that she has not a handsome Independence of her own" (Letters, May 29, 1811). After 1815, when Byron cites* Vathek *in his romances, Beckford enjoyed a revival and republished the novel in both French and English. He died at age eighty-four, a recluse in a new tower he built on a hill outside of Bath which he called Lansdown Baghdad.*

from Vathek[1]

The caliph, not daring to object, abandoned himself to grief and the wind that ravaged his entrails, whilst his mother went forwad with the requisite operations. Phials of serpents' oil, mummies, and bones, were soon set in order on the balustrde of the tower. The pile began to rise, and in three hours was twenty cubits high. At length darkness approached, and Carathis, having stripped herself to her inmost garment, clapped her hands in an impulse of ecstasy; the mutes followed her example; but Vathek, extenuated with hunger and impatience, was unable to support himself, and fell down in a swoon. The sparks had already kindled the dry wood; the venomous oil burst into a thousand blue flames; the mummies, dissolving, emitted a thick dun vapour; and the rhinoceros' horns, beginning to consume, all together diffused such a stench, that the caliph, recovering, started from his trance, and gazed wildly on the scene in full blaze around him. The oil gushed forth in a plenitude of streams; and the negresses, who supplied it without intermission, united their cries to those of the princess. At last the fire became so violent, and the flames reflected from the polished marble so dazzling, that the caliph, unable to withstand the heat and the blaze, effected his escape, and took shelter under the imperial standard.

In the meantime, the inhabitants of Samarah, scared at the light which shone over the city, arose in haste, ascended their roofs, beheld the tower on fire, and hurried, half naked, to the square. Their love for their sovereign immediately awoke; and, apprehending him in danger of perishing in his tower, their whole thoughts were occupied with the means of his safety. Morakanabad flew from his retirement, wiped

[1]Collated from the Bentley Standard Authors editions (London, 1834, 1849, and 1852); ed. Richard Garnett (London: Lawrence and Bullen, 1893).

away his tears, and cried out for water like the rest. Bababalouk, whose olfactory nerves were more familiarized to magical odours, readily conjecturing that Carathis was engaged in her favourite amusements, strenuously exhorted them not to be alarmed. Him, however, they treated as an old poltroon, and styled him a rascally traitor. The camels and dromedaries were advancing with water; but no one knew by which way to enter the tower. Whilst the populace was obstinate in forcing the doors, a violent north-east wind drove an immense volume of flame against them. At first they recoiled, but soon came back with redoubled zeal. At the same time, the stench of the horns and mummies increasing, most of the crowd fell backwards in a state of suffocation. Those that kept their feet mutually wondered at the cause of the smell, and admonished each other to retire. Morakanabad, more sick than the rest, remained in a piteous condition. Holding his nose with one hand, every one persisted in his efforts with the other to burst open the doors and obtain admission. A hundred and forty of the strongest and most resolute at length accomplished their purpose. Having gained the staircase, by their violent exertions, they attained a great height in a quarter of an hour.

Carathis, alarmed at the signs of her mutes, advanced to the staircase, went down a few steps, and heard several voices calling out from below, "You shall in a moment have water!" Being rather alert, considering her age, she presently regained the top of the tower, and bade her son suspend the sacrifice for some minutes; adding, "We shall soon be enabled to render it more grateful. Certain dolts of your subjects, imagining, no doubt, that we were on fire, have been rash enough to break through those doors which had hitherto remained inviolate, for the sake of bringing up water. They are very kind, you must allow, so soon to forget the wrongs you have done them; but that is of little moment. Let us offer them to the Giaour; let them come up; our mutes, who neither want strength nor experience, will soon dispatch them, exhausted as they are with fatigue."—"Be it so," answered the caliph, "provided we finish, and I dine." In fact, these good people, out of breath from ascending fifteen hundred stairs in such haste, and chagrined at having spilt by the way the water they had taken, were no sooner arrived at the top, than the blaze of the flames and the fumes of the mummies at once overpowered their senses. It was a pity! for they beheld not the agreeable smile with which the mutes and negresses adjusted the cord to their necks: these amiable personages rejoiced, however, no less at the scene. Never before had the ceremony of strangling been performed with so much facility. They all fell, without the least resistance or struggle: so that Vathek, in the space of a few moments, found himself surrounded by the dead bodies of the most faithful of his subjects; all which were thrown on the top of the pile. Carathis, whose presence of mind never forsook her, perceiving that she had carcasses sufficient to complete her oblation, commanded the chains to be stretched across the staircase, and the iron doors barricadoed, that no more might come up.

No sooner were these orders obeyed, than the tower shook; the dead bodies vanished in the flames, which at once changed from a swarthy crimson to a bright rose colour; an ambient vapour emitted the most exquisite fragrance; the marble columns rang with harmonious sounds, and the liquefied horns diffused a delicious perfume. Carathis, in transports, anticipated the success of her enterprise; whilst her mutes and negresses, to whom these sweets had given the colic, retired grumbling to their cells.

Matthew Gregory Lewis (1775–1818)

In 1796, when Matthew Gregory Lewis, age twenty-one, replaced Beckford as a Member of Parliament (to 1802), he had already anonymously published The Monk, *written, he claimed, in only ten weeks, inspired by reading* The Mysteries of Udolpho *(see Contexts, p. 225), which, in a letter to his mother, he called "one of the most interesting Books that ever have been published."* The Monk, *on the other hand, a lurid mix of religion and sex, horror and comedy, rape, necrophilia, incest, and matricide, was universally condemned as obscene and blasphemous. It sold out immediately, eliciting a second edition within a few months under his own name as an MP, and a tamer fourth edition in response to public outcry and a threatened lawsuit in 1798. Thorpe reveals his taste and character when he calls* The Monk *"the only tolerably decent [novel] to come out since* Tom Jones.*"*

Lewis brought the gothic conventions to the stage with six dramas, starting with the successful and profitable The Castle Spectre *(1797–98), a true spectacle that challenged dramatic form and set the precedent for a generation of gothic melodrama (plays set to music appearing in the un-licensed theaters). A talented man of letters, Lewis also collaborated with Sir Walter Scott on* Tales of Wonder *(1801), a collection of translations and original stories that inspired the cartoon by Gillray on the cover. Unlike Beckford, Lewis was a social catalyst, someone who connected people: he knew Goethe in Weimar in 1792, and in the summer of 1816 he translated* Faust *for Byron, Polidori, and Mary and Percy Shelley, during that great gothic gathering in Villa Diodati, where Mary Shelley wrote* Frankenstein *and Polidori* The Vampyre. *Like Beckford, Lewis's wealth was based on the many slaves who worked his Jamaican sugar plantations. Opposed to slavery, he made several journeys to Jamaica to improve the lives of his slaves; in 1818, during a return voyage, he died of a fever and was buried at sea.*

Set in Madrid, The Monk *is ostensibly about Ambrosio, a foundling raised as a Capuchin monk and a charismatic preacher whose virtue is corrupted by a demonic figure who enters the monastery disguised as Rosario, a young novice, and then reveals herself as Matilda. Seducing Ambrosio, she awakens insatiable sexual appetites: "Matilda gluts me with enjoyment even to loathing. . . ." He then seduces the naïve Antonia, who has turned to him for protection, murders her and her mother, who turn out to be his own sister and mother, for which he is brought before the Inquisition. In a subplot, an imprisoned pregnant nun is later discovered with the maggot-covered body of her dead infant whom she could not feed, while the Prioress, after confessing her fault, is stoned and dismembered by a riotous crowd. Ambrosio, rescued by the "The Fiend" from the Inquisition, is flown to the mountains, where the following spectacular conclusion occurs.*

from *The Monk*[1]

"What more did I promise than to save you from your prison? Have I not done so? Are you not safe from the Inquisition—safe from all but from me? Fool that you were to confide yourself to a Devil! Why did you not stipulate for life, and power, and pleasure? Then all would have been granted: Now, your reflections come too late. Miscreant, prepare for death; You have not many hours to live!"

On hearing this sentence, dreadful were the feelings of the devoted Wretch! He sank upon his knees, and raised his hands towards heaven. The Fiend read his intention and prevented it—

"What?" He cried, darting at him a look of fury: "Dare you still implore the Eternal's mercy? Would you feign penitence, and again act an Hypocrite's part? Villain, resign your hopes of pardon. Thus I secure my prey!"

[1]Matthew Gregory Lewis, *Ambrosio; or, The Monk: A Romance,* 3 vols., 4th ed., (London: J. Bell, 1798).

As He said this, darting his talons into the Monk's shaven crown, He sprang with him from the rock. The Caves and mountains rang with Ambrosio's shrieks. The Dæmon continued to soar aloft, till reaching a dreadful height, he released the sufferer. Headlong fell the Monk through the airy waste. The sharp point of a rock received him; and he rolled from precipice to precipice, till bruised and mangled, he rested on the river's banks. Life still exsisted in his miserable frame: he attempted in vain to raise himself. His broken and dislocated limbs refused to perform their office, nor was he able to quit the spot where he had first fallen. The sun now rose above the horizon. Its scorching beams darted full upon the head of the expiring Sinner. Myriads of insects were called forth by the warmth. They drank the blood which trickled from Ambrosio's wounds; he had no power to drive them from him, and they fastened upon his sores, darted their stings into his body, covered him with their multitudes, and inflicted on him tortures the most exquisite and insupportable. The eagles of the rock tore his flesh piecemeal, and dug out his eye-balls with their crooked beaks. A burning thirst tormented him; he heard the river's murmur as it rolled beside him, but strove in vain to drag himself towards the sound. Blind, maimed, helpless, and despairing, venting his rage in blasphemy and curses, execrating his existence, yet dreading the arrival of death destined to yield him up to greater torments, six miserable days did the Villain languish. On the seventh a violent storm arose: The winds in fury rent up rocks and forests: The sky was now black with clouds, now sheeted with fire: The rain fell in torrents; It swelled the stream; The waves overflowed their banks; They reached the spot where Ambrosio lay, and when they abated carried with them into the river the corpse of the despairing Monk.

Samuel Taylor Coleridge
from *Biographia Literaria*

In the following passage from the *Biographia Literaria* (1817), Coleridge recalls his collaboration with Wordsworth for their forthcoming *Lyrical Ballads* (1798). The timeline as well as the principles Coleridge recalls illuminate not only *The Mysteries of Udolpho* but also *Northanger Abbey.*

> During the first year that Mr. Wordsworth and I were neighbors, our conversations turned frequently on the two cardinal points of poetry, the power of exciting the sympathy of the reader by a faithful adherence to the truth of nature, and the power of giving the interest of novelty by the modifying colors of imagination. The sudden charm, which accidents of light and shade, which moonlight or sun-set diffused over a known and familiar landscape, appeared to represent the practicability of combining both. These are the poetry of nature. The thought suggested itself (to which of us I do not recollect) that a series of poems might be composed of two sorts. In the one, the incidents and agents were to be, in part at least, supernatural; and the excellence aimed at was to consist in the interesting of the affections by the dramatic truth of such emotions as would naturally accompany such situations, supposing them real. And real in this sense they have been to every human being who, from whatever source of delusion, has at any time believed himself under supernatural agency. For the second class, subjects were to be chosen from ordinary life; the characters and incidents were to be such, as will be found in every village and its vicinity, where there is a meditative and feeling mind to seek after them, or to notice them, when they present themselves.
>
> In this idea originated the plan of the "Lyrical Ballads"; in which it was agreed, that my endeavors should be directed to persons and characters supernatural, or at least romantic, yet so as to transfer from our inward nature a human interest and a semblance of truth sufficient to procure for these shadows of imagination that willing suspension of disbelief for the moment, which constitutes poetic faith. Mr. Wordsworth on the other hand was to propose to himself as his object, to give the charm of novelty to things of every day, and to excite a feeling analogous to the supernatural, by awakening the mind's attention from the lethargy of custom, and directing it to the loveliness and the wonders of the world before us; an inexhaustible treasure, but for which in consequence of the film of familiarity and selfish solicitude we have eyes, yet see not, ears that hear not, and hearts that neither feel nor understand. (Chapter XIV)

Sensibility

In *The Rhyme of the Ancient Mariner* and in *Christabel*, like *The Mysteries of Udolpho* and *Northanger Abbey*, the emphasis is not so much on what happens, on the action, but on the response, on how characters react to objects and events. However rational the explanation for supernatural or mysterious events, the characters who experience them are often irrational, emotional adventurers, such as Emily St. Aubert, suffering from a common and fashionable personality affliction that was called *sensibility*.

Sensibility as a personal attribute appered early in the eighteenth century, formulated by philosophers and poets who believed that feelings, emotions, sympathy are, should be, or could become the basis of action, for charitable behavior, for social progress. This identification of sympathy and virtue characterizes some of the best poetry, starting with James Thomson, who is often quoted in gothic novels and in parodies such as *Northanger Abbey*, and culminating in Wordsworth, *The Prelude*, Book VIII, subtitled, "Love of Nature leading to Love of Mankind." In *Mysteries of Udolpho*, Valancourt, the bereft hero, progresses from self-indulgent feeling to altruism: from the "delicious melancholy" of twilight "which no person, who had felt it once, would resign for the gayest pleasures," a melancholy that awakens "our best and purest feelings; disposing us to benevolence, pity and friendship."

Early in *The Mysteries of Udolpho*, Emily's father warns her against such excess.

> I have endeavoured to teach you, from your earliest youth, the duty of self-command; I have pointed out to you the great importance of it through life, not only as it preserves us in the various and dangerous temptations that call us from rectitude and virtue, but as it limits the indulgences which are termed virtuous, yet which, extended beyond a certain boundary, are vicious, for their consequence is evil. All excess is vicious; even that sorrow, which is amiable in its origin, becomes a selfish and unjust passion, if indulged at the expense of our duties –by our duties I mean what we owe to ourselves, as well as to others. The indulgence of excessive grief enervates the mind, and almost incapacitates it for again partaking of those various

innocent enjoyments which a benevolent God designed to be the sun-shine of our lives. My dear Emily, recollect and practice the precepts I have so often given you, and which your own experience has so often shown you to be wise.

On his deathbed, he again advises, "Those who really possess sensibility ought early to be taught that it is a dangerous quality, which is continually extracting the excess of misery, or delight, from every surrounding circumstance. . . . We become the victims of our feelings unless we can in some degree command them." But Emily pursues sensation for its own sake: "a faint degree of terror . . . occupies and expands the mind," she says, "and elevates it to high expectations . . . and leads us, by a kind of fascination, to seek even the object from which we appear to shrink."

If there is a moral or value to *The Mysteries of Udolpho*, it is the self-control that Emily acquires. After multiple fits of fainting, weeping, and paragraphs of emotional inventories, she unconvincingly admits: "I do indeed perceive how much more valuable is the strength of fortitude than the grace of sensibility, and I will also endeavor to fulfill the promise I then made; I will not indulge in unavailing lamentation, but will try to endure, with firmness the oppression I cannot elude" (214). In *Northanger Abbey*, Catherine, in turn, came to recognize, that she had "an imagination resolved on alarm," a "craving to be frightened," which she "traced" to the influence of reading Mrs. Radcliffe.

The Sublime

The capacity for feeling is stirred by "sublime" events and scenes. Originally a classical rhetorical form, the sublime in the eighteenth century was associated with nature, the irregular, powerful, unpredictable, terrifying aspects of the landscape such as mountains, earthquakes, volcanoes, storms, tidal waves, gloomy oceans. Such events expressed divine power and wrath, lift the mind and heart and leave the observer transported—but also feeling small and helpless. Wild animals, wars, famines, fires, plagues, tidal waves, the new astronomy and geology with their allusions to infinity, mysterious and frightening phenomena of all sorts convey the sublime or awaken sublime effects. According to Edmund Burke in *Enquiry into the Origin of our Ideas of the Sublime and Beautiful* (1757): "Whatever is fitted in any sort to excite the ideas of pain, and danger, that is to say, whatever is in any sort terrible, or is conversant about terrible objects, or operates in a manner analogous to terror . . . productive of the strongest emotion which the mind is capable of feeling."

The impulse to seek the sublime, Burke begins, is curiosity, that same ambiguous faculty on which so much gothic transgression and its archetypal predecessors depend. "The first and the simplest emotion which we discover in the human mind, is Curiosity. By curiosity, I mean whatever desire we have for, or whatever pleasure we take in, novelty."

Like sensibility, however, the pursuit of the sublime became a social affectation, especially in the fine distinctions and self-observation it encouraged, as Peacock depicts in *Nightmare Abbey* (1818): Scythrop the young hero, having discovered a strange lady in his tower, "either was or ought to have been frightened; at all events, he was astonished; and astonishment, though not in itself fear, is nevertheless a good stage towards it, and is, indeed, as it were, the half-way house between respect and terror, according to Mr. Burke's graduated scale of the sublime."

Ann Radcliffe (1764–1823)

Ann Radcliffe was the most successful and influential of all the gothic novelists, but, unlike the others, she was an outsider, the sheltered and isolated wife of a lawyer and newspaper editor, who occupied her long evenings alone writing stories that reflected her own fantasy life while they captured and shaped the fantasies of readers and other authors. So reclusive was she that for the last thirteen years of her life, she was reputed to be dead or driven mad by an excess of imagination. In fact, after six novels, a verse romance, a travel diary, and some poems, all in eight years, following The Italian *(1797), she stopped writing.*

Universally admired, Radcliffe brought the gothic novel to a peak of popularity and of craft in part because she could tell a compelling story in an appropriate style, reconciled the universal and eternal romance plot with contemporary manners, characters, and popular motifs such as sensibility, the picturesque, and the sublime, and projected them onto sixteenth-century French and Italian characters. Unlike other gothic writers, Radcliffe focused on rational explanations for the supernatural, the psychological sources of terror, exhibiting the aesthetic principles that Coleridge and Wordsworth were formulating for their poetry during the same period.

from *The Mysteries of Udolpho*

In the "willing suspension of disbelief" that *The Mysteries of Udolpho* induces, the excesses of the sublime effects and of social sensibility seem appropriate. Emily's father dies early in the novel, leaving her in the care of a foolish and fashionable aunt who separates her from Valancourt, her true love. With her aunt's new husband, the mysterious and morose Montoni, captain of a band of thieves, they travel to Udolpho, the castle in the Apennines, where Montoni tricks her into giving up her property then tries to marry her off to the evil Count Moreno. While searching for her aunt, whom Emily believes Montoni has killed, she encounters mysteries such as the disappearance of Laurentini di Udolpho, who turns up later on as a nun, Sister Agnes, having taken on this identity after she murdered Emily's other aunt because she had been in love with her husband, the Marquis de Villeroi, who owns the chateau in the South of France to which Emily escapes with Valancourt. And so, in its cumulative and convoluted way, it goes on. However dangerous Emily's situation, most of the terrors are self-induced; she imagines supernatural causes for rationally explained events. The following passage inspired the parody of Catherine's arrival at Northanger, the smooth path, the uneventful trip, during which time Henry amuses her with his own version of *Udolpho*.

At length, the travelers began to ascend among the Apennines. The immense pine-forests, which, at that period, overhung these mountains, and between which the road wound, excluded all views but of the cliffs aspiring above, except, that, now and then, an opening through the dark woods allowed the eye a momentary glimpse of the country below. The gloom of these shades, their solitary silence, except when the breeze swept over their summits, the tremendous precipices of the mountains, that came partially to the eye, each assisted to raise the solemnity of Emily's feelings into awe; she saw only images of gloomy grandeur, or of dreadful sublimity, around her; other images, equally gloomy and equally terrible, gleamed on her imagination. She was going she scarcely knew whither, under the dominion of a person, from whose arbitrary disposition she had already suffered so much, to marry, perhaps, a man who possessed neither her affection, or esteem; or to endure, beyond the hope of succour, whatever punishment revenge, and that Italian revenge, might dictate.—The more she considered what might be the motive of the journey, the more she became convinced, that it was for the purpose of concluding her nuptials with Count Morano, with that secrecy which her resolute resistance had made necessary to the honour, if not to the safety, of Montoni. From the deep solitudes, . . . and from the gloomy castle, of which she had heard some mysterious hints, her sick heart recoiled in despair, and she experienced, that, though her mind was already occupied by peculiar distress, it was still alive to the influence of new and local circumstance; why else did she shudder at the idea of this desolate castle?

As the travelers still ascended among the pine forests, steep rose over steep, the mountains seemed to multiply, as they went, and what was the summit of one eminence proved to be only the base of another. At length, they reached a little plain, where the drivers stopped to rest the mules, whence a scene of such extent and magnificence opened below, as drew even from Madame Montoni a note of admiration. Emily lost, for a moment, her sorrows, in the immensity of nature. Beyond the amphitheatre of mountains, that stretched below, whose tops appeared as numerous almost, as the waves of the sea, and whose feet were concealed by the forests extended the Campagna of Italy, where cities and rivers, and woods and all the glow of cultivation were mingled in gay confusion. . . .

Wild and romantic as were these scenes, their character had far less of the sublime, than had those of the Alps, which guard the entrance of Italy. Emily was often elevated, but seldom felt those emotions of indescribable awe which she had so continually experienced, in her passage over the Alps.

Towards the close of day, the road wound into a deep valley. Mountains, whose shaggy steeps appeared to be inaccessible, almost surrounded it. To the east, a vista opened, that exhibited the Apennines in their darkest horrors; and the long perspective of retiring summits, rising over each other, their ridges clothed with pines, exhibited a stronger image of grandeur, than any that Emily had yet seen. The sun had just sunk below the top of the mountains she was descending, whose long shadow stretched opening of the cliffs, touched with a yellow gleam the summits of the forest, that hung upon the opposite steeps, and streamed in full splendour upon the towers and battlements of a castle, that spread its extensive ramparts along the brow of a precipice above. The splendour of these illumined objects was heightened by the contrasted shade, which involved the valley below.

"There," said Montoni, speaking for the first time in several hours, "is Udolpho."

Emily gazed with melancholy awe upon the castle, which she understood to be Montoni's; for, though it was now lighted up by the setting sun, the gothic greatness of its features, and its mouldering dark grey stone, rendered it a gloomy and sublime object, gazed, the light died away on its walls, leaving a melancholy purple tint, which spread deeper and deeper, as the thin vapour crept up the mountain, while the battlements above were still tipped with splendour. From those too, the rays soon faded, and the whole edifice was invested with the solemn duskiness of evening. Silent, lonely and sublime, it seemed to stand the sovereign of the scene, and to frown defiance on all, who dared to invade its solitary reign. As the twilight deepened, its features became more awful in obscurity, and Emily continued to gaze, till its clustering towers were alone seen, rising over the tops of the woods, beneath whose thick shade the carriages soon after began to ascend.[1]

Radcliffe's last gothic romance, *The Italian: Or the Confessional of the Black Penitents,* is also the last of the great gothic novels, some say the best, responding to *The Monk* just as that novel responded

---

[1]Quoted from the four-volume edition published in London by G. G. and J. Robinson, 1794, Vol II, Chapter 5.

to *The Mysteries of Udolpho*. The villain, Schedoni, an evil monk, is victimized by his past, by the conflict between his instincts and his actions, and by his superhuman ambitions and his mortal limitations—a character reminiscent of Milton's Satan, reflecting the popular view of Napoleon, anticipating Byron's villain-heroes, and invading the dreams and fantasies of British audiences through many afterlives in the popular stage adaptations of gothic melodrama. In *The Italian Monk* (1798), for example, James Boaden set Schedoni to music and ended with his redemption in the obligatory penitential scene with which melodramas end.

from *The Italian*

There lived in the Dominican convent of the Spirito Santo, at Naples, a man called father Schedoni, an Italian, as his name imported, but whose family was unknown, and from some circumstances, it appeared, what he wished to throw an impenetrable veil over his origin. For whatever reason, he was never heard to mention a relative, or the place of his nativity, and he had artfully eluded every enquiry that approached the subject, which the curiosity of his associates had occasionally prompted. There were circumstances, however, which appeared to indicate him to be a man of birth, and of fallen fortune; his spirit, as it had sometimes looked forth from under the disguise of his manners, seemed lofty; it showed not, however, the aspirings of a generous mind, but rather the gloomy pride of a disappointed one. Some few persons in the convent, who had been interested by his appearance, believed that the peculiarities of his manners, his severe reserve and unconquerable silence, his solitary habits and frequent penances, were the effect of misfortunes preying upon a haughty and disordered spirit; while others conjectured them the consequence of some hideous crime gnawing upon an awakened conscience.

He would sometimes abstract himself from the society for whole days together, or when with such a disposition he was compelled to mingle with it, he seemed unconscious where he was, and continued shrouded in meditation and silence till he was again alone. There were times when it was unknown whither he had retired, notwithstanding that his steps had been watched, and his customary haunts examined. No one ever heard him complain. The elder brothers of the convent said that he had talents, but denied him learning; they applauded him for the profound subtlety which he occasionally discovered in argument, but observed that he seldom perceived truth when it lay on the surface; he could follow it through all the labyrinths of disquisition, but overlooked it, when it was undisguised before him. In fact he cared not for truth, nor sought it by bold and broad argument, but loved to exert the wily cunning of his nature in hunting it through artificial perplexities. At length, from a habit of intricacy and suspicion, his vitiated mind could receive nothing for truth, which was simple and easily comprehended.

Among his associates no one loved him, many disliked him, and more feared him. His figure was striking, but not so from grace; it was tall, and, though extremely thin, his limbs were large and uncouth, and as he stalked along, wrapt in the black garments of his order, there was something terrible in its air; something almost super-human. His cowl, too, as it threw a shade over the livid paleness of his face, encreased its severe character, and gave an effect to his large melancholy eye, which approached to horror. His was not the melancholy of a sensible and wounded heart, but apparently that of a gloomy and ferocious disposition. There was something in his physiognomy extremely singular, and that can not easily be defined. It bore the traces of many passions, which seemed to have fixed the features they no longer animated. An habitual gloom and severity prevailed over the deep lines of his countenance; and his eyes were so piercing that they seemed to penetrate, at a single glance, into the hearts of men, and to read their most secret thoughts; few persons could support their scrutiny, or even endure to meet them twice. Yet, notwithstanding all this gloom and austerity, some rare occasions of interest had called forth a character upon his countenance entirely different; and he could adapt himself to the tempers and passions of persons, whom he wished to conciliate, with astonishing facility, and generally with complete triumph.

Gothic Decline
and Gothic Parody

Gothic Decline

Between Ann Radcliffe's *The Italian* (1797) and Mary Shelley's *Frankenstein* (1818), between the conception of *Northanger Abbey* and its publication, no significant new gothic novels appear, first, because the form was exhausted, the public overwhelmed with "ghosts, goblins, and skeletons . . . till even the devil himself . . . became too base, common, and popular for its surfeited appetite," as Thomas Love Peacock says in *Nightmare Abbey* (Everyman Edition [1910] 179). Secondly, gothic romances migrated to the stage where they became the action movies of the 1790's, inducing that collective experience of terror that is missing from reading novels even aloud in groups. Radcliffe and Lewis, whose *Castle Spectre* was written for the stage (1797), found a new audience among the illiterate or semi-literate working classes who could not afford to buy the novels but who delighted in images of a suffering, deprived, helpless, and corrupt aristocracy and clergy, heroes or villains, all answering to ultimate powers that had no interest in their titles or fashions.

Adapting tricks and themes from *The Monk* and *Vathek,* in 1798, the year they were published as novels, George Colman the Younger produced *Blue-Beard; or Female Curiosity*, a spectacle of oriental pageantry, live animals, and visual drama. Both contemporary and timeless, it introduced an archetypal motif: a tomb with a huge skeleton under the inscription "The Punishment of Curiosity." Supposedly, Jane Austen attended an intimate production of *Blue-Beard* in the small Orchard Street theater in Bath in 1799.

Third, the gothic romance found a new home in serials appearing next to fashions, recipes, and domestic advice in magazines such as the *Lady's Monthly Museum* and the *Lady's Magazine*, or even in six-penny chap-book condensations. Finally, however, for those twenty years, the gothic horror of real life overcame the artificial terror on which the novels depended. King George III was mad, blind, and sequestered in Windsor Castle conversing with the dead while his children, their friends and mistresses, amused themselves with gambling, gluttony, public adulteries, pet monkeys, tropical gardens, and exotic architecture. For this ruling class, the army and navy were ornamental, an excuse for elaborate uniforms and imaginary heroic pasts, or, like the Duke of York's mistress, exchanging military commissions for bribes and sexual favors.

While the aristocracy and some clergy enjoyed the personal liberties of a gothic villain, dramatists were prohibited by law from presenting them on the stage, while journalists and publishers were imprisoned, sometimes without trial, for protesting their loss of freedom, or the hunger and deprivations of the working classes. As the war escalated, so did domestic crime and poverty among the lower classes: discharged soldiers, wounded and deranged, criminals, vagrants, widows and abandoned children brought misery to the public roads, the very roads on which Catherine was sent home alone in a rented carriage. Excluded from villages by discriminatory "poor" laws, dispossessed by enclosures, displaced by machinery, they could be hanged for stealing a turnip. For every Northanger Abbey, a hobby for the idle rich, there was a Ruined Cottage, a monument to neglect and despair.

Even the new sciences had gothic dimensions: human beings became victims of nature, born into an expanded universe of infinite histories and spaces, an earth that catastrophic geology depicted as a multi-layered ruin—a more sublime scene than any novelist could produce. Gas, steam, and electricity that powered and moved the inanimate world enslaved the people who discovered and applied them. Galvanism made corpses smile, mesmerism made live people look dead, and Jeremy Bentham, one of the greatest philosophical minds of his generation, spent most of his lifetime perfecting that image of gothic punishment, the perfect prison. Manchester and Birmingham, the most advanced industrial cities in the world, lay under such a pall of smoke that Gustave Doré used them to illustrate the sublime terrors of Dante's *Inferno*. The practice of medicine was so demonized that some accused medical schools of starting epidemics to replenish their supply of patients and of corpses, which were regularly robbed from their new graves. In this context of genuine horror, suffering, danger, and the seclusion of the ruling classes, the gossip, betrayals, and injustices, Tilney's admonition to Catherine serves as a chilling reminder of the political environment in which the novel was written, and in which it was being read:

> Remember the country and the age in which we live. Remember that we are English, that we are Christians. Consult your own understanding, your own sense of the probable, your own observation of what is passing around you—Does our education prepare us for such atrocities? Do our laws connive at them? Could they be perpetrated without being known, in a country like this, where social and literary intercourse is on such a footing; where every man is surrounded by a neighbourhood of voluntary spies . . . ? (p. 157)

In the years of war and recovery, everyone was a gothic victim and Catherine, everyone, had a great deal to fear.

Gothic Parody

Victims, the helpless and hopeless, take comfort in parody; it is the last and sometimes only weapon against arbitrary power and overwhelming odds. Essentially, parody is caricature, imitation, exaggerated, simplified, and juxtaposed often with whatever might be considered normal. On stage, in books, magazines, newspapers, and cartoons, parodies became as fashionable as the gothic novels they often ridiculed.

Thomas Love Peacock (1785–1866)

Published in 1818, the same year as Northanger Abbey, *Peacock's* Nightmare Abbey *addresses the same audience as Wordsworth, Scott, and Austen, with the same goal: "To reconcile man as he is to the world as it is," as Mr. Hilary says in* Nightmare Abbey. *He blames contemporary despair and frustration on the writers and philosophers themselves who created the false ideals that then betrayed them: "To rail against humanity for not being abstract perfection, and against human love for not realizing all the splendid visions of the poets of chivalry, is to rail at the summer for not being all sunshine, and at the rose for not being always in bloom."* Like Northanger Abbey, *however,* Nightmare Abbey *is more than a parody or a message; it is clever, entertaining, and, in the caricatures of writers, all of whom Peacock knew and influenced, a critique of contemporary literature.*

The setting is the Abbey. Mr. Glowry and his son, Scythrop (who resembles Peacock's friend, Shelley) entertain an assortment of guests who make up the complex conversation of the novel: Mr. Flossky (Coleridge), a "lachrymose and morbid gentleman" who "lived in the midst of that visionary world in which nothing is but what is not" and who is truly indecipherable; Mr. Toobad, "the Manichaean Millenarian" who believed that the world "had been given over for awhile to the Evil Principle"; the Reverend Mr. Larynx, the vicar of Claydyke, a "good-natured accommodating divine" who had no opinions of his own; the Honourable Mr. Listless, an exhausted "dandy" and his ridiculous French butler, Fatout; the "merry-hearted" cousin Marionetta Celestina O'Carroll, whom Scythrop terrifies by proposing that they drink each other's blood; Celinda Toobad, who has run away from her father to escape a bad marriage and ends up at the Abbey anyway; and Mr. Asterias, the ichthyologist, whose goal in life is to find a mermaid. The following passage is from the opening chapter.

from Nightmare Abbey[1]

Nightmare Abbey, a venerable family-mansion, in a highly picturesque state of semi-dilapidation, pleasantly situated on a strip of dry land between the sea and the fens at the verge of the county of Lincoln, had the honour to be the seat of Christopher Glowry, Esquire. This gentleman was naturally of an atrabilarious temperament, and much troubled with those phantoms of indigestion which are commonly called *blue devils.* He had been deceived in an early friendship: he had been crossed in love; and had offered his hand, from pique, to a lady, who accepted it from interest, and who, in so doing, violently tore asunder the bonds of a tried and youthful attachment. Her vanity was gratified by being the mistress of a very

[1]Bentley's Standard Authors (London: 1837), Volume LVII.

extensive, if not very lively establishment; but all the springs of her sympathies were frozen. Riches she possessed, but that which enriches them, the participation of affection, was wanting. All that they could purchase for her became indifferent to her, because that which they could not purchase, and which was more valuable than themselves, she had, for their sake, thrown away. She discovered, when it was too late, that she had mistaken the means for the end—that riches, rightly used, are instruments of happiness, but are not in themselves happiness. In this wilful blight of her affections, she found them valueless as means: they had been the end to which she had immolated all her affections, and were now the only end that remained to her. She did not confess this to herself as a principle of action, but it operated through the medium of unconscious self-deception, and terminated in inveterate avarice. She laid on external things the blame of her mind's internal disorder, and thus became by degrees an accomplished scold. She often went her daily rounds through a series of deserted apartments, every creature in the house vanishing at the creak of her shoe, much more at the sound of her voice, to which the nature of things affords no simile; for, as far as the voice of woman, when attuned by gentleness and love, transcends all other sounds in harmony, so far does it surpass all others in discord when stretched into unnatural shrillness by anger and impatience.

Mr. Glowry used to say that his house was no better than a spacious kennel, for every one in it led the life of a dog. Disappointed both in love and in friendship, and looking upon human learning as vanity, he had come to a conclusion that there was but one good thing in the world, *videlicet*, a good dinner; and this his parsimonious lady seldom suffered him to enjoy: but one morning, like Sir Leoline, in "Christabel," "he woke and found his lady dead," and remained a very consolate widower, with one small child.

This only son and heir Mr. Glowry had christened Scythrop, from the name of a maternal ancestor, who had hanged himself one rainy day in a fit of *tædium vitæ*, and had been eulogized by a coroner's jury in the comprehensive phrase of *felo de se*; on which account Mr. Glowry held his memory in high honour, and made a punchbowl of his scull.

When Scythrop gew up, he was sent, as usual, to a public school, where a little learning was painfully beaten into him, and thence to the University, where it was carefully taken out of him;

and he was sent home, like a well-threshed ear of corn, with nothing in his head: having finished his education to the high satisfaction of the master and fellows of his college, who had, in testimony of their approbation, presented him with a silver fish-slice, on which his name figured at the head of a laudatory inscription in some semi-barbarous dialect of Anglo-Saxonized Latin.

His fellow-students, however, who drove tandem and random in great perfection, and were connoisseurs in good inns, had taught him to drink deep ere he departed. He had passed much of his time with these choice spirits, and had seen the rays of the midnight lamp tremble on many a lengthening file of empty bottles. He passed his vacations sometimes in Nightmare Abbey, sometimes in London, at the house of his uncle, Mr. Hilary, a very cheerful and elastic gentleman, who had married the sister of the melancholy Mr. Glowry. The company that frequented his house was the gayest of the gay. Scythrop danced with the ladies and drank with the gentlemen, and was pronounced by both a very accomplished, charming fellow and an honour to the university.

At the house of Mr. Hilary, Scythrop first saw the beautiful Miss Emily Girouette. He fell in love; which is nothing new. He was favourably received; which is nothing strange. Mr. Glowry and Mr. Girouette had a meeting on the occasion, and quarrelled about the terms of the bargain; which is neither new nor strange. The lovers were torn asunder, weeping and vowing everlasting constancy; and, in three weeks after this tragical event, the lady was led a smiling bride to the altar, by the Honourable Mr. Lackwit; which is neither strange nor new.

Scythrop received this intelligence at Nightmare Abbey, and was half distracted on the occasion. It was his first disappointment, and preyed deeply on his sensitive spirit. His father, to comfort him, read him a Commentary on Ecclesiastes, which he had himself composed, and which demonstrated incontrovertibly that all is vanity. He insisted particularly on the text, "One man among a thousand have I found, but a woman amongst all those have I not found."

"How would he expect it," said Scythrop, "when the whole thousand were locked up in his seraglio? His experience is no precedent for a free state of society like that in which we live."

"Locked up or at large," said Mr. Glowry, "the result is the same: their minds are always locked up, and vanity and interest keep the key. I speak feelingly, Scythrop."

Illustration of a Dandy

Robert Dighton, "Portrait of George 'Beau' Brummell" (1778–1849), 1805 (water-color on paper).

"I am sorry for it, sir," said Scythrop. "But how is it that their minds are locked up? The fault is in their artiificial education, which studiously models them into mere musical dolls, to be set out for sale in the great toy-shop of society."

"To be sure," said Mr. Glowry, "their education is not so well finished as yours has been; and your idea of a musical doll is good. I bought one myself, but it was confoundedly out of tune; but, whatever be the cause, Scythrop, the effect is certainly this, that one is pretty nearly as good as another, as far as any judgment can be formed of them before marriage. It is only after marriage that they show their true qualities, as I know by bitter experience. Marriage is, therefore, a lottery, and the less choice and selection a man bestows on his ticket the better; for if he has incurred considerable pains and expense to obtain a lucky number, and his lucky number proves a blank, he experiences not a simple, but a complicated disappointment; the loss of labour and money being superadded to the disappointment of drawing a blank, which, constituting simply and entirely the grievance of him who has chosen his ticket at random, is, from its simplicity, the more endurable." This very excellent reasoning was thrown away upon Scythrop, who retired to his tower as dismal and disconsolate as before.

The tower which Scythrop inhabited stood at the south-eastern angle of the Abbey; and, on the southern side, the foot of the tower opened on a terrace, which was called the garden, though nothing grew on it but ivy, and a few amphibious weeds. The south-western tower, which was ruinous and full of owls, might, with equal propriety, have been called the aviary. This terrace or garden, or terrace-garden, or garden-terrace (the reader may name it *ad libitum*), took in an oblique view of the open sea, and fronted a long tract of level sea-coast, and a fine monotony of fens and windmills.

The reader will judge, from what we have said, that this building was a sort of castellated abbey; and it will, probably, occur to him to inquire if it had been one of the strongholds of the ancient church militant. Whether this was the case, or how far it had been indebted to the taste of Mr. Glowry's ancestors for any transmutations from its original state, are, unfortunately, circumstances not within the pale of our knowledge.

The north-western tower contained the apartments of Mr. Glowry. The moat at its base, and the fens beyond, comprised the whole of his prospect. The moat surrounded the Abbey, and was in immediate contact with the walls on every side but the south.

The north-eastern tower was appropriated to the domestics, whom Mr. Glowry always chose by one of two criterions,—a long face or a dismal name. His butler was Raven; his steward was Crow; his valet was Skellet. Mr. Glowry maintained that the valet was of French extraction, and that his name was Squelette. His grooms were Mattocks and Graves. On one occasion, being in want of a footman, he receivd a letter from a person signing himself Diggory Deathshead, and lost no time in securing his acquisition; but on Diggory's arrival, Mr. Glowry was horror-struck by the sight of a round ruddy face, and a pair of laughing eyes. Deathshead was always grinning—not a ghastly smile, but the grin of a comic mask; and disturbed the echoes of the hall with so much unhallowed laughter, that Mr. Glowry gave him his discharge. Diggory, however, had stayed long enough to make conquests of all the old gentleman's maids, and left him a flourishing colony of young Deathsheads to join chorus with the owls, that had before been the exclusive choristers of Nightmare Abbey.

The main body of the building was divided into rooms of state, spacious apartments for feasting, and numerous bedrooms for visitors, who, however, were few and far between.

Family interests compelled Mr. Glowry to receive occasional visits from Mr. and Mrs. Hilary, who paid them from the same motive, and, as the lively gentleman on these occasions found few conductors for his exuberant gaiety, he became like a double-charged electric jar, which often exploded in some burst of outragious merriment to the signal discomposure of Mr. Glowry's nerves.

Another occasional visitor, much more to Mr. Glowry's taste, was Mr. Flosky,[2] a very lachrymose and morbid gentleman, of some note in the literary world, but in his own estimation of much more merit than name. The part of his character which recommended him to Mr. Glowry, was his very fine sense of the grim and the tearful. No one could relate a dismal story with so many minutiæ of supererogatory wretchedness. No one could call up a *raw head* and *bloody bones* with so many adjuncts and circumstances of ghastliness. Mystery was his mental element. He lived in the midst of that visionary world in which nothing is but what

---

[2] A corruption of Filosky, quasi a lover, or sectator, of shadows.

is not. He dreamed with his eyes open, and saw ghosts dancing round him at noon-tide. He had been in his youth an enthusiast for liberty, and had hailed the dawn of the French Revolution as the promise of a day that was to banish war and slavery, and every form of vice and misery, from the face of the earth. Because all this was not done, he deduced that nothing was done; and from this deduction, according to his system of logic, he drew a conclusion that worse than nothing was done; that the overthrow of the feudal fortresses of tyranny and superstition was the greatest calamity that had ever befallen mankind; and that their only hope now was to rake the rubbish together, and rebuild it without any of those loopholes by which the light had originally crept in. To qualify himself for a coadjutor in this laudable task, he plunged into the central opacity of Kantian metaphysics, and lay *perdu* several years in transcendental darkness, till the common daylight of common sense became intolerable to his eyes. He called the sun an *ignis fatuus*; and exhorted all who would listen to his friendly voice, which were about as many as called "God save King Richard," to shelter themselves from its delusive radiance in the obscure haunt of Old Philosophy. This word Old had great charms for him. The good old times were always on his lips; meaning the days when polemic theology was in its prime, and rival prelates beat the drum ecclesiastic with Herculean vigour, till the one wound up his series of syllogisms with the very orthodox conclusion of roasting the other.

But the dearest friend of Mr. Glowry, and his most welcome guest, was Mr. Toobad, the Manichæan Millenarian. The twelfth verse of the twelfth chapter of Revelations was always in his mouth: "Woe to the inhabiters of the earth and of the sea! for the devil is come among you, having great wrath, because he knoweth that he hath but a short time." He maintained that the supreme dominion of the world was, for wise purposes, given over for a while to the Evil Principle; and that this precise period of time, commonly called the enlightened age, was the point of his plenitude of power. He used to add that by-and-by he would be cast down, and a high and happy order of things succeed; but he never omitted the saving clause, "Not in our time:" which last words were always echoed in doleful response by the sympathetic Mr. Glowry.

The GRACES in a high Wind. — a scene taken from Nature, in Kensington Gardens;

Three Graces in a High Wind, James Gillray, 1810.

Another and very frequent visitor, was the Reverend Mr. Larynx, the vicar of Claydyke, a village about ten miles distant;—a good-natured accommodating divine, who was always most obligingly ready to take a dinner and a bed at the house of any country gentleman in distress for a companion. Nothing came amiss to him,—a game at billiards, at chess, at draughts, at backgammon, at piquet, or at all-fours in a *tête-à-tête*,—or any game on the cards, round, square, or triangular, in a party of any number exceeding two. He would even dance among friends, rather than that a lady, even if she were on the wrong side of thirty, should sit still for want of a partner. For a ride, a walk, or a sail, in the morning,—a song after dinner, a ghost story after supper,—a bottle of port with the squire, or a cup of green tea with his lady,—for all or any of these, or for anything else that was agreeable to any one else, consistently with the dye of his coat, the Reverend Mr. Larynx was at all times equally ready. When at Nightmare Abbey, he would condole with Mr. Glowry,—drink Madeira with Scythrop,—crack jokes with Mr. Hilary,—hand Mrs. Hilary to the piano, take charge of her fan and gloves, and turn over her music with surprising dexterity,—quote Revelations with Mr. Toobad,—and lament the good old times of feudal darkness with the transcendental Mr. Flosky.

Bath
"Faery lands forlorn"

While Samuel Johnson couldn't imagine who could get tired of London, Catherine Morland naïvely wondered, "who can ever be tired of Bath," and the more sensible Anne Elliot in *Persuasion* "persisted in a very determined disinclination for it." Jane Austen visited Bath with her mother in 1797, again in 1799 with her brother Edward, who was ill, his wife, and two of their five children. In 1801, after her father retired as Rector at Steventon, they moved to Bath, as many elderly people did. She left without remorse a year after her father died of fever in 1805.

More than half of *Northanger Abbey* is set in Bath. Considered, after London, the most beautiful city in England, Bath was nestled in a western valley, surrounded by hills and downs, in a damp and rainy part of the country, awash in mud most of the year, fetid in the summer, icy in the winter, a place as full of contradictions as the age itself, the best and worst of it: ancient pagan superstition survived along with bizarre forms of Christian revivalism, scientific speculation, and a social experiment that went terribly wrong. A "rendezvous of the diseased," as Tobias Smollett called it in *Humphry Clinker* (1771), "a national hospital [where] none but lunatics are admitted," where people died of fevers from the waters that were supposed to save them and caught the sexual diseases they had gone there to cure—as R. S. Neale points out in his indispensable *Bath 1680–1850* (1981), with the revealing subtitle: *A Valley of Pleasure Yet a Sink of Iniquity*.

The history of Bath is rich with legend and superstition. The Celts founded Bath in 700 B.C. and dedicated the sacred springs to Sul, the sun goddess. After 43 A.D., the Romans turned them into a spa called Sul Minerva, in honor of both cultures. Tracing the springs to 10,000 B.C., geologists believe they have been spouting water at a constant temperature of 120 degrees ever since, acquiring over the centuries a reputation for treating infertility, joint pain, gout, and skin disorders. Bath became a Christian center first in 676 with a convent, then a church in 757, and then, after burning and rebuilding several times, completed as one of the last great Cathedrals in 1572. Even with the religious fervor of the Middle Ages, however, Bath remained a center for erotic and commercial activity, famous for producing lace, wool, and Chaucer's Wife of Bath. After Queen Elizabeth passed a statute authorizing free use of the waters by the poor and diseased, Bath attracted encampments of beggars, vagrants, prostitutes, and thieves, who dominated the landscape through the eighteenth century.

Re-discovered by Richard "Beau" Nash in 1702, Bath became a social center again, a remarkable mix of the elderly, sick, and dying, the infertile and the insane: young men and women looking for pleasure, romance, or mates; criminals, imposters, and eccentrics looking for money and social connections; and an odd assortment of creative intellectuals, religious fanatics, and natural historians. Nash introduced street lighting, night-watches, regulated bathing, dancing, gambling, drinking, fashion, and instituted a code of manners that included strictures against gossip and against swords and dueling. His eleven requirements posted in the Pump Room reveal the raucous atmosphere he was trying to control.

1. That a visit of ceremony at first coming, and another at going away, are all that are expected or desired by ladies of quality and fashion—except impertinents.
2. That ladies coming to the ball appoint a time for their footmen coming to wait on them home, to prevent disturbance and inconvenience to themselves and others.
3. That gentlemen of fashion never appear in a morning before the ladies in gowns and caps, show breeding and respect.
4. That no person take it ill that anyone goes to another's play or breakfast and not theirs; except captious by nature.
5. That no gentleman give his ticket for the balls to any but gentlewomen. N.B.—Unless he has none of his acquaintance.

6. That gentlemen crowding before the ladies at the ball show ill manners; and that none do so for the future except such as respect nobody but themselves.
7. That no gentleman or lady takes it ill that another dances before them—except such as have no pretence to dance at all.
8. That the elder ladies and children be content with a second bench at a ball, as being past or not come to perfection.
9. That the younger ladies take notice how many eyes observe them.
10. That all whisperers of lies or scandal be taken for their authors.
11. That all repeaters of such lies and scandal be shunned by all company; except such as have been guilty of the same crime. N.B.—Several men of no character, old women and young ones of questioned reputation, are great authors of lies in these places. . . .

In spite of the pettiness, gossip, envy, and potential violence, Bath attracted crowds of people for the performance, the display of possessions, the conspicuous leisure, therapeutic benefits, courtship rituals, or the opportunities to live off others' false hopes and naïve expectations. By the end of the eighteenth century, Bath had also become a political and intellectual center, with an excellent grammar school, a Philosophical Society, Royal Theater, circulating libraries, book sellers, and trade in obscene literature. Inevitably, Bath attracted Christian revivalists such as John Wesley and George Whitfield, who found the city in dire need of redemption. It was a last resort for the aged and terminally ill who came to die and a first hope for parents of sick children such as the young Edward Gibbon, Samuel Johnson, Sir Walter Scott, Robert Southey, and De Quincey, whose widowed mother moved there, changed her name, and like so many started a new life.

In 1791, excavations for the new houses and canals revealed the Roman remains, some statuary and mosaics that showed the erotic, recreational, and therapeutic uses which the baths had once and still served. This subterranean history, like the geological strata that William Smith discovered, placed the social life of Bath in perspective: against the huge tracts of time, the quality of muslin, the size of one's carriage, the cost of fish became trivial, the very essence of satire. Bath, then, with all its absurdities and

A Spill on the Slopes
Thomas Rowlandson (1756–1827), "The Bath Races," plate 12, *Comforts of Bath*, 1798 (watercolor on paper).

illusions was a satire waiting for an author. In Christopher Anstey's *New Bath Guide* (1766, first of eleven editions), Simkin Blunderhead visiting Bath with his sister Prudence, cousin Jenny, and their maid Tabitha Runt, describes, in verse, the physicians, Methodist preachers, and pretenders of all sorts, including himself. Cultivating his celebrity, Anstey lived in Bath from 1770 to 1805, his style and characters influencing Tobias Smollett's *The Expedition of Humphry Clinker* (1771) and dozens of ephemeral productions, all epistolary in style, innocent in perspective, and satirical in tone. Thomas Brown's *Bath: A Satirical Novel with Portraits* and Pierce Egan's *Walks Through Bath* both appeared in 1818, the same year as *Northanger Abbey*.

By the 1790's, when Jane Austen visited, the wealthy had begun to migrate to seaside resorts such as Brighton, and Bath was socially in decline. Architecturally, however, it was at its peak: everywhere, new buildings, new addresses, and, in the transient world of the sick and the pleasure-seekers, new neighbors all the time. While the population had expanded from 3,000 in 1699 to

34,000 in 1799, it had also shifted from an aristocracy seeking recreation among their own kind, to a new affluent class of uneducated merchants and manufacturers who had the money to pay for the architectural revival, and the middle classes and social predators who rented from them. Status shifted from birth and blood to possessions and style. Anyone with the right clothes, manners, and a good address found a place in the assembly halls, the pump rooms, the streets, shops, coffee houses, dances, and card games. When gambling was forbidden in public, the rich held private parties in their homes while only the disreputable or the socially unconnected such as the Thorpes, Mrs. Allen, and Catherine in *Northanger Abbey* would go to the Pump Room, where "not a genteel face [was] to be seen."

With no real productivity, the economy was based on service and consumption, an array of people who cleaned houses, streets, and shoes, who cooked and served food, the fishmongers, butchers, and peddlers who delivered it and took away the garbage, the dressmakers, hairdressers, shopkeepers of every sort (about which Mrs. Allen comments to Tilney), the musicians, clergy, and muscle-men who carried the sedan chairs or hauled huge stones from the quarries up the hills for the new terraced houses, the construction workers and furniture makers, coal-men and chimney sweeps, the undertakers and physicians, some of them celebrities: Dr. Parry, who treated Jane Austen's friends for gout with a "Lowering system," a regimen of bread and meat, blood-letting, exercise, and drinking the "waters," in 1814 tended Coleridge through the worst drug overdose of his life and the suicidal anguish that followed. Jane's brother Edward was "tied down" to Dr. Fellowes, Physician Extraordinary to the Prince of Wales, whereas she preferred Dr. Mapleton—"not a Physician in the place who writes so many prescriptions as he does," as "everybody" knows—an apothecary concluded that Edward's fever came from something he ate, while the "occasional particular glow in the hands & feet," a symptom of gout, "he only calls the effect of the Water in promoting a better circulation of the blood" (Letter, June 19, 1999).

While air and exercise were part of the cure, walking was unpleasant: animal droppings everywhere, prostitutes, beggars and thieves, open sewers where chamber pots were emptied, rotting garbage, and heaps of mud from the constant construction. In

Taking the Waters
Thomas Rowlandson (1756–1827), "The King's Bath," plate 7, *Comforts of Bath*, 1798 (hand-coloured engraving).

Northanger Abbey, after a rainstorm, Isabella complains: "I never saw so much dirt in my life. Walk! You could no more walk than you could fly! It has not been so dirty the whole winter; it is ankle deep everywhere." The steeply sloping streets were slippery and windy, a favorite image for cartoons of Bath.

"Taking the Waters" was also a demanding and unpleasant ritual. Dressed in billowing yellow canvas bathing-clothes distributed at the bath, men and women, children and the aged, bobbed around together, observed by a gallery of spectators and an officer of the bath whose job it was to preserve order. After the bath, exhausted by the heat, they were wrapped in flannel, carried through the cold streets in sedan chairs to the Pump Rooms, where an orchestra played while they drank more water or, if they were well enough, gambled and gossiped before moving on to the public gardens for breakfast. Dinner was at three, then the Pump Room again or a coffee house, and then the Assembly Halls for dancing or the theater. So long as guests didn't injure themselves or anyone else, formalities, manners, and social rituals were all relaxed and improvisational.

Ironically, while Jane Austen satirized almost every aspect of Bath and was glad to escape, she is now enshrined there in the Jane Austen Center, which boasts, rightfully, that most of the buildings in her novels, in spite of the destructive bombing in World War II, have been restored, scrubbed clean, and the city itself, "the elegant well-ordered world" of her novels, according to the Center's website, is "still very much as Jane Austen knew it."

Tobias Smollett (1721–1771)

After publishing two novels, Roderick Random *(1748) and* Peregrine Pickle *(1751), and earning a medical degree in 1750, Tobias Smollett came to Bath to be a surgeon. Alienating both colleagues and potential patients with an essay on the dangerous waters, he left, returning twice, nonetheless, to take the cure himself.* Humphry Clinker *(1771), is an epistolary novel consisting of letters by Matthew Bramble, his sister Tabitha, his niece Lydia, his nephew Jery, and their semi-literate servant, Winifred Jenkins, describing the same events and scenes from different perspectives as they travel around England visiting spas to restore Matthew's health. Arriving in Bath after thirty years, Bramble (Smollett's fictional voice) writes in the letter of April 23 to Dr. Lewis that he finds "nothing but disappointment": the streets are "mean, dirty, dangerous, and indirect, crowded with carriages, sedan-chairs, horses, grooms, shouting, colliding, tipping here and there." The Circus, at the heart of the new town, is at too "great a distance from all the markets, baths and places of public entertainment. The only entrance to it, through Gay-Street, is so difficult, steep and slippery, that in wet weather, it must be exceedingly dangerous, both for those that ride in carriages, and those that walk a-foot; and when the street is covered with snow, as it was for fifteen days successively this very winter, I don't see how any individual could go either up or down, without the most imminent hazard of broken bones." He complains about the damp leather inside the sedan chairs, the unsteady footmen who carry them, and their double-duty in the morning taking the sick home from the baths, sometimes accidentally spilling them out on the street, and carrying the ladies (such as Catherine and Mrs. Allen) to the balls at night.*

A Visit from the Doctor
Thomas Rowlandson (1756–1827), "The Doctors," plate 1, *Comforts of Bath*, 1798 (hand-coloured engraving).

from *The Expedition of Humphry Clinker*[1]

Moving up to what will be the Crescent, along which Catherine and Eleanor walk in *Northanger Abbey*, Bramble writes:

> . . . when that is finished, we shall probably have a Star; and those who are living thirty years hence may, perhaps, see all the signs of the Zodiac exhibited in architecture at Bath. These, however fantastical, are still designs that denote some ingenuity and knowledge in the architect; but the rage of building has laid hold on such a number of adventurers, that one sees new houses starting up in every out-let and every corner of Bath; contrived without judgment, executed without solidity, and stuck together with so little regard to plan and propriety, that the different lines of the new rows and buildings interfere with, and intersect one another in every different angle of conjunction.

[1]*The Expedition of Humphry Clinker* (London: 1831).

They look like the wreck of streets and squares disjointed by an earthquake, which hath broken the ground into a variety of holes and hillocks; or as if some Gothic devil had stuffed them altogether in a bag, and left them to stand higgedly piggedly, just as chance directed. What sort of a monster Bath will become in a few years, with those growing excrescences, may be easily conceived: but the want of beauty and proportion is not the worst effect of these new mansions; they are built so slight, with the soft crumbling stone found in this neighbourhood, that I shall never sleep quietly in one of them, when it blowed (as the sailors say) a cap-full of wind; and, I am persuaded, that my hind, Roger Williams, or any man of equal strength, would be able to push his foot through the strongest part of their walls, without any great exertion of his muscles.

The people are as objectionable as the architecture, the same ones who will fill the Assembly halls in *Northanger Abbey*:

All these absurdities arise from the general tide of luxury, which hath overspread the nation, and swept away all, even the very dregs of the people. Every upstart of fortune, harnessed in the trappings of the mode, presents himself at Bath, as in the very focus of observation—Clerks and factors from the East Indies, loaded with the spoil of plundered provinces; planters, negro-drivers, and hucksters, from our American plantations, enriched they know not how; agents, commissaries, and contractors, who have fattened, in two successive wars, on the blood of the nation; usurers, brokers, and jobbers of every kind; men of low birth, and no breeding, have found themselves suddenly translated into a state of affluence, unknown to former ages; and no wonder that their brains should be intoxicated with pride, vanity, and pre-sumption. Knowing no other criterion of greatness, but the osten-tation of wealth, they discharge their affluence without taste or conduct, through every channel of the most absurd extravagance; and all of them hurry to Bath, because here, without any further qualification, they can mingle with the princes and the nobles of the land. Even the wives and daughters of low tradesmen, who, like shovel-nosed sharks, prey upon the blubber of those uncouth whales of fortune, are infected with the same rage of displaying their importance; and the slightest indisposition serves them for a pretext to insist upon being conveyed to Bath, where they may hobble country-dances and cotillions among lordlings, squires, counselors, and clergy. These delicate creatures from Bedford-bury, Butcher-row, Crutched-friers, and Botolph-lane, cannot breathe in the gross air of the Lower Town, or conform to the vulgar rules of a common lodging-house; the husband, therefore, must provide an entire house, or elegant apartments in the new buildings. Such is the composition of what is called the fashionable company at Bath; where a very inconsiderable proportion of genteel people are lost in a mob of impudent plebeians, who have neither understanding nor judgment, nor the least idea of propriety and decorum; and seem to enjoy nothing so much as an opportunity of insulting their betters. . . .

. . . This, I own, is a subject on which I cannot write with any degree of patience; for the mob is a monster I never could abide, either in its head, tail, midriff or members; I detest the whole of it, as a mass of ignorance, presumption, malice, and brutality; and, in this term of reprobation, I include, without respect of rank, station, or quality all those of both sexes, who affect its manners, and court its society.

As for the baths, at least a hundred years before germ theory, Smollett recognized that the water was a medium for spreading the diseases it was supposed to cure and that many of the doctors were charlatans and predators. On April 28, Bramble writes:

I have done with the waters. . . . Two days ago I went into the King's Bath by the advice of our friend . . . , in order to clear the strainer of the skin, for the benefit of a free perspiration; and the first object that saluted my eye, was a child full of scrophulous ulcers, carried in the arms of one of the guides, under the very noses of the bathers. I was so shocked at the sight that I retired immediately with indignation and disgust—Suppose the matter of those ulcers, floating on the water, comes in contact with my skin, when the pores are all open, I would ask you what must be the consequence?—Good Heaven, the very thought makes my blood run cold! We know not what sores may be running into the water while we are bathing, and what sort of matter we may thus

A Ball in the Assembly Rooms
Thomas Rowlandson (1756–1827), "An Assembly Ball," plate 10, *Comforts of Bath*, 1798 (hand-coloured engraving).

imbibe; the king's-evil [scrofula, swollen lymph glands], the scurvy, the cancer, and the pox; and, no doubt, the heat will render the virus the more volatile and penetrating. . . .

But I am now as much afraid of drinking, as of bathing; for after a long conversation with the Doctor, about the construction of the Pump and the cistern, it is very far from being clear to me, that the patients in the Pump Room don't swallow the scourings of the bathers. I can't help suspecting, that there is, or may be, some regurgitation from the bath into the cistern of the pump. In that case, what a delicate beverage is every day quaffed by the drinkers; medicated with the sweat and dirt, and dandruff; and the abominable discharges of various kinds, from twenty different diseased bodies, parboiling in the kettle below. In order to avoid this filthy composition, I had recourse to the spring that supplies the private baths on the Abbey Green; but I at once perceived something extraordinary in the taste and smell; and, upon inquiry, I find that the Roman baths in this quarter, were found covered by an old burying ground, belong-ing to the Abbey; through which, in all probability, the water drains in its passage: so that as we drink the decoction of living bodies at the Pump Room, we swallow the strainings of rotten bones and carcasses at the private bath—I vow to God, the very idea turns my stomach!

Indoors, wherever it was crowded, the assemblies, the Pump Room, the air was so bad that, on May 8, Matthew Bramble reported fainting from

an accidental impression of fetid effluvia upon nerves of uncom-mon sensibility . . . it was, indeed, a compound of *villainous smells*, in which the most violent stinks, and the most powerful perfumes, contended for the mastery. Imagine to yourself a high exalted essence of mingled odours, arising from putrid gums, imposthumated lungs, sour flatulencies, rank armpits, sweating feet, running sores and issues, plasters, ointments, and embro-cations, hungry-water, spirit of lavender, assafoetida drops, musk, hartshorn and sal-volatile; besides a thousand frowzy steams, which I could not analyze. O Dick! Is this the fragrant aether we breathe in the polite assemblies of Bath?

From Gothic Romance
to Historical Novel

Sir Walter Scott (1771–1832)

"Walter Scott has no business to write novels, especially good ones. It is not fair. He has fame and profit enough as a poet, and should not be taking the bread out of the mouths of other people. I do not like him, and do not mean to like 'Waverley' if I can help it, but fear I must," Jane Austen complained to Cassandra *(Letter, September 28, 1814). However different on the surface, Austen and Scott admired each other's work and shared the same audience. Answering the Prince Regent's request for an historical novel, Austen writes, "I could no more write a romance than an epic poem. . . . I must keep to my own style and go on in my own way; and though I may never succeed again in that, I am convinced that I should totally fail in any other." Similarly, Scott, one of her best readers, appreciated her unique talent: "The big bow-wow strain I can do myself like any now going; but the exquisite touch, which renders ordinary commonplace things and characters interesting, from the truth of the description and the sentiment, is denied to me" ("The Journal . . ." March 1826). He admired* Emma *for, among other things, moving away from "romance" to "real life," the author (who was anonymous), "the first . . . of a new class," "copying from nature as she really exists in the common walks of life, and presenting to the reader . . . a correct and striking representation of that which is daily taking place around him"* (Quarterly Review, *March 1816, dated October 1815).*

Influenced by Ann Radcliffe's gothic romances, both Northanger Abbey *and* Waverley *rejected the misleading ideals of love and heroism. They each created domestic heroes, a man and a woman, reconciled to reality, or, as Hazlitt wrote of Scott in* The Spirit of the Age, *both had found that "facts are better than fiction; . . . there is no romance like the romance of real life." They were both impatient with pretension, pomposity, and jargon, and both, out of a familiar and colloquial language, developed a compelling prose style. Both fictionalized history and historicized fiction: in* Northanger Abbey, *for example, fictional events take place in historical Bath, including real calendars, street names, and buildings, while at the fictional Abbey there are authentic period touches such as the china, the stoves, and the window panes. Scott and Austen even share the experience of anonymous and delayed publication.* Waverley, *begun in 1805, was published in 1814. And each, however imaginary and imaginative, obliquely reflects and comments on the time of publication as well as the time they were written.*

Waverley; or, 'Tis Sixty Years Since *places the fictional Edward Waverley in the historic rebellion of "Bonnie" Prince Charlie against the British in 1745. Waverley, the young English protagonist, assigned to a regiment in Scotland, takes leave to visit the estate of a family friend, Baron Bradwardine, and falls in love with the Baron's daughter, Rose. She takes him to the rebel camp where he also falls in love with Flora MacIvor, sister of a young chieftain, Fergus. Accused of disloyalty, he is arrested, imprisoned, rescued by Rose, and later, after rescuing Colonel Talbot, in the battle of Culloden, he and the Bradwardines are pardoned; Fergus executed; Flora joins a convent; Waverley marries Rose and helps her father rebuild the estate.*

from Waverley[1]

1– Introductory

The title of this work has not been chosen without the grave and solid deliberation, which matters of importance demand from the prudent. Even its first, or general denomination, was the result of no common research or selection, although, according to the example of my predecessors, I had only to seize upon the most sounding and euphonic surname that English history or topography affords, and elect it at once as the title of my work, and the name of my hero. But, alas! what could my readers have expected from the chivalrous epithets of Howard, Mordaunt, Mortimer, or Stanley, or from the softer and more sentimental sounds of Belmour, Belville, Belfield, and Belgrave, but pages of inanity, similar to those which have been so christened for half a century past? I must modestly admit I am too diffident of my own merit to place it in unnecessary opposition to

---

[1]The quotations are from the Centennial Edition of 1870, identified by the section or chapter.

preconceived associations; I have, therefore, like a maiden knight with his white shield, assumed for my hero, Waverley, an uncontaminated name, bearing with its sound little of good or evil, excepting what the reader shall hereafter be pleased to affix to it.

But my second or supplemental title was a matter of much more difficult election, since that, short as it is, may be held as pledging the author to some special mode of laying his scene, drawing his characters, and managing his adventures. Had I, for example, announced in my frontispiece, "Waverley, a Tale of other Days," must not every novel reader have anticipated a castle scarce less than that of Udolpho, of which the eastern wing had long been uninhabited, and the keys either lost, or consigned to the care of some aged butler or housekeeper, whose trembling steps, about the middle of the second volume, were doomed to guide the hero, or heroine, to the ruinous precincts? Would not the owl have shrieked and the cricket cried in my very title-page? and could it have been possible for me, with a moderate attention to decorum, to introduce any scene more lively than might be produced by the jocularity of a clownish but faithful valet, or the garrulous narrative of the heroine's *fille-de-chamber* [maid], when rehearsing the stories of blood and horror which she had heard in the servants' hall? Again, had my title borne "Waverley, a Romance from the German," what head so obtuse as not to image forth a profligate abbot, an oppressive duke, a secret and mysterious association of Rosicrucians and Illuminati, with all their properties of black cowls, caverns, daggers, electrical machines, trap-doors, and dark-lanterns? Or if I had rather chosen to call my work a "Sentimental Tale," would it not have been a sufficient presage of a heroine with a profusion of auburn hair, and a harp, the soft solace of her solitary hours, which she fortunately finds always the means of transporting from castle to cottage, although she herself be sometimes obliged to jump out of a two-pair-of-stairs window, and is more than once bewildered on her journey, alone and on foot, without any guide but a blowzy peasant girl, whose jargon she hardly can understand? Or again, if my Waverley had been entitled "A Tale of the Times," wouldst thou not, gentle reader, have demanded from me a dashing sketch of the fashionable world, a few anecdotes of private scandal thinly veiled, and if lusciously painted, so much the better? a heroine from Grosvenor Square, and a hero from the Barouche Club or the Four-in-hand, with a set of subordinate characters from the *elegantes* of Queen Anne Street East, or the dashing heroes of the Bow Street Office? I could proceed in proving the importance of a title-page, and displaying at the same time my own intimate knowledge of the particular ingredients necessary to the composition of romances and novels of various descriptions: but it is enough, and I scorn to tyrannize longer over the impatience of my reader, who is doubtless already anxious to know the choice made by an author so profoundly versed in the different branches of his art.

By fixing, then, the date of my story Sixty Years before the present November, 1, 1805, I would have my readers understand, that they will meet in the following pages neither a romance of chivalry, nor a tale of modern manners; that my hero will neither have iron on his shoulders, as of yore, nor on the heels of his boots, as is the present fashion of Bond Street; and that my damsels will neither be clothed "in purple and in pall," like the Lady Alice of an old ballad, nor reduced to the primitive nakedness of a modern fashionable at a rout. From this my choice of an era the understanding critic may further presage, that the object of my tale is more a description of men than manners. A tale of manners, to be interesting, must either refer to antiquity so great as to have become venerable, or it must bear a vivid reflection of those scenes which are passing daily before our eyes, and are interesting from their novelty. Thus the coat- of-mail of our ancestors, and the triple-furred pelisse of our modern beaux, may, though for very different reasons, be equally fit for the array of a fictitious character; but who, meaning the costume of his hero to be impressive, would willingly attire him in the court dress of George the Second's reign, with its no collar, large sleeves, and low pocket-holes? The same may be urged, with equal truth, of the Gothic hall, which, with its darkened and tinted windows, its elevated and gloomy roof, and massive oaken table garnished with boar's-head and rosemary, pheasants and peacocks, cranes and cygnets, has an excellent effect in fictitious description. Much may also be gained by a lively display of a modern fete, such as we have daily recorded in that part of a newspaper entitled the *Mirror of Fashion*, if we contrast these, or either of them, with the splendid formality of an entertainment given Sixty Years since; and thus it will be readily seen how much the painter of antique or of fashionable manners gains over him who delineates those of the last generation.

Considering the disadvantages inseparable from this part of my subject, I must be understood to have resolved to avoid them as much as possible, by throwing the force of my narrative upon the characters and passions of the actors;—those passions common to men in all stages of society, and which have alike agitated the human heart, whether it throbbed under the steel corselet of the fifteenth century, the brocaded coat of the eighteenth, or the blue frock and white dimity waistcoat of the present day. (Alas! that attire, respectable and gentlemanlike in 1805, or thereabouts, is now as antiquated as the Author of Waverley has himself become since that period! The reader of fashion will please to fill up the costume with an embroidered waistcoat of purple velvet or silk, and a coat of whatever colour he pleases.) Upon these passions it is no doubt true that the state of manners and laws casts a necessary colouring; but the bearings, to use the language of heraldry, remain the same, though the tincture may be not only different, but opposed in strong contradistinction. . . .

from Chapter 52

"For mere fighting," answered Flora, "I believe all men (that is, who deserve the name) are pretty much alike; there is generally more courage required to run away. They have, besides, when confronted with each other, a certain instinct for strife, as we see in other male animals, such as dogs, bulls, and so forth. But high and perilous enterprise is not Waverley's forte. He would never have been his celebrated ancestor Sir Nigel, but only Sir Nigel's eulogist and poet. I will tell you where he will be at home, my dear, and in his place,—in the quiet circle of domestic happiness, lettered indolence, and elegant enjoyments, of Waverley-Honour. And he will refit the old library in the most exquisite Gothic taste, and garnish its shelves, with the rarest and most valuable volumes; and he will draw plans and landscapes, and write verses, and rear temples, and dig grottoes;—and he will stand in a clear summer night in the colonnade before the hall, and gaze on the deer as they stray in the moonlight, or lie shadowed by the boughs of the huge old fantastic oaks;—and he will repeat verses to his beautiful wife, who will hang upon his arm;—and he will be a happy man."

"And she will be a happy woman," thought poor Rose. But she only sighed, and dropped the conversation.

The Picturesque, Enclosures, and the Anti-Pastoral

The Picturesque

"Picturesque" is another large and complicated theme in which Jane Austen plays an unexpected but important role. The picturesque refers to natural scenery which looks as if it might appear in a painting, especially by one of three eighteenth-century European artists, Claude Lorrain, Nicholas Poussin, and Salvator Rosa. It also refers to paintings that include specific elements of the picturesque: mountains, small figures, a winding stream, a dot of red, a weathered tree, sometimes from a hilltop (a prospect piece), all carefully layered into a fore-ground, middle distance, side-screen, and so on. The picturesque also refers to a literary description capturing such a scene as in Thomson's *Seasons*, Gray's *Elegy in a Country Churchyard*, Wordsworth's *Tintern Abbey*, and in Radcliffe's description of Emily's approach to Udolpho, which also displays characteristics of the sublime. William Gilpin, among others, encouraged picturesque tours in which travelers visited sequences of places that connoisseurs identified as picturesque, published in a guide book with advice on where to stand (stations), how to observe, even the emotions that the scene was supposed to awaken: awe, admiration, melancholy, fear, and so on. If one were on such a tour, the ideal way to view this landscape was backwards, over the shoulder, reflected in a small, smoked, oval mirror called a Claude Glass, which composed the scenery as if it were a painting by Claude Lorrain. Then, the good picturesque traveler would sketch it, describe it in a letter, and publish it in a journal or another guide book.

Before England and France were at war, young British gentlemen toured the Continent, especially the Alps, searching for the picturesque, and after, they looked for it in Great Britain, a more sedate landscape to be sure, with opportunities in Wales, the Lake District, and Scotland. Picturesque travel led to the discovery of Great Britain, new roads and inns, books and maps, a new consciousness of local dialects, native customs, birds, plants, animals, architecture, and a new school of British painting that included John Constable and William Turner. Even the new sciences came into play; instruments developed for trade or war to measure speed, distance, and time became toys of the leisured: John Thorpe concludes on the basis of his watch, the town clock at Tetbury, and the speed of his horse, that they had traveled twenty-five miles, while Morland claims it was twenty-three, on "the authority of road-books, innkeepers, and milestones" (Chapter VII).

By 1798, when Jane Austen was writing *Northanger Abbey*, the satirical reaction against the picturesque mania had begun, reflected in James Plumptre's *The Lakers* (1798) and William Combe's *Tour of Dr. Syntax in Search of the Picturesque*, illustrated by Thomas Rowlandson in *Poetical Magazine*, starting in 1809, and Thomas Love Peacock's *Headlong Hall* (1816). Like Austen, they exposed the inappropriate use of the picturesque, the judgmental behavior it encouraged, the way that an alien language obscured the landscape they were describing. Even Wordsworth, whose love of nature was immediate and unmediated, confessed in *The Prelude* to having fallen victim to the "rules of mimic art transferred / To things above all art," "a strong infection of the age," comparing "scene with scene, / Bent overmuch on superficial things," until "the eye was master of the heart." He recovered and wrote a *Guide to the Lakes* (1810), which is still used by travelers in the Lake District.

Among the many writers engaged with the picturesque, Gilpin was the most influential. According to Henry Austen, in the "Biographical Memoir" in *Northanger Abbey*, Jane Austen "was enamoured of Gilpin on the Picturesque; and she seldom changed her opinions either on books or men." In the novels, however, the picturesque is another artificial concept that substitutes for genuine experience. In *Northanger Abbey*, after Henry's lecture on the

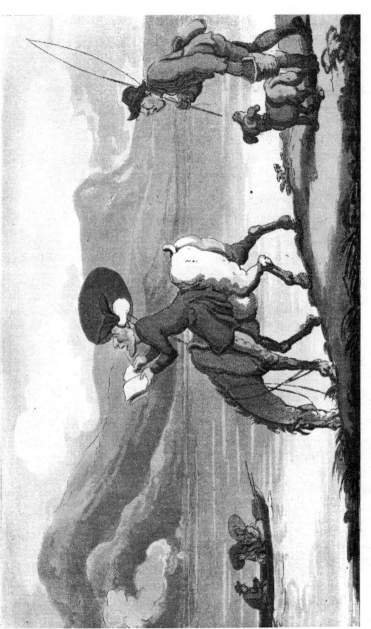

Thomas Rowlandson, *Dr. Syntax sketching the lake* (1756–1827).

picturesque, Catherine dismisses the entire city of Bath as "unworthy" of the landscape, as Austen herself was tempted to dismiss it on her first view, "all vapour, shadow, smoke, and confusion" (Letter, May 5, 1801).

In *Sense and Sensibility*, Edward reveals the paradox of the picturesque, a search for natural beauty which is judged on the basis of art:

> . . . remember I have no knowledge in the picturesque, and I shall offend you by my ignorance and want of taste if we come to particulars. I shall call hills steep, which ought to be bold; surfaces strange and uncouth, which ought to be irregular and rugged; and distant objects out of sight, which ought only to be indistinct through the soft medium of a hazy atmosphere. You must be satisfied with such admiration as I can honestly give. I call it a very fine country—the hills are steep, the woods seem full of fine timber, and the valley looks comfortable and snug—with rich meadows and several neat farm houses scattered here and there. It exactly answers my idea of a fine country, because it unites beauty with utility—and I dare say it is a picturesque one too, because you admire it; I can easily believe it to be full of rocks and promontories, grey moss and brush wood, but these are all lost on me. I know nothing of the picturesque. . . . (Chapter XVIII)

William Gilpin (1813–1894)

In Observations on the River Wye, and Several Parts of South Wales, &c. Relative Chiefly to Picturesque Beauty; Made in the Summer of the Year 1770, *Gilpin describes a scene that became the basis for Wordsworth's meditations in* Tintern Abbey *(1798).*

from *Observations on the River Wye*

But if *Tintern-abbey* be less striking as a *distant* object, it exhibits, on a *nearer* view (when the whole together cannot be seen) a very enchanting piece of ruin. The eye settles upon some of its nobler parts. Nature has now made it her own. Time has worn off all traces of the chisel: it has blunted the sharp edges of the rule and compass, and broken the regularity of opposing parts. The figured ornaments of the east-window are gone; those of the west-window are left. Most of the other windows, with their principal ornaments, remain.

To these were superadded the ornaments of time. Ivy, in masses uncommonly large, had taken possession of many parts of the wall; and given a happy contrast to the grey-coloured stone of which the building is composed: nor was this undecorated. Mosses of various hues, with lichens, maiden-hair, penny-leaf, and other humble plants, had over-spread the surface, or hung from every joint and crevice. Some of them were in flower, others only in leaf; but all together gave those full-blown tints which add the richest finishing to a ruin. . . .

When we stood at one end of this awful piece of ruin, and surveyed the whole in one view—the elements of air and earth, its only covering and pavement; and the grand and venerable remains which terminated both; perfect enough to form the perspective, yet broken enough to destroy the regularity—the eye was above measure delighted with the beauty, the greatness, and the novelty of the scene. More *picturesque* it certainly would have been, if the area, unadorned, had been left with all its rough fragments of ruin scattered round; and bold was the hand that removed them: yet as the outside of the ruin, which is the chief object of *picturesque curiosity*, is still left in all its wild and native rudeness, we excuse, perhaps we approve, the neatness that is introduced within: it *may* add to the *beauty* of the scene; to its *novelty* it undoubtedly *does*.

Among other things in this scene of desolation, the poverty and wretchedness of the inhabitants were remarkable. They occupy little huts, raised among the ruins of the monastery, and seem to have no employment but begging; as if a place once devoted to indolence could never again become the seat of industry. As we left the abbey, we found the whole hamlet at the gate, either openly soliciting alms, or covertly, under the pretence of carrying us to some part of the ruins, which each could shew; and which was far superior to anything which could be shewn by anyone else. The most lucrative occasion could not have excited more jealousy and contention.

James Plumptre (1770–1832)

from *The Lakers*[1]

In 1798, after two tours of the Lake District, the Reverend James Plumptre composed The Lakers, *a comic opera and parody of Gilpin's principles of picturesque touring and the odd uses to which it could be put as well as the fashionable interest in contemporary botany. Geology and entomology, collecting rocks and shells, butterflies and beetles, indeed, all the sciences that encouraged observation and collecting specimens, were well suited to both picturesque travel and to the perennial concerns of mating. With Linnaeus's classification of plants according to sexual parts and Erasmus Darwin's celebration of them in the erotic* Loves of Plants, *studying botany was as lurid, popular, and controversial for women as reading* The Monk. *Botany, Plumptre writes in the preface, should be discouraged: it represents "the false taste of a licentious age," "corrupting the soft and elegant manners of the otherwise loveliest part of the creation."*

"Lakers" was the derisive term applied to picturesque travelers in the Lake District, such as the heroine, Beccabunga Veronica, a botanist on tour with her niece Lydia, looking for a mate and planning her next gothic romance:

I think I shall lay the scene of my next upon Derwent-water, make Sir Herbert to have murdered a pilgrim, who shall turn out to be his brother, and I shall call it 'The Horrors of the Hermitage.' I can introduce a mysterious monk of Borrowdale, and shall have fine opportunities of describing luxuriant groves and bowery lanes in all the pomp of foliage of beech, birch, mountain ash, and holly. It shall be a romance of the fourteenth century; the castle upon Lord's island shall be haunted by an armed head: and, I believe, Lydia, I shall draw my heroine from either you or myself, and make her passionately fond of drawing and botany; she shall be mistress of the Linnaean system, and then, if I should make her stop, in the midst of her distresses, to admire the scenery, or gather a plant, it will be perfectly natural.

Arriving at a mountain scene, Beccabunga cries:

Oh! Claude and Poussin are nothing. By the bye, where's my Claude-Lorrain? I must throw a Gilpin tint over these magic

---

[1]James Plumptre, *The Lakers* (1798), ed. Jonathan Wordsworth (Oxford, UK: Woodstock Books. 1990), 18–20.

scenes of beauty. (*Looks through the glass*). How gorgeously glowing! Now for the darker (*Looks through the glass*). How gloomily glaring! Now the blue. (*Pretends to shiver with cold*). How frigidly frozen! What illusions of visions! The effect is inexpressibly interesting. The amphitheatrical perspective of the long landscape; the peeping points of the man-coloured crags of the head-long mountains, looking out most interestingly from the picturesque luxuriance of the bowery foliage, margining their ruggedness and feathering the fells; the delightful differences of the heterogeneous masses, the horrific mountains, such scenes of ruin and privation! The turfy hillocks, the umbrageous and reposing hue of the copsy lawns, so touchingly beautiful; the limpid lapse of Lowdore, the islands coroneting the flood; the water, the soft purple of the pigeon's neck,—are so many circumstances of imagery, which all together combine a picture, which for its sentimental beauty and assemblages of sublimity, I never exceeded in the warmest glow of my fancied descriptions. And then the incomparable verdure of the turfy slope we are upon; the water bickering at the base; the sultry low of the cattle, sipping the clear wave, add a sweet pathos to the magical effect of the surrounding scenery. And now the effulgence of the sunshine landscape is fading way, and the blue distances, stealing on the nearer view, soften the sublime severity. . . .

Beccabunga concludes this endless speech with the demand that her companions "form . . . into a picturesque group." Having lost her intended mate, the titled Sir Charles Portinscale, to Lydia, she settles for Speedwell, the simple butler: "I fear I shall never get another offer half so good. . . . He's a vastly clever fellow, he's a botanist, he's picturesque—I'll throw a Gilpin tint over him (looks through her glass). Yes, he's gorgeously glowing. . . ."

Writing gothic romances in the Lake District among the simpletons Plumptre depicts is as absurd as Catherine's expecting to find Radcliffe's Italian or Swiss "horrors" in the "midland counties of England" or, for that matter, as judging the English landscape by aesthetic principles drawn from French and Italian paintings. England had its own rural gothic, and writers who were trying to get the attention of the reading public.

Enclosures and the Anti-Pastoral

Henry's Tilney's lecture on the picturesque on Beechen Cliff concludes with an allusion to "inclosure," the political dark side of the picturesque in which the landed gentry, as they had for centuries, accelerated their conversion of arable land into pasture, ornamental gardens, hunting grounds, and "landscapes" while the poor were starving, or imprisoned for rioting against recurrent food shortages and rising prices. Austen recognized the injustice of enclosure in *Sense and Sensibility*, when, John Dashwood, inheriting the family estate, displaces the surviving women and later the tenants, appropriates or purchases the common land, cuts down an old grove of walnut trees to build a greenhouse for exotic fruits, and the native hawthorn, "the ancestor of the Maypole," to improve his view. But enclosures were also profitable: landlords and farmers appropriated small tracts of common land, the personal cottage gardens that often had supported a whole family, sometimes for generations, to make pastures for raising sheep and forcing the tenants into cities, factories, or into exile. Given the importance of rustic life, of the pastoral ideal in Western literature, writers responded in a variety of voices, especially the poets that Jane Austen most admired, William Cowper in *The Task*, Oliver Goldsmith in *The Deserted Village*, George Crabbe with satire in *The Village*, and Wordsworth in *The Ruined Cottage* with an unrelenting realism.

George Crabbe (1754–1832)

George Crabbe began life as a day-laborer, then a doctor, and finally a vicar. Throughout his life, he wrote highly regarded, mostly satiric verse narratives, The Village, The Newspaper, The Parish Register, *and* Tales in Verse, *which won the admiration and friendship of such powerful figures as Edmund Burke and Sir Walter Scott. To Austen, he was a family joke, a fictional suitor she claims in letters to Cassandra "not" to have seen in London, a joke that turns callous when Mrs. Crabbe dies: "I have only just been making out from one of his prefaces that he probably was married. It is almost ridiculous. Poor woman. I will comfort him as well as I can, but I do not undertake to be good to her children" (Letters, October 21, 1813).*

Crabbe's satiric technique is similar to Austen's, and he may have influenced her narrative style: literal, realistic, juxtaposing conventional beliefs against real experience, incorporating traditional pastoral language, imitating the literary form he is satirizing. Like Austen, he is impatient with hypocrisy, pretension, the failure of authority, even gothic romances—which he undermines, as she does, with gothic realities.

In The Village *(1783), he attacks the sentimental pastoral tradition, especially Goldsmith's maudlin and idealized representation of rustic life in* The Deserted Village, *lamenting the depopulation of the imaginary village of Auburn, the hedges and fences that enclosed the common lands, the forced emigration, and with it the loss of native customs and manners. Crabbe includes the poets who write about the pastoral, laws and legislators, the landed gentry, the decorative priests, and the exploitive landlords.*

from *The Village*,[1] Book One

The Village Life, and every care that reigns
O'er youthful peasants and declining swains;
What labour yields, and what, that labour past,
Age, in its hour of languor, finds at last;
What form the real Picture of the Poor,   5
Demand a song—the Muse can give no more.
   Fled are those times, when, in harmonious strains,
The rustic poet praised his native plains:
No Shepherds now, in smooth alternate verse,[1]
Their country's beauty or their nymph's rehearse;   10
Yet still for these we frame the tender strain,
Still in our lays fond Corydons[2] complain,
And shepherds' boys their amorous pains reveal,
The only pains, alas! they never feel. [1–14]

. . .

   I grant indeed that fields and flocks have charms
For him that grazes or for him that farms;   40
But when amid such pleasing scenes I trace
The poor laborious natives of the place,
And see the mid-day sun, with fervid ray,

[1]*The Traveller, The Deserted Village, and Other Poems* (London: 1819).

[1]Sung in turn by two.
[2]For Shepherd poet named in Virgil's seventh eclogue.

On their bare heads and dewy temples play;
While some, with feebler heads and fainter hearts,   45
Deplore their fortune, yet sustain their parts;
Then shall I dare these real ills to hide
In tinsel trappings of poetic pride?
  No; cast by Fortune on a frowning coast,
Which neither groves nor happy valleys boast;   50
Where other cares than those the Muse relates,
And other shepherds dwell with other mates;
By such examples taught, I paint the Cot,
As Truth will paint it, and as Bards will not:
Nor you, ye Poor, of letter'd scorn complain,   55
To you the smoothest song is smooth in vain;
O'ercome by labour, and bow'd down by time,
Feel you the barren flattery of a rhyme?
Can poets soothe you, when you pine for bread,
By winding myrtles round your ruin'd shed?   60
Can their light tales your weighty griefs o'erpower,
Or glad with airy mirth the toilsome hour? [39–62]

Reviews of
Northanger Abbey

Book reviewing was so brutal during the Romantic period that Byron and Shelley both thought the young John Keats had been killed by a review in *The Quarterly*. Even the best reviews didn't help sales: paid by the line, reviewers often summarized in such detail that no one needed to buy the book even if the reviewer liked it. The following two anonymous reviews appeared in major periodicals and are exceptionally good for the times.

British Critic n.s. 9 (March 1818): 293–301

With respect to the talents of Jane Austen, they need no other voucher, than the works which she has left behind her; which in some of the best qualities of the best sort of novels, display a degree of excellence that has not often been surpassed. In imagination, of all kinds, she appears to have been extremely deficient; not only her stories are utterly and entirely devoid of invention, but her characters, her incidents, her sentiments, are obviously all drawn exclusively from experience. The sentiments which she puts into the mouths of her actors, are the sentiments, which we are every day in the habit of hearing; and as to her actors themselves, we are persuaded that fancy, strictly so called, has had much less to do with them, than with the characters of Julius Caesar, Hannibal, or Alexander, as represented to us by historians.

At description she seldom aims; at that vivid and poetical sort of description, which we have of late been accustomed to, (in the novels of a celebrated anonymous writer) never; she seems to have no other object in view, than simply to paint some of those scenes which she has herself seen, and which every one, indeed, may witness daily. Not only her characters are all of them belonging to the middle size, and with a tendency, in fact, rather to fall below, than to rise above the common standard, but even the incidents of her novels, are of the same description. Her heroes and heroines, make love and are married, just as her readers make love, and were or will be, married; no unexpected ill fortune occurs to prevent, not any unexpected good fortune, to ring about the events on which her novels hinge. She seems to be describing such people as meet together every night, in every respectable house in London; and to relate such incidents as have probably happened, one time or another, to half the families in the United Kingdom. And yet, by a singular good judgment, almost every individual represents a class; not a class of humourists, or of any of the rarer specimens in our species, but one of those classes to which we ourselves, and every acquaintance we have, in all probability belong. . . .

Her merit consists altogether in her remarkable talent for observation; no ridiculous phrase, no affected sentiment, no foolish pretension seems to escape her notice. It is scarcely possible to read her novels, without meeting with some of one's own absurdities reflected back upon one's conscience; and this, just in the light in which they ought to appear. For in recording the customs and manners of common-place people in the commonplace intercourse of life, our authoress never dips her pen in satire; the follies which she holds up to us, are, for the most part, mere follies, or else natural imperfections; and she treats them, as such, with good-humoured pleasantry; mimicking them so exactly, that we always laugh at the ridiculous truth of the imitation, but without ever being incited to indulge in feelings, that might tend to render us ill-natured, and intolerant in society. This is the result of that good sense which seems ever to keep complete possession over all the other qualities of the mind of our authoress; she sees every thing just as it is; even her want of imagination (which is the principal defect of her writings) is useful to her in this respect, that it enables her to keep clear of all exaggeration, in a mode of writing where the least exaggeration would be fatal; for if the people and the scenes which she has chosen, as the subjects of her composition, be not painted with perfect truth, with exact and striking resemblance, the whole effect ceases; her characters have no merit in themselvs, and whatever interest they excite in the mind of the reader, results almost entirely, from the unaccountable pleasure, which, by a peculiarity in our nature, we derive from a simple imitation of any object, without any reference to the abstract value or importance of the object itself. This fact is notorious in painting; and the novels of Miss Austen alone, would be sufficient to prove, were proof required, that the same is true in the department of literature, which she has adorned. . . . Be their merit what it may, it is not founded upon the interest of a narrative. In fact, so little narrative is there in either of the two novels . . . that it is difficult to give any thing like an abstract of their contents.

"Northanger Abbey and Persuasion," Blackwood's Edinburgh Magazine n.s.2 (May 1818): 453–55

We are happy to receive two other novels from the pen of this amiable and agreeable authoress, though our satisfaction is much alloyed, from the feeling, that they must be the last. We have always regarded her works as possessing a higher claim to public estimation than perhaps they have yet attained. They have fallen, indeed, upon an age whose taste can only be gratified with the highest seasoned food. This, as we have already hinted, may be partly owing to the wonderful realities which it has been our lot to witness. We have been spoiled for the tranquil enjoyment of common interests, and nothing now will satisfy us in fiction, any more than in real life, but grand movements and striking characters. A singular union has, accordingly, been attempted between history, and poetry. The periods of great events have been seized on as a ground work for the display of powerful or fantastic characters: correct and instructive pictures of national peculiarities have been exhibited; and even in those fictions which are altogether wild and monstrous, some insight has been given into the passions and theories which have convulsed and bewildered this our 'age of Reason'. In the poetry of Mr. Scott and Lord Byron, in the novels of Miss Edgeworth, Mr. Godwin, and the author of *Waverley*, we see exemplified in different forms this influence of the spirit of the times,—the prevailing love of historical, and at the same time romantic incident,—dark and high-wrought passions,—the delineations, chiefly of national character,—the pursuit of some substance, in short, yet of an existence more fanciful often than absolute fiction,—the dislike of a cloud, yet the form which is embraced, nothing short of a Juno. In this raised state of our imaginations, we cannot, it may be supposed, all at once descend to the simple representations of common life, to incidents which have no truth, except that of universal nature, and have nothing of fiction except in not having really happened,—yet the time, probably, will return, when we shall take a more permanent delight in those familiar cabinet pictures, than even in the great historical pieces of our more eminent modern masters; when our sons and daughters will deign once more to laugh over the Partridges and the Trullibers, and to weep over the Clementinas and Clarissas of past times, as we have some distant recollection of having been able to do ourselves, before we were so entirely engrossed with the Napoleons of real life, or the Corsairs of poetry; and while we could enjoy a work that was all written in pure English, without ever dreaming how great would be the embellishment to have at least one half of it in the dialect of Scotland or of Ireland.

When this period arrives, we have no hesitation in saying, that the delightful writer of the works now before us, will be one of the most popular of English novelists, and if, indeed, we could point out the individual who, within a certain limited range, has attained the highest perfection of the art of novel writing, we should have little scruple in fixing upon her. She has confined herself, no doubt, to a narrow walk. She never operates among deep interests, uncommon characters, or vehement passions. The singular merit of her writings is, that we could conceive, without the slightest strain of imagination, any one of her fictions to be realised in any town or village in England, (for it is only English manners that she paints,) that we think we are reading the history of people whom we have seen thousands of times, and that with all this perfect commonness, both of incident and character, perhaps not one of her characters is to be found in any other book, portrayed at least in so lively and interesting a manner. She has much observation,—much fine sense,—much delicate humour,—many pathetic touches,—and throughout all her works, a most charitable view of human nature, and a tone of gentleness and purity that are almost unequalled. . . .

Further Reading

Primary Sources

Chapman, R. W., ed. *The Novels of Jane Austen*, 3rd ed. 5 vols. London: Oxford University Press, 1932–34.

Le Faye, Deirdre, ed. *Jane Austen's Letters*, 3rd ed. Oxford: Oxford University Press, 1995.

Biographies

Austen-Leigh, James Edward. *A Memoir of Jane Austen*. London: Richard Bentley and Son, 1870.

Fergus, Jan S. *Jane Austen: A Literary Life*. London: Macmillan, 1991.

Halperin, John. *The Life of Jane Austen*. Baltimore, MD: The Johns Hopkins University Press, 1984; rev. 1996.

Honan, Park. *Jane Austen: Her Life*, rev. ed. London: Phoenix, 1997.

Le Faye, Deirdre. *Jane Austen: A Family Record*. London: British Library, 1989; rev. Cambridge: Cambridge University Press, 2004.

Nokes, David. *Jane Austen: A Life*. London: Fourth Estate, 1997.

Pilgrim, Constance. *Dear Jane: A Biographical Study*. Durham, SC: Pentland Press, 1991.

Tomalin, Clare. *Jane Austen: A Life*. Harmondsworth, UK: Viking Press, 1997.

Bibliographies and Reference Tools

Cooper, Patrick, compiler. "Television, Film, and Radio Productions of Austen." In *Jane Austen and Co.*, eds. Suzanne R. Pucci and James Thompson. Albany: SUNY Press, 2003, 261–66.

Dabundo, Laura, ed. "Representative Chronology of English Novels by Women of the Romantic Period." In *Jane Austen and Mary Shelley and Their Sisters*, ed. Laura Dabundo. Lanham, MD: University Press of America, 2000, 159–69.

Gilson, David. *A Bibliography of Jane Austen.* Oxford: Oxford University Press, 1982; rev. 1997.

Roth, Barry. *An Annotated Bibliography of Jane Austen Studies 1984–94.* Columbus, OH: Ohio State University Press, 1996.

Southam, B. C. *Jane Austen: The Critical Heritage.* 2 vols. London: Routledge, vol. I, 1968; vol. II, 1987.

———. *Jane Austen's Literary Manuscripts: A Study of the Novelist's Development through the Surviving Papers.* London: Oxford University Press, 1964.

Tracy, Ann B. *The Gothic Novel, 1790–1830: Plot Summaries and Index to Motifs.* Lexington, KY: University Press of Kentucky, 1981.

http://www.perberley.com. (texts, links, allusions, illustrations, biography, letters, novels, chronologies, jokes, songs, and information about films.)

Critical and Scholarly Studies

Andrews, Malcolm. *The Search for the Picturesque: Landscape Aesthetics and Tourism in Britain, 1760–1800.* Stanford: Stanford University Press, 1989.

Axelrod, Arthur M. "Jane Austen's 'Susan' Restored." *Persuasions: Journal of the Jane Austen Society* 15:1 (1993): 44–45.

Barker-Benfield, G. J. *The Culture of Sensibility: Sex and Society in Eighteenth-Century Britain.* Chicago: University of Chicago Press, 1992; rev. 1996.

Bermingham, Ann. *Landscape and Ideology: The English Rustic Tradition, 1740–1860.* Berkeley: University of California Press, 1986.

Bradbrook, Frank. *Jane Austen and Her Predecessors.* Cambridge: Cambridge University Press, 1966.

Brown, Julia Prewitt. *Jane Austen's Novels: Social Change and Literary Form.* Cambridge: Cambridge University Press, 1966.

Brown, Lloyd. *Bits of Ivory: Narrative Techniques in Jane Austen's Fiction.* Baton Rouge: Louisiana State University Press, 1973.

Brownstein, Rachel M. "*Northanger Abbey, Sense and Sensibility, Pride and Prejudice.*" In *The Cambridge Companion to Jane Austen,* eds. Edward Copeland and Juliet McMaster. Cambridge: Cambridge University Press, 1997, 32–57.

———. *Becoming a Heroine: Reading about Women in Novels.* New York: Viking Press, 1982.

Butler, Marilyn. *Romantics, Rebels, and Reactionaries: English Literature and Its Backgrounds, 1760–1830.* Oxford: Oxford University Press, 1981.

———. *Peacock Displayed: A Satirist in His Context.* London: Routledge and Keegan Paul, 1979.

———. *Jane Austen and the War of Ideas.* Oxford: Oxford University Press, 1975.

Byrne, Paula. *Jane Austen and the Theatre.* London: Hambledon and London, 2002.

Colley, Linda. *Britons: Forging the Nation, 1707–1837.* New Haven, CT: Yale University Press, 1992.

Collins, Irene. *Jane Austen and the Clergy.* London: Hambledon and London, 1994.

Copeland, Edward. *Women Writing about Money: Women's Fiction in England 1790–1820.* Cambridge: Cambridge University Press, 1995.

———, and Juliet McMaster, eds. *The Cambridge Companion to Jane Austen.* Cambridge: Cambridge University Press, 1997.

Cotton, Daniel. *The Civilized Imagination: A Study of Ann Radcliffe, Jane Austen, and Sir Walter Scott.* Cambridge: Cambridge University Press, 1985.

Dabundo, Laura. "Jane Austen's Opacities." In *Jane Austen and Mary Shelley and Their Sisters,* ed. Laura Dabundo. Lanham, MD: University Press of America, 2000.

Devlin, David. *Jane Austen and Education.* Tottowa, NJ: Barnes and Noble, 1975.

Doody, Margaret. "Jane Austen's Reading." In *The Jane Austen Handbook,* ed. J. E. Grey. London: Athlone Press, 1986.

Duckworth, Alistair M. *The Improvement of the Estate: A Study of Jane Austen's Novels*. Baltimore: The Johns Hopkins University Press, 1971.

Fergus, Jan. *Jane Austen and the Didactic Novel: Northanger Abbey, Sense and Sensibility, and Pride and Prejudice*. London: Macmillan, 1983.

Galperin, William H. *The Historical Austen*. Philadelphia: University of Pennsylvania Press, 2003.

Gard, Roger. *Jane Austen's Novels: The Art of Clarity*. New Haven: Yale University Press, 1936; rev. 1992.

Gaull, Marilyn. *English Romanticism: The Human Context*. New York: W. W. Norton, 1988.

Gay, Penny. *Jane Austen and the Theatre*. Cambridge: Cambridge University Press, 2000.

Giffin, Michael. *Jane Austen and Religion: Salvation and Society in Georgian England*. New York: Palgrave, 2002.

Gilbert, Sandra, and Susan Gubar. *The Madwoman in the Attic: The Woman Writer and the Nineteenth-Century Literary Imagination*. New Haven: Yale University Press, 1979.

Gill, Richard, and Susan Gregory. *Mastering the Novels of Jane Austen*. New York: Palgrave, 2003.

Grey, David J., ed. *The Jane Austen Companion*. New York: Macmillan, 1986.

Griffin, Dustin. *Satire: A Critical Reintroduction*. Lexington: The University Press of Kentucky, 1994.

Harding, D. W. *Regulated Hatred and Other Essays on Jane Austen*. London: Athlone Press, 1998.

Hardy, Barbara Nathan. *A Reading of Jane Austen*. London: Owen, 1975.

Harris, Jocelyn. *Jane Austen's Art of Memory*. Cambridge: Cambridge University Press, 1989.

Heydt-Stevenson, Jill. *Jane Austen: Comedies of the Flesh*. New York: Palgrave, 2004.

Janowitz, Anne. *England's Ruins: Poetic Purpose and the National Landscape*. Oxford: Blackwell, 1990.

Johnson, Claudia L. *Equivocal Beings: Politics, Gender, and Sentimentality in the 1790's: Wollstonecraft, Radcliffe, Burney, Austen*. Chicago: University of Chicago Press, 1995.

———. *Jane Austen: Women, Politics, and the Novel*. Chicago: University of Chicago Press, 1988.

Jones, Steven E. *Satire and Romanticism*. New York: Palgrave, 2000.

Kaplan, Deborah. *Jane Austen Among Women*. Baltimore: The Johns Hopkins University Press, 1992.

Kelly, Gary. *English Fiction of the Romantic Period, 1789–1830*. New York: Longman, 1989.

Kiely, Robert. *The Romantic Novel in England*. Cambridge: Harvard University Press, 1973.

Kowalski-Wallace, Elizabeth. *Consuming Subjects: Women, Shopping, and Business in the Eighteenth Century*. New York: Columbia University Press, 1997.

Kroeber, Karl. "Jane Austen's *Northanger Abbey*: Self-Reflexive Satire and Biopoetics." In *The Satiric Eye: Forms of Satire in the Romantic Period*, ed. Steven E. Jones. New York: Palgrave, 2003, 91–114.

———. *Styles in Fictional Structures: The Art of Jane Austen, Charlotte Brontë, and George Eliot*. Princeton: Princeton University Press, 1971.

Landes, David. *Revolution in Time*. Cambridge: Harvard University Press, 1983.

Lane, Maggie. *Jane Austen and Food*. London: Hambledon and London, 2003.

Langford, Paul. *Englishness Identified: Manners and Character 1650–1850*. Oxford: Oxford University Press, 2000.

Lascelles, Mary. *Jane Austen and Her Art*. Oxford: Oxford University Press, 1939.

Lau, Beth. "Madeline at *Northanger Abbey*: Keats's Anti-Romances and Gothic Satire." *Journal of English and German Philology* 84:1 (1985): 30–50.

Litz, A. Walton. *Jane Austen: A Study of Her Artistic Development*. New York: Oxford University Press, 1965.

Lodge, David. *Changing Places: A Tale of Two Campuses*. London: Secker and Warburg, 1975.

Looser, Devoney, ed. *Jane Austen and Discourses of Feminism*. New York: St. Martin's Press, 1995.

Lynch, Deidre. *The Economy of Character: Novels, Market Culture, and the Business of Inner Meaning*. Chicago: University of Chicago Press, 1998.

MacDonagh, Oliver. *Jane Austen: Real and Imagined Worlds*. New Haven, CT: Yale University Press, 1991.

McCalman, Iain. *Radical Underworld: Prophets, Revolutionaries and Pornographers in London, 1795–1840*. Cambridge: Cambridge University Press, 1988.

McMaster, Juliet. "Clothing the Thought in the Word: The Speakers of *Northanger Abbey*." *Persuasions: Journal of the Jane Austen Society* 20 (1998): 207–21.

———. *Jane Austen the Novelist*. New York: St. Martin's Press, 1996.

———. *Jane Austen on Love*. Victoria, BC: University of Victoria Press, 1978.

———, ed. *Jane Austen's Achievement*. London: Macmillan, 1973.

McMaster, Juliet, and Bruce Stoval, eds. *Jane Austen's Business: Her World and Her Profession*. London: Macmillan, 1996.

Mellor, Anne K. *Romanticism and Gender*. New York: Routledge, 1993.

Miall, David. S. "The Preceptor as Fiend: Radcliffe's Psychology of the Gothic." In *Jane Austen and Mary Shelley and Their Sisters*, ed. Laura Dabundo. Lanham, MD: University Press of America, 2000.

Miles, Robert. *Gothic Writing: 1750–1820: A Genealogy*, 2nd ed. Manchester: Manchester University Press, 1993; rev. 2002.

Moler, Kenneth L. *Jane Austen's Art of Allusion*. Lincoln: University of Nebraska Press, 1968.

Monaghan, David, ed. *Jane Austen in Social Context*. London: Macmillan, 1981.

———. *Jane Austen: Structure and Social Vision*. London: Macmillan, 1980.

Morgan, Susan. *In the Meantime: Character and Perception in Jane Austen's Fiction*. Chicago: University of Chicago Press, 1980.

Mudrick, Marvin. *Jane Austen: Irony as Defense and Discovery*. Princeton: Princeton University Press, 1952.

Mullan, John. *Sentiment and Sociability: The Language of Feeling in the Eighteenth Century*. Oxford: Clarendon Press, 1988.

Murray, Venetia. *An Elegant Madness: High Society in Regency England*. New York: Viking Press, 1998.

Neale, R. S. *Bath 1680–1850: A Social History or A Valley of Pleasure Yet a Sink of Iniquity*. London: Routledge and Keegan Paul, 1981.

Neill, Edward. "The Secret of *Northanger Abbey.*" *Essays in Criticism* 47:1 (1997): 13–32.

Norton, Rictor, ed. *Gothic Readings: The First Wave, 1764–1840.* London: Leicester University Press, 2000.

Pearson, Jacqueline. *Women's Reading in Britain, 1750–1835: Dangerous Recreation.* Cambridge: Cambridge University Press, 1999.

Phillips, Mark Salber. *Society and Sentiment: Genres of Historical Writing in Britain.* Princeton: Princeton University Press, 2000.

Poovey, Mary. *The Proper Lady and the Woman Writer: Ideology as Style in the Works of Mary Wollstonecraft, Mary Shelley, and Jane Austen.* Chicago: University of Chicago Press, 1984.

Punter, David. "The Picturesque and the Sublime: Two Worldscapes." In *The Politics of the Picturesque*, eds. Stephen Copley and Peter Garside. Cambridge: Cambridge University Press, 1994, 220–39.

———. *The Literature of Terror: A History of Gothic Fictions from 1765 to the Present Day.* London: Longmans, 1980.

Regis, Pamela. *A Natural History of the Romance Novel.* Philadelphia: University of Pennsylvania Press, 2003.

Roberts, Warren. *Jane Austen and the French Revolution.* New York: St. Martin's Press, 1979.

Sales, Roger. *Jane Austen and the Representations of Regency England.* London: Routledge, 1996.

———. *English Literature in History: 1780–1830, Pastoral and Politics.* London: Hutchinson, 1983.

Selwyn, David. *Jane Austen and Leisure.* London: Hambledon, 1999.

Shaw, Philip. *Waterloo and the Romantic Imagination.* New York: Palgrave, 2002.

———. *Romantic Wars: Studies in Culture and Conflict, 1793–1822.* Burlington, VT: Ashgate, 2000.

Simpson, David. *Romanticism, Nationalism, and the Revolt Against Theory.* Chicago: University of Chicago Press, 1993.

Siskin, Clifford. *The Historicity of Romantic Discourse.* Oxford: Oxford University Press, 1988.

Southam, Brian C. *Jane Austen and The Navy.* London: Hambledon, 2000.

———. *Jane Austen: Northanger Abbey and Persuasion: A Casebook.* London: Macmillan, 1976.

————. *Jane Austen: A Selection of Critical Essays*. London: MacMillan, 1976.

————, ed. *Critical Essays on Jane Austen*. London: Routledge, 1968.

Spencer, Jane. *The Rise of the Woman Novelist: From Aphra Behn to Jane Austen*. Oxford: Blackwell, 1986.

Spender, Dale. *100 Good Women Novelists Before Jane Austen*. London: Pandora, 1986.

Stabler, Jane. *Burke to Byron, Barbauld to Baillie, 1790–1830*. New York: Palgrave, 2001.

Stewart, Maaja. *Domestic Realities and Imperial Fictions: Jane Austen's Novels in Eighteenth-Century Contexts*. Athens: University of Georgia Press, 1993.

Stovel, Bruce. "*Northanger Abbey* at the Movies." *Persuasions: Journal of the Jane Austen Society* 20 (1998): 236–47.

Sulloway, Alison. *Jane Austen and the Province of Womanhood*. Philadelphia: University of Pennsylvania Press, 1989.

Tanner, Tony. *Jane Austen*. Cambridge: Harvard University Press, 1986.

Tave, Stuart. *Some Words of Jane Austen*. Chicago: University of Chicago Press, 1973.

Thompson, James. "How to Do Things with Austen." In *Jane Austen and Co.*, eds. Suzanne R. Pucci and James Thompson. Albany: SUNY Press, 2003.

————. *Between Self and World: The Novels of Jane Austen*. University Park: Pennsylvania State University Press, 1988.

Thorslev, Peter. *The Byronic Hero: Types and Prototypes*. Minneapolis: University of Minnesota Press, 1962.

Troost, Linda, and Sayre Greenfield, eds. *Jane Austen in Hollywood*. Lexington: University Press of Kentucky, 1998.

Tucker, George Holbert. *Jane Austen the Woman: Some Biographical Insights*. New York: St. Martin's Press, 1994.

————. *A Goodly Heritage: A History of Jane Austen's Family*. Manchester: Carcanet New Press, 1983.

Tuite, Claire. *Romantic Austen: Sexual Politics and the Literary Canon*. Cambridge: Cambridge University Press, 2002.